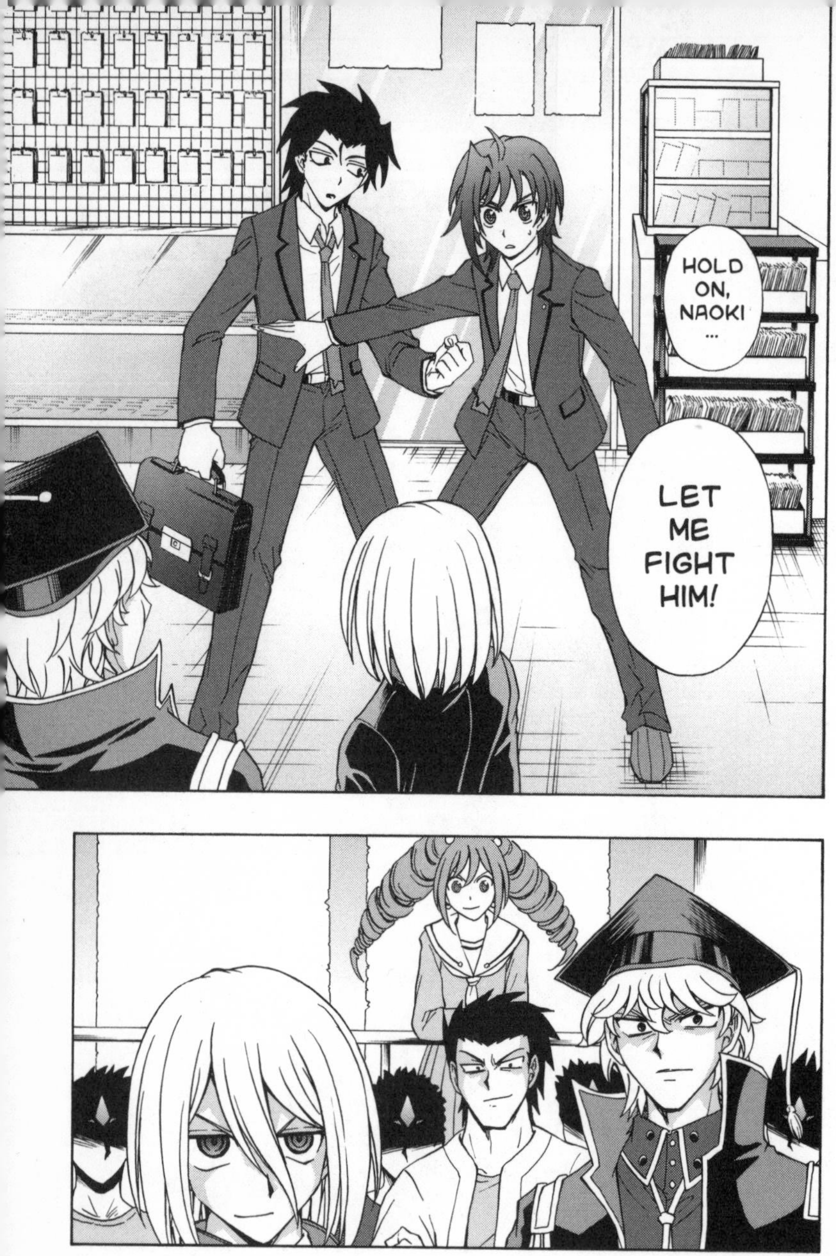
HOLD ON, NAOKI ...
LET ME FIGHT HIM!

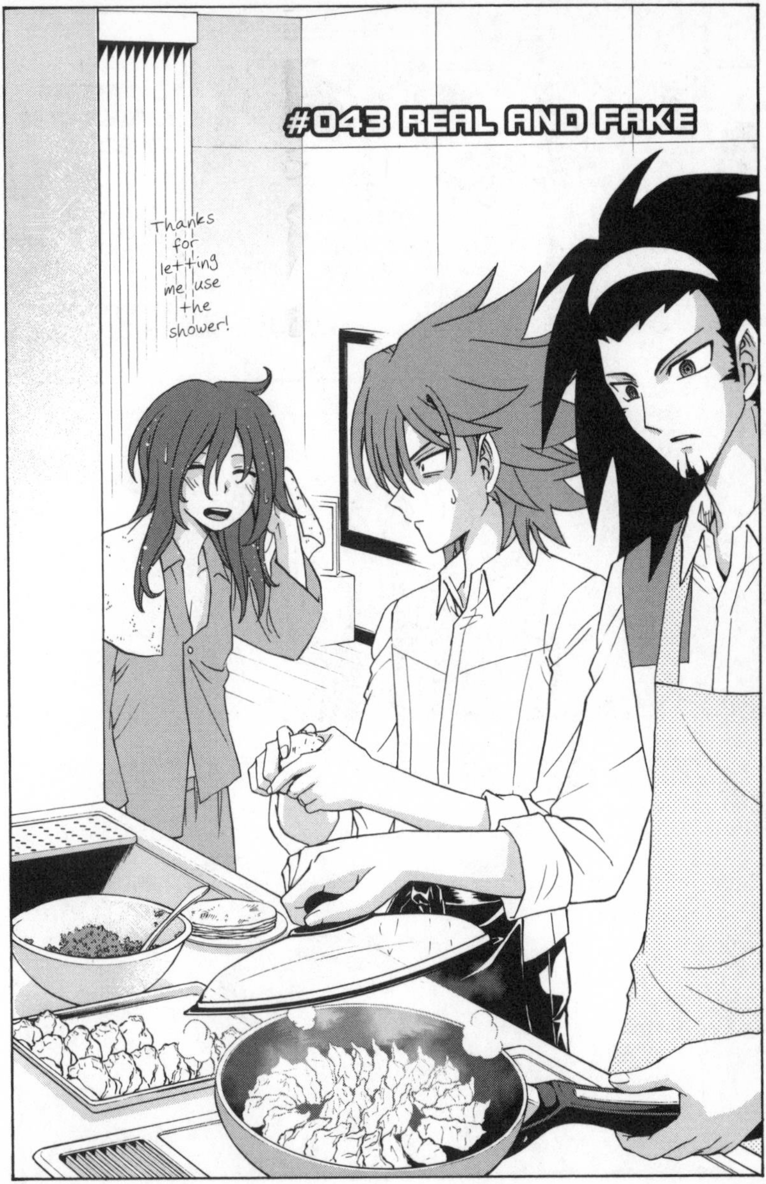
#043 REAL AND FAKE
Thanks for letting me use the shower!

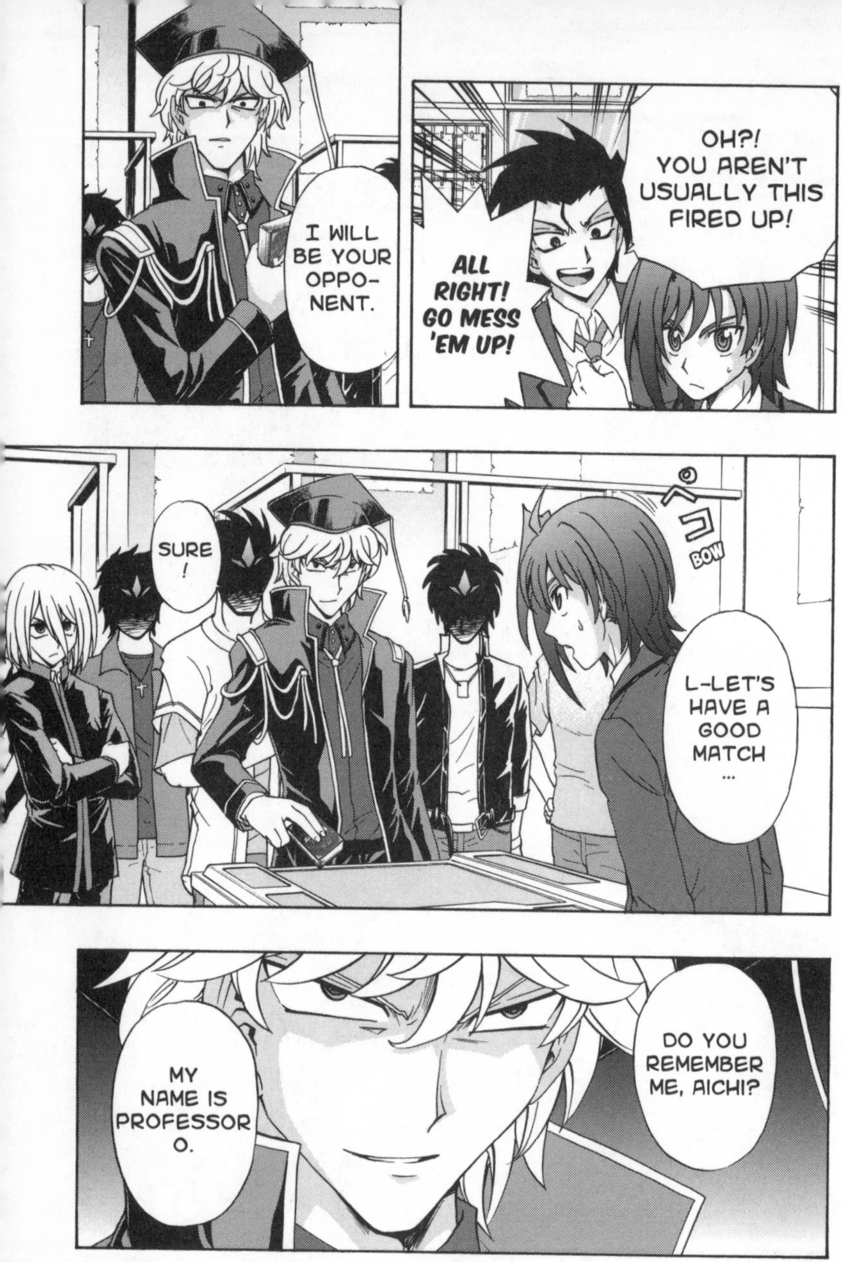
OH?! YOU AREN'T USUALLY THIS FIRED UP!
ALL RIGHT! GO MESS 'EM UP!
I WILL BE YOUR OPPO- NENT.
ペコ
BOW
L-LET'S HAVE A GOOD MATCH ...
SURE !
DO YOU REMEMBER ME, AICHI?
MY NAME IS PROFESSOR O.

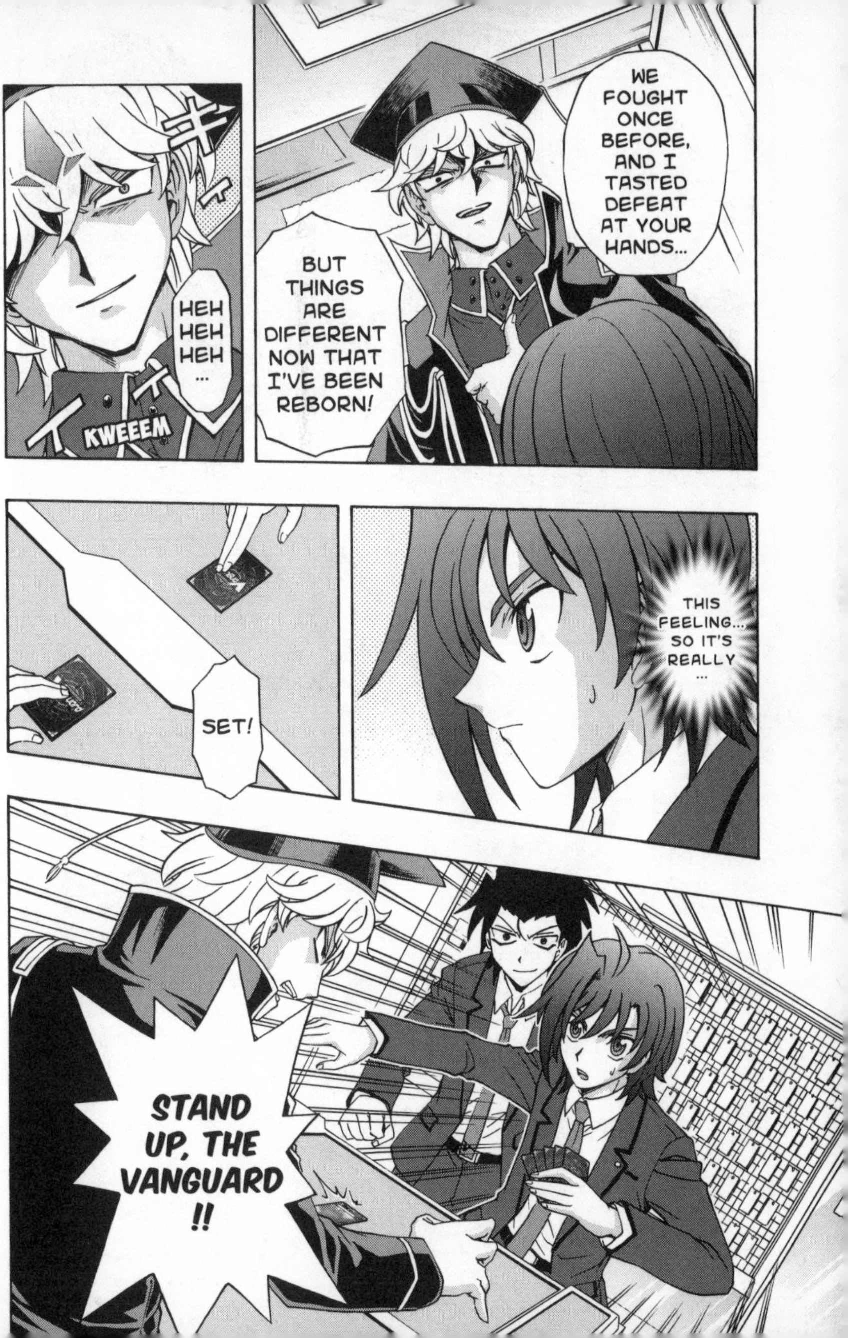
WE FOUGHT ONCE BEFORE, AND I TASTED DEFEAT AT YOUR HANDS...
BUT THINGS ARE DIFFERENT NOW THAT I'VE BEEN REBORN!
HEH HEH HEH ...
KWEEEM
THIS FEELING... SO IT'S REALLY ...
SET!
STAND UP, THE VANGUARD !!

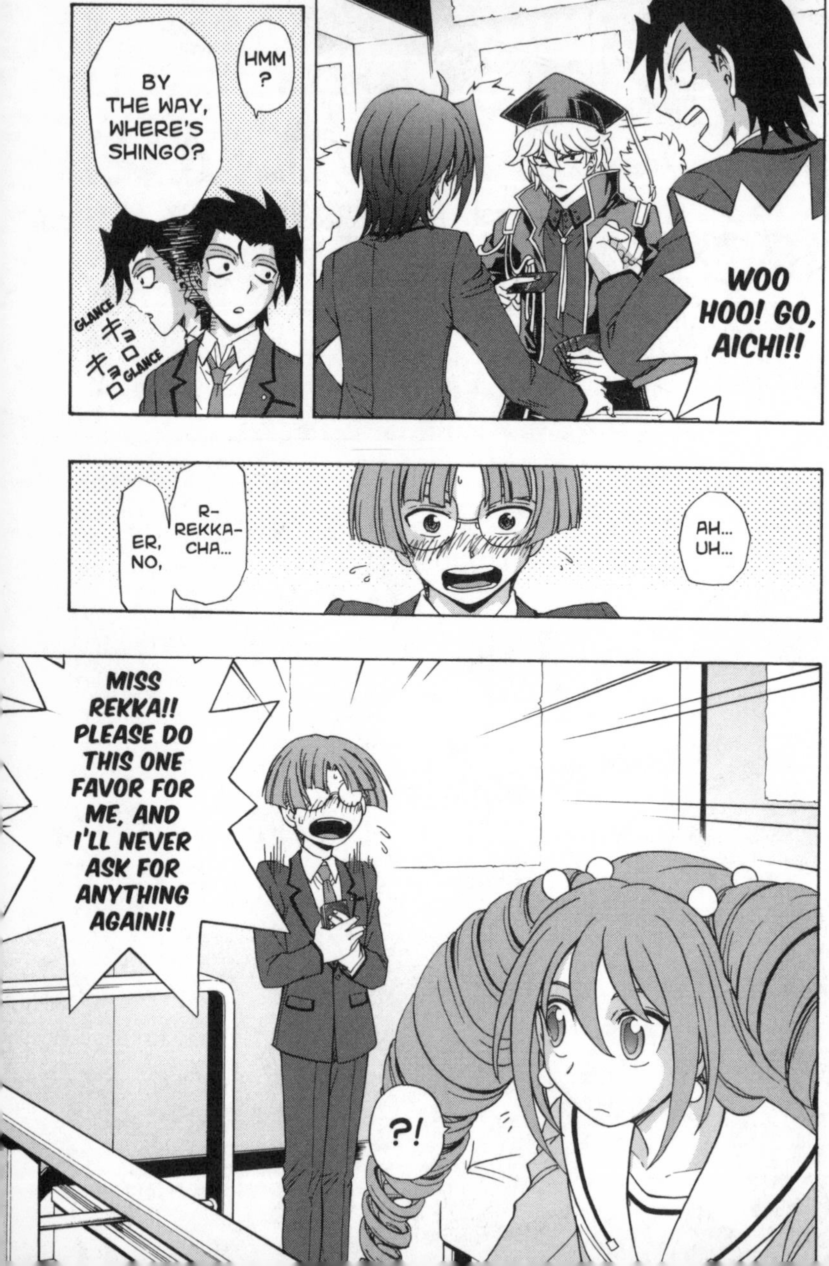
WOO HOO! GO, AICHI!!
HMM?
BY THE WAY, WHERE'S SHINGO?
キョロ GLANCE
キョロ GLANCE
AH... UH...
R-REKKA-CHA...
ER, NO,
MISS REKKA!! PLEASE DO THIS ONE FAVOR FOR ME, AND I'LL NEVER ASK FOR ANYTHING AGAIN!!
?!

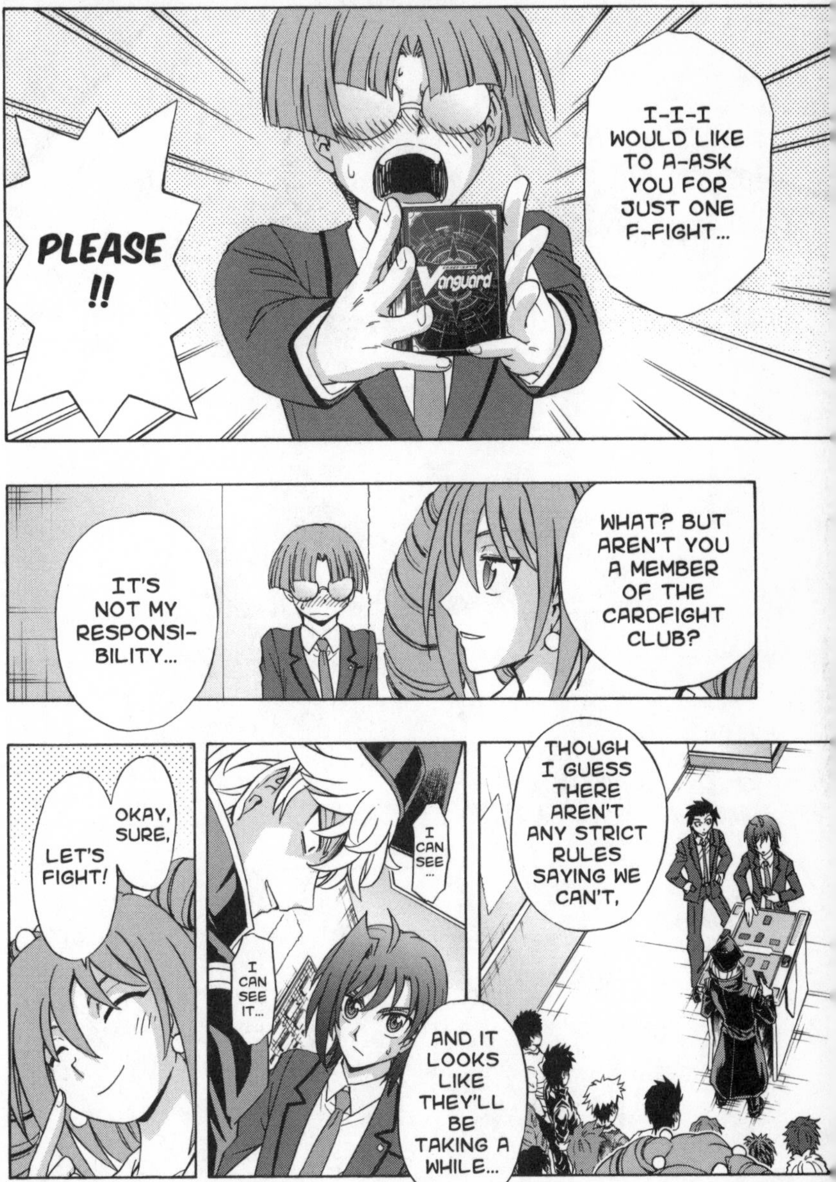
I-I-I WOULD LIKE TO A-ASK YOU FOR JUST ONE F-FIGHT...
PLEASE !!
WHAT? BUT AREN'T YOU A MEMBER OF THE CARDFIGHT CLUB?
IT'S NOT MY RESPONSI-BILITY...
THOUGH I GUESS THERE AREN'T ANY STRICT RULES SAYING WE CAN'T,
AND IT LOOKS LIKE THEY'LL BE TAKING A WHILE...
I CAN SEE...
I CAN SEE IT...
OKAY, SURE, LET'S FIGHT!

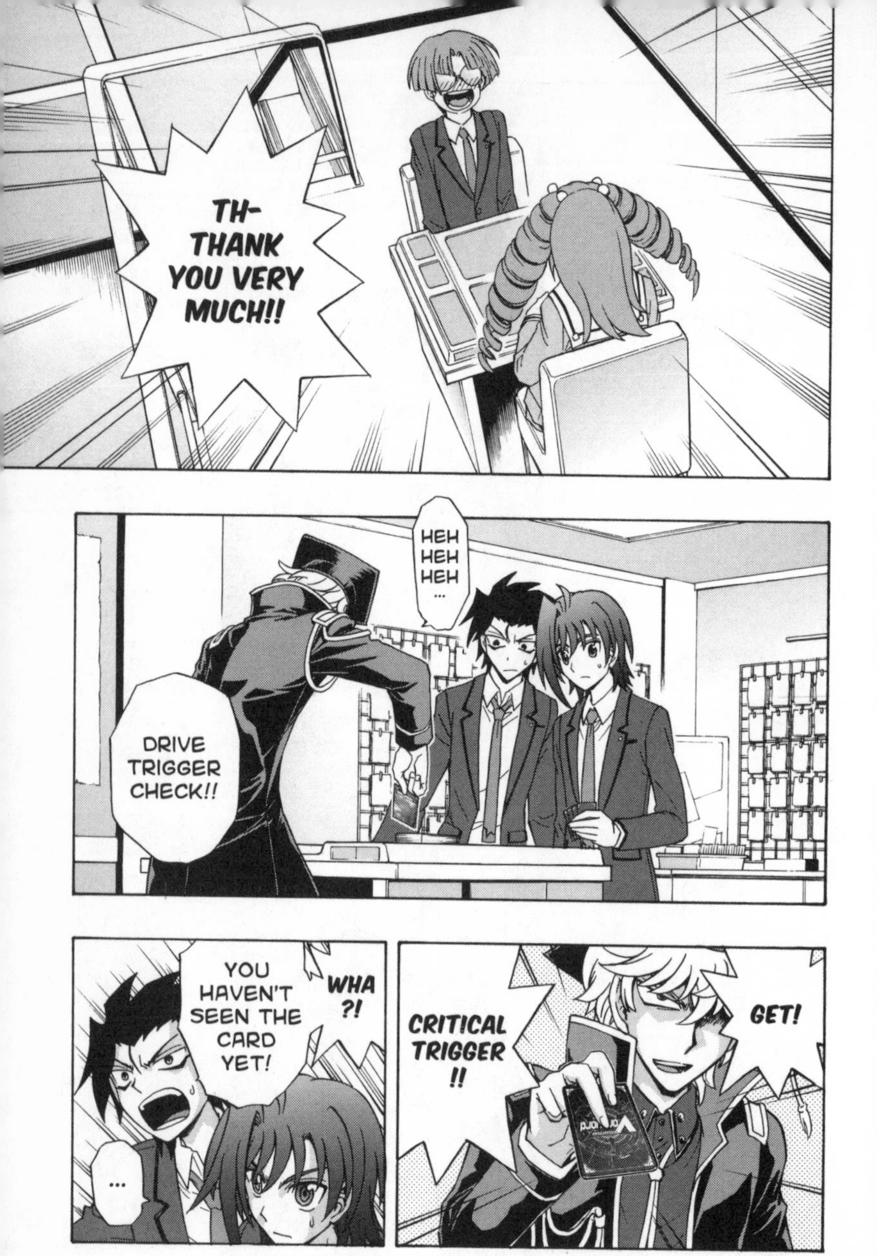
TH-
THANK
YOU VERY
MUCH!!
HEH
HEH
HEH
...
DRIVE
TRIGGER
CHECK!!
GET!
CRITICAL
TRIGGER
!!
WHA
?!
YOU
HAVEN'T
SEEN THE
CARD
YET!
...

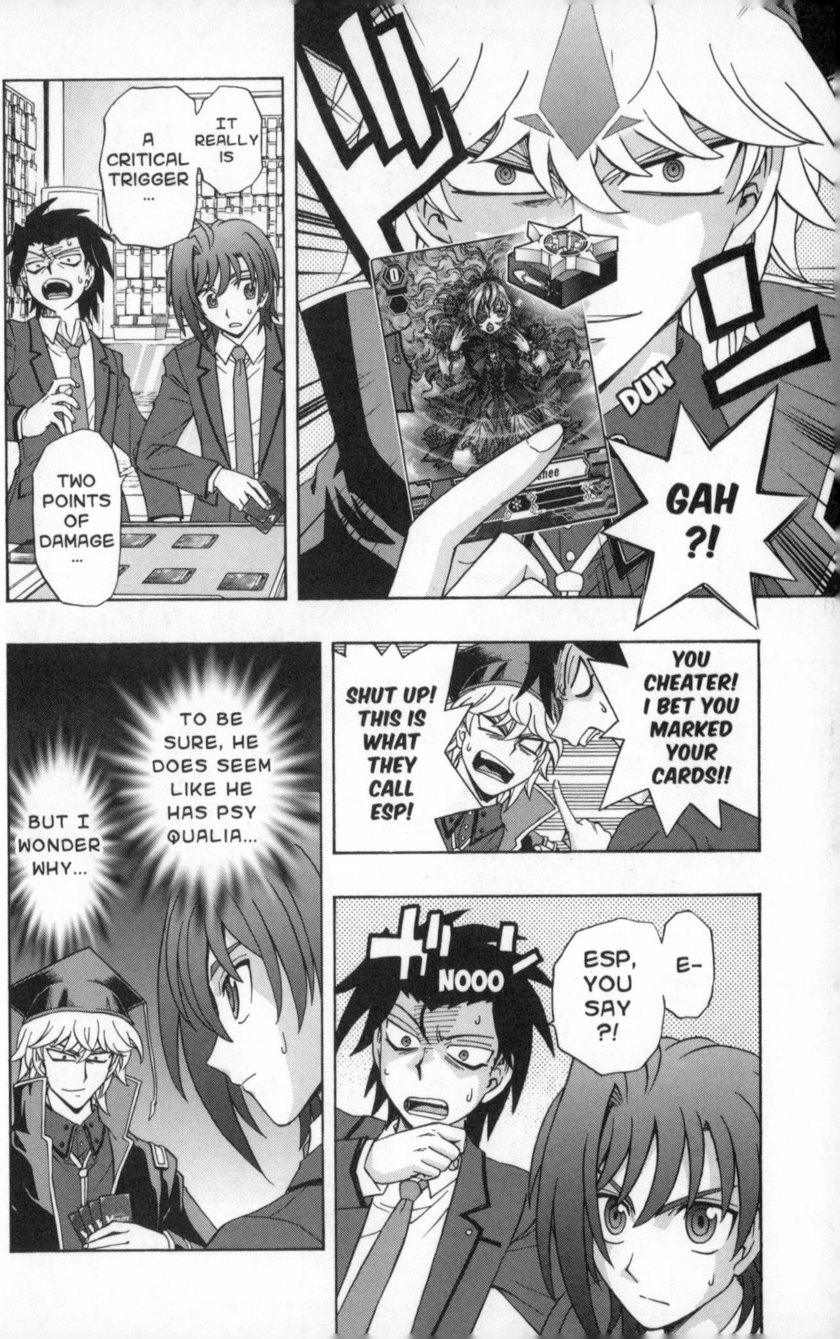
DUN
GAH ?!
IT REALLY IS
A CRITICAL TRIGGER ...
TWO POINTS OF DAMAGE ...
YOU CHEATER! I BET YOU MARKED YOUR CARDS!!
SHUT UP! THIS IS WHAT THEY CALL ESP!
E-
ESP, YOU SAY ?!
NOOO
TO BE SURE, HE DOES SEEM LIKE HE HAS PSY QUALIA...
BUT I WONDER WHY...

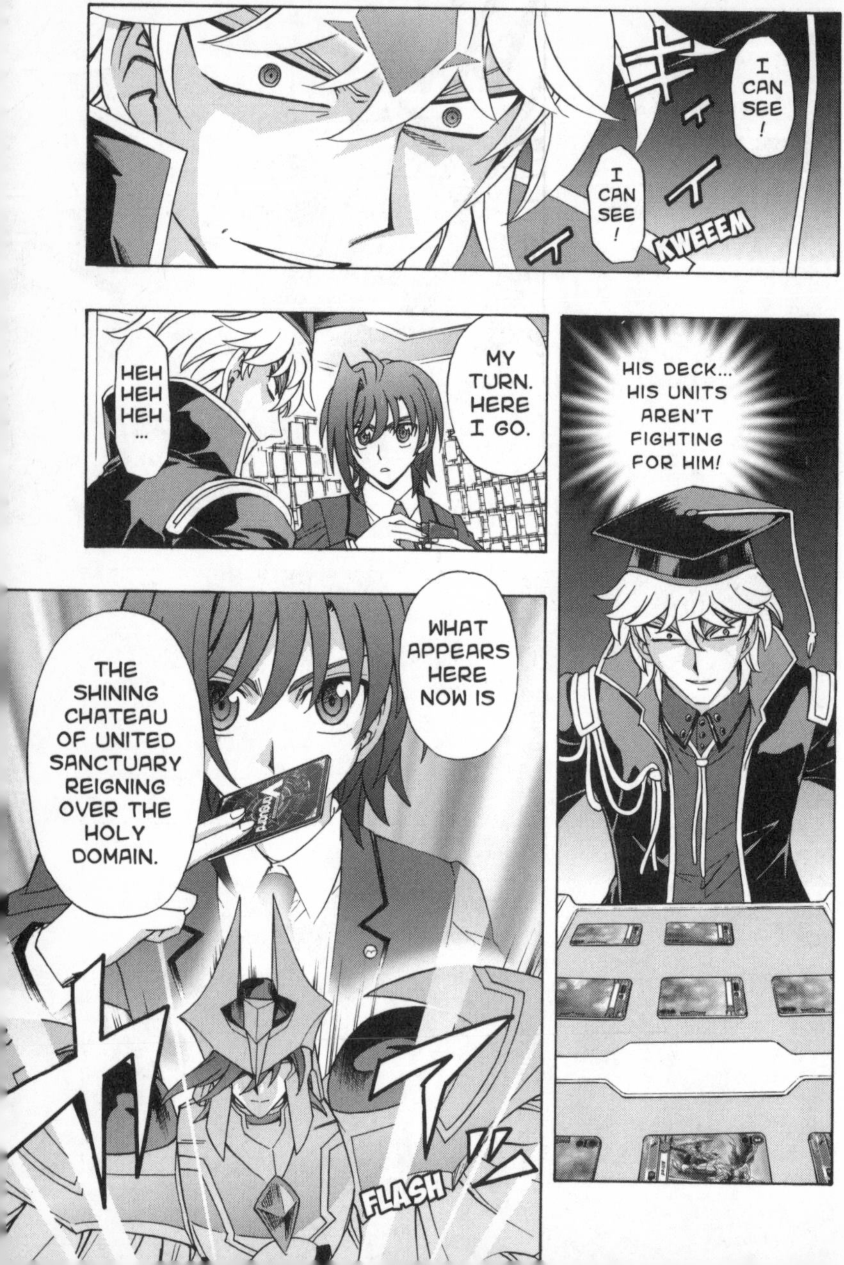
I CAN SEE!
I CAN SEE!
KWEEEM
HIS DECK... HIS UNITS AREN'T FIGHTING FOR HIM!
MY TURN. HERE I GO.
HEH HEH HEH ...
WHAT APPEARS HERE NOW IS
THE SHINING CHATEAU OF UNITED SANCTUARY REIGNING OVER THE HOLY DOMAIN.
FLASH

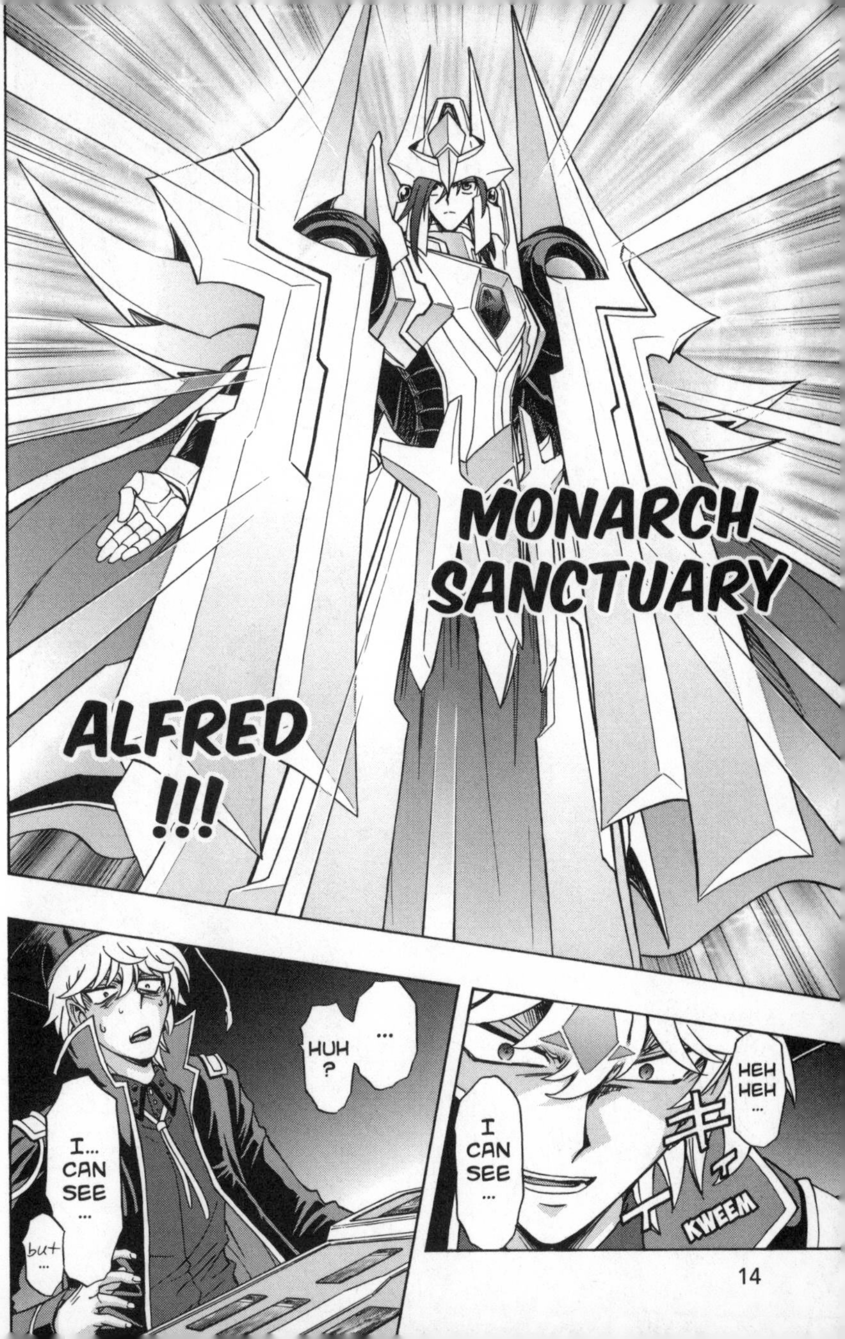
MONARCH SANCTUARY
ALFRED !!!
HEH HEH ...
I CAN SEE ...
KWEEM
... HUH?
I... CAN SEE ...
but ...

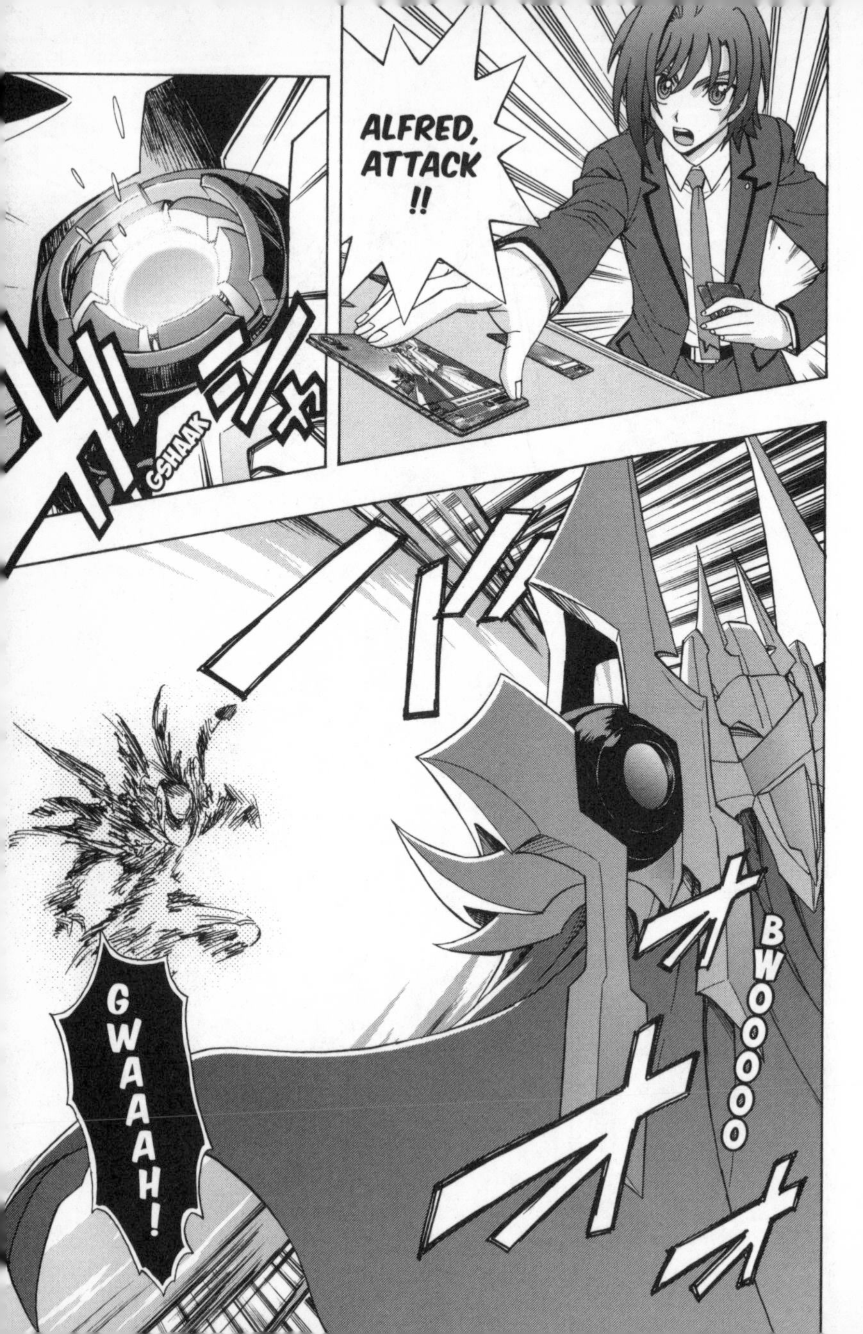
ALFRED, ATTACK !!
GSHAAK
BWOOOOOOO
GWAAAH!

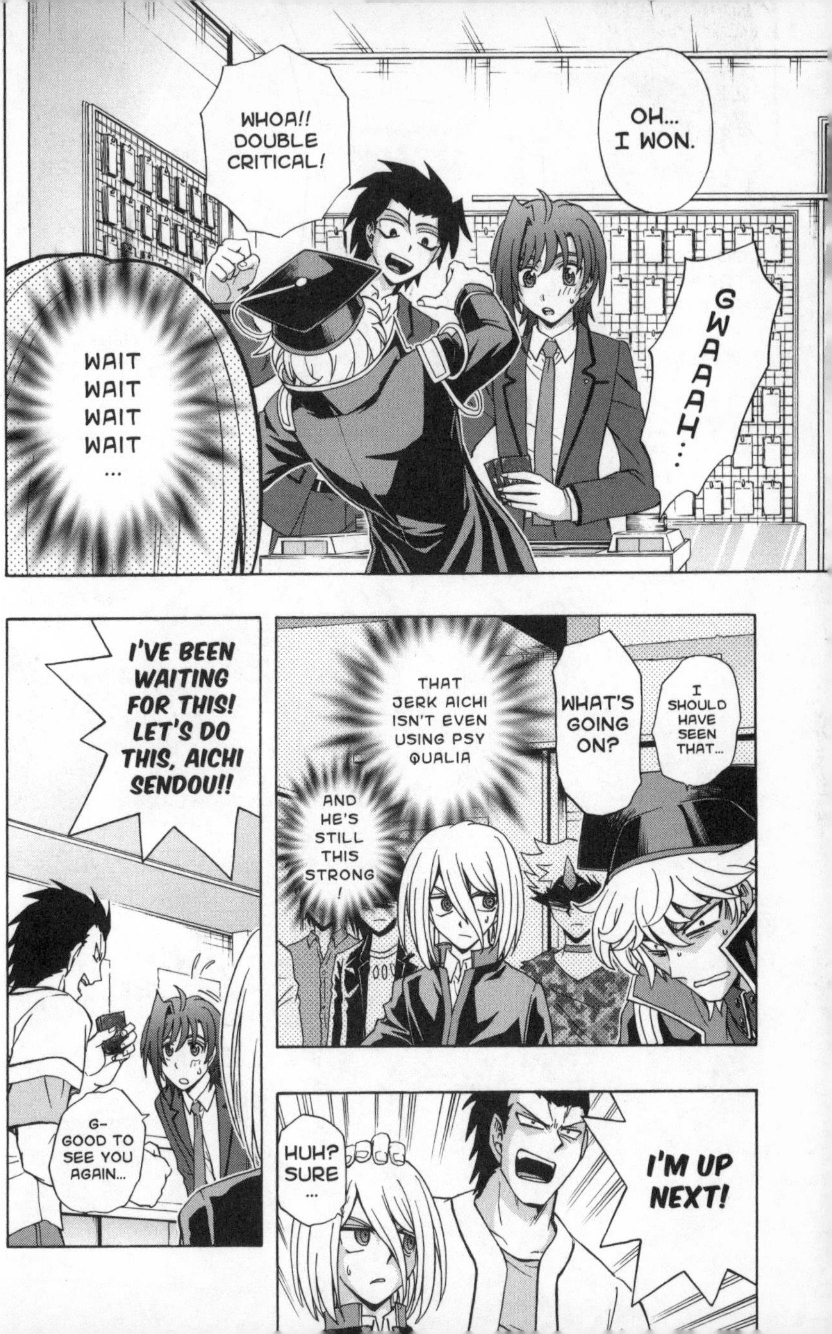
OH... I WON.
WHOA!! DOUBLE CRITICAL!
GWAAAAH...
WAIT WAIT WAIT WAIT ...
I SHOULD HAVE SEEN THAT...
WHAT'S GOING ON?
THAT JERK AICHI ISN'T EVEN USING PSY QUALIA
AND HE'S STILL THIS STRONG!
I'M UP NEXT!
HUH? SURE ...
I'VE BEEN WAITING FOR THIS! LET'S DO THIS, AICHI SENDOU!!
G-GOOD TO SEE YOU AGAIN...

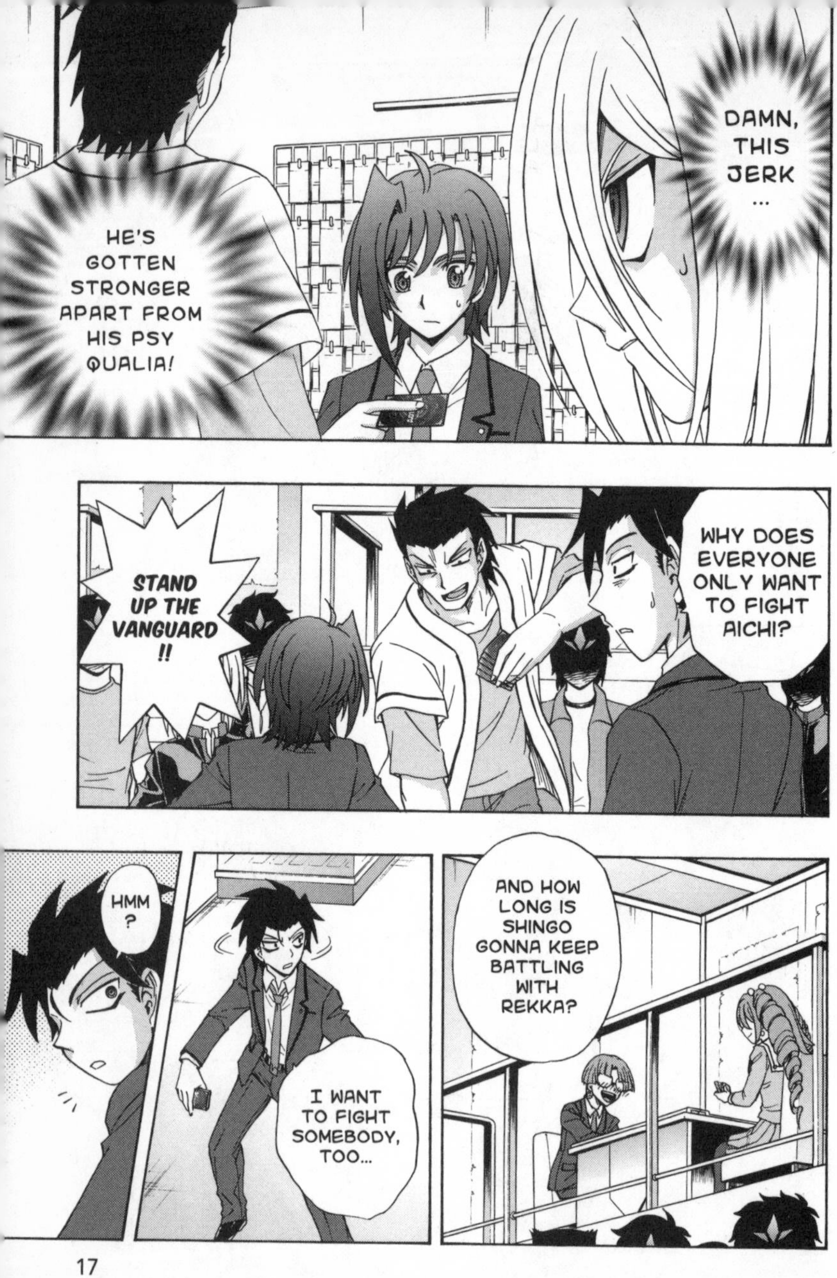
DAMN, THIS JERK ...
HE'S GOTTEN STRONGER APART FROM HIS PSY QUALIA!
WHY DOES EVERYONE ONLY WANT TO FIGHT AICHI?
STAND UP THE VANGUARD !!
AND HOW LONG IS SHINGO GONNA KEEP BATTLING WITH REKKA?
I WANT TO FIGHT SOMEBODY, TOO...
HMM ?

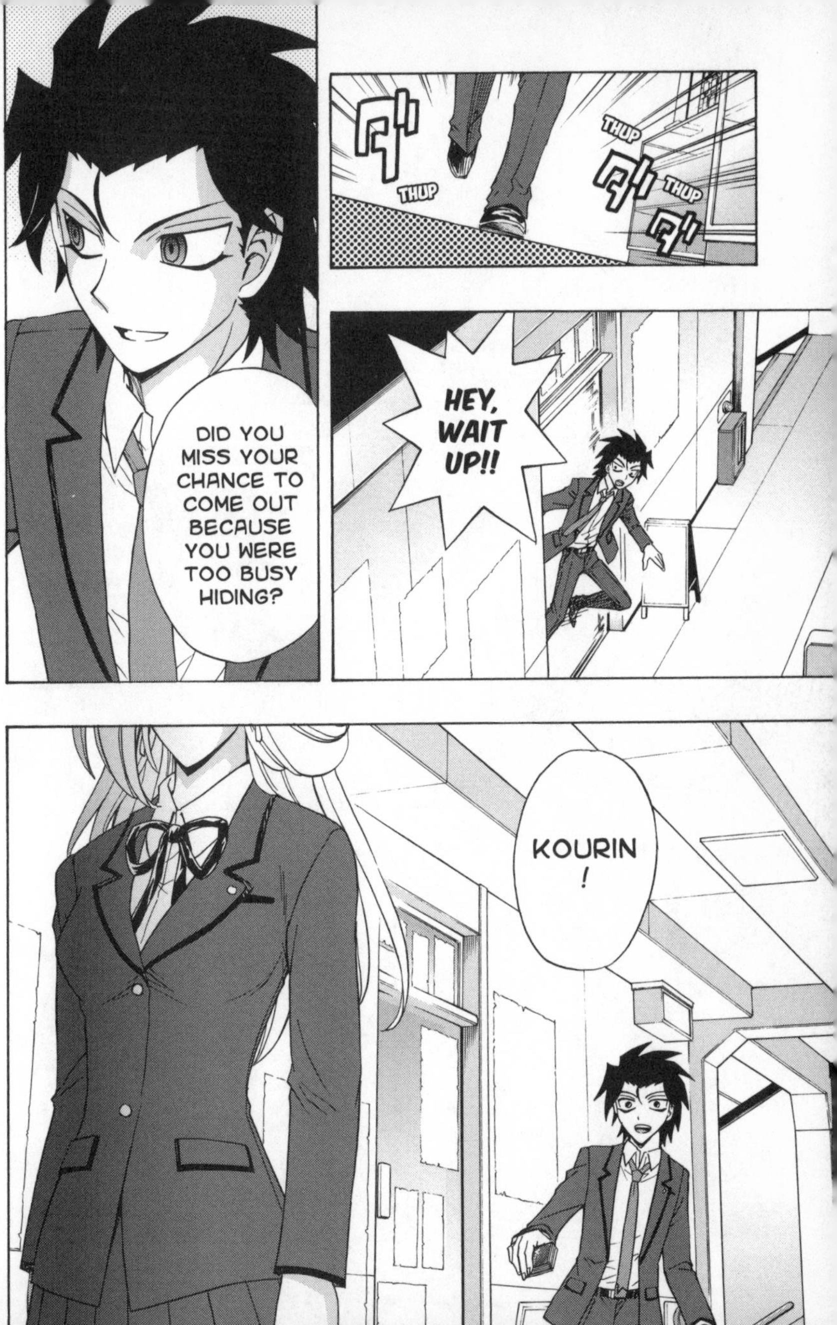
THUP
THUP
THUP
HEY, WAIT UP!!
DID YOU MISS YOUR CHANCE TO COME OUT BECAUSE YOU WERE TOO BUSY HIDING?
KOURIN!

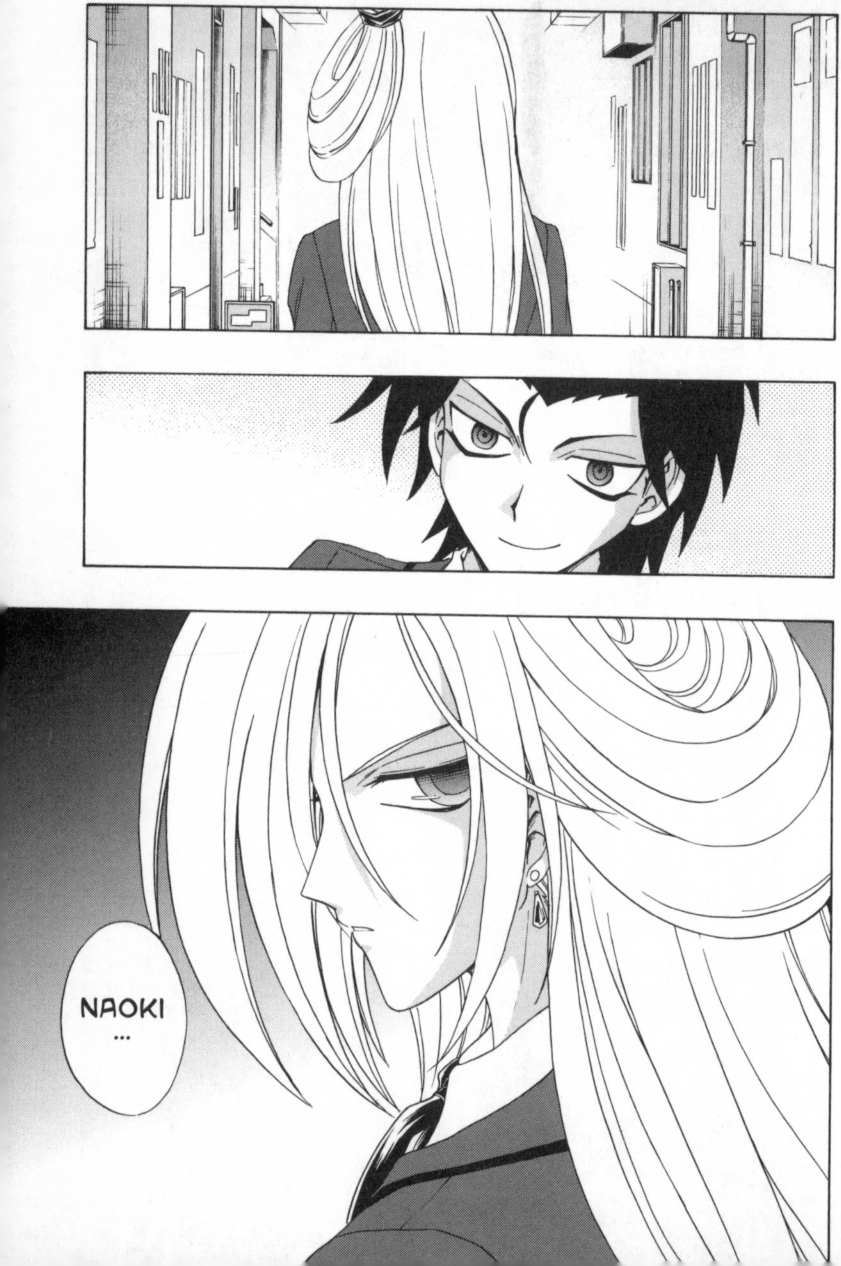
NAOKI
...

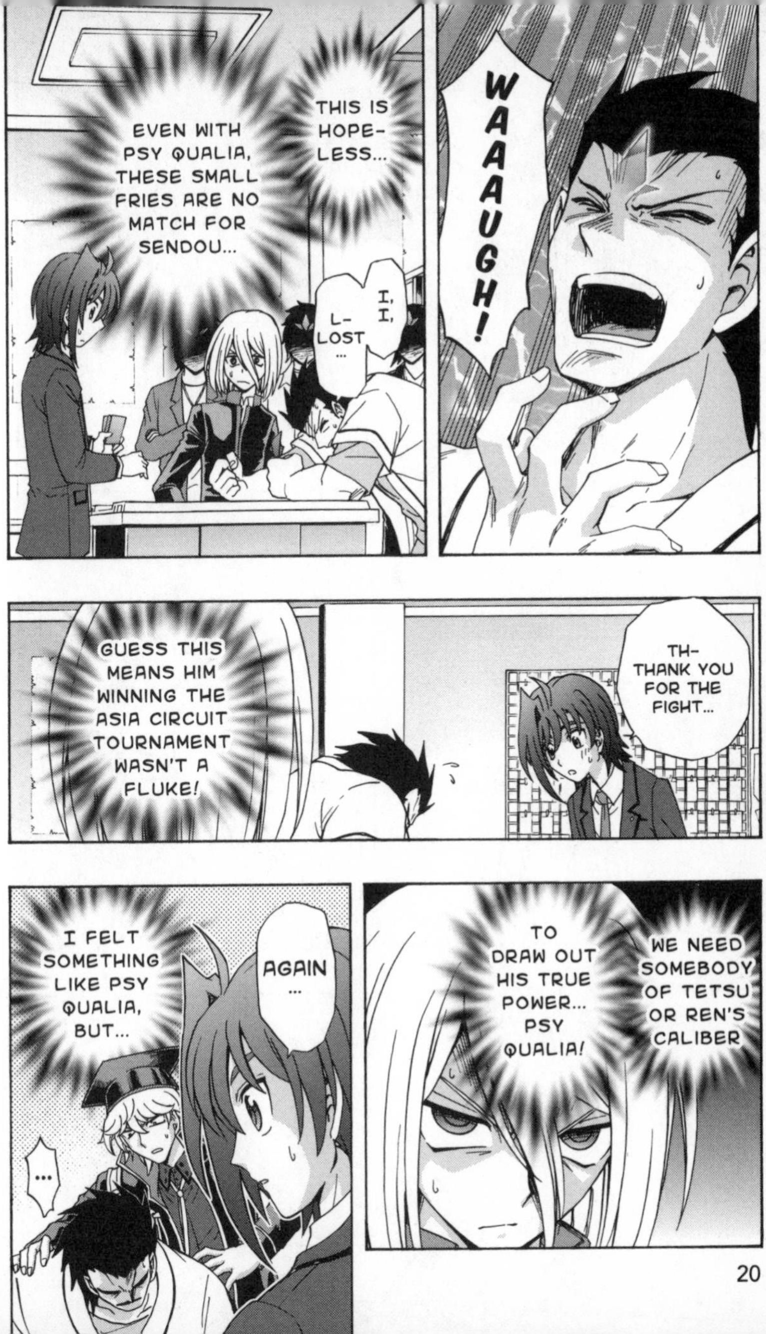
WAAAAUGH!
THIS IS HOPELESS...
EVEN WITH PSY QUALIA, THESE SMALL FRIES ARE NO MATCH FOR SENDOU...
I, I, L-LOST ...
TH-THANK YOU FOR THE FIGHT...
GUESS THIS MEANS HIM WINNING THE ASIA CIRCUIT TOURNAMENT WASN'T A FLUKE!
WE NEED SOMEBODY OF TETSU OR REN'S CALIBER
TO DRAW OUT HIS TRUE POWER... PSY QUALIA!
AGAIN ...
I FELT SOMETHING LIKE PSY QUALIA, BUT...
...

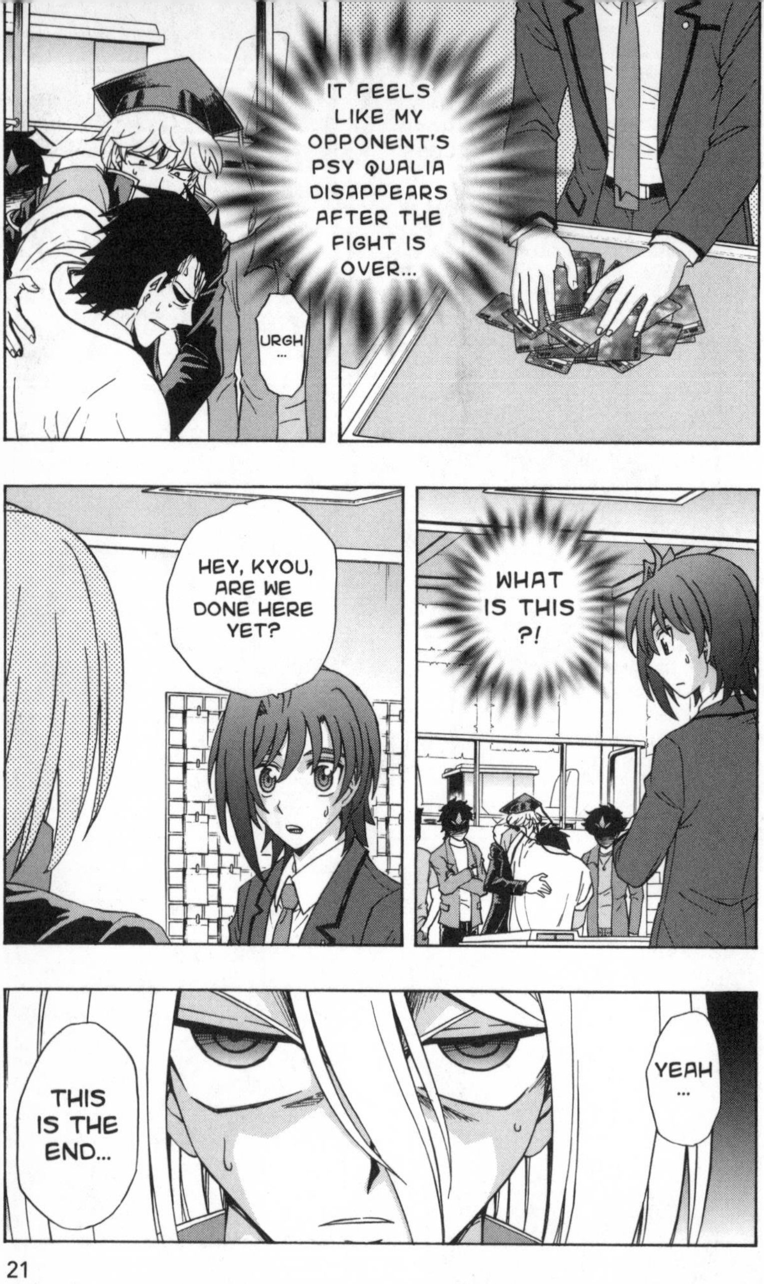
IT FEELS LIKE MY OPPONENT'S PSY QUALIA DISAPPEARS AFTER THE FIGHT IS OVER...
URGH...
WHAT IS THIS?!
HEY, KYOU, ARE WE DONE HERE YET?
YEAH...
THIS IS THE END...

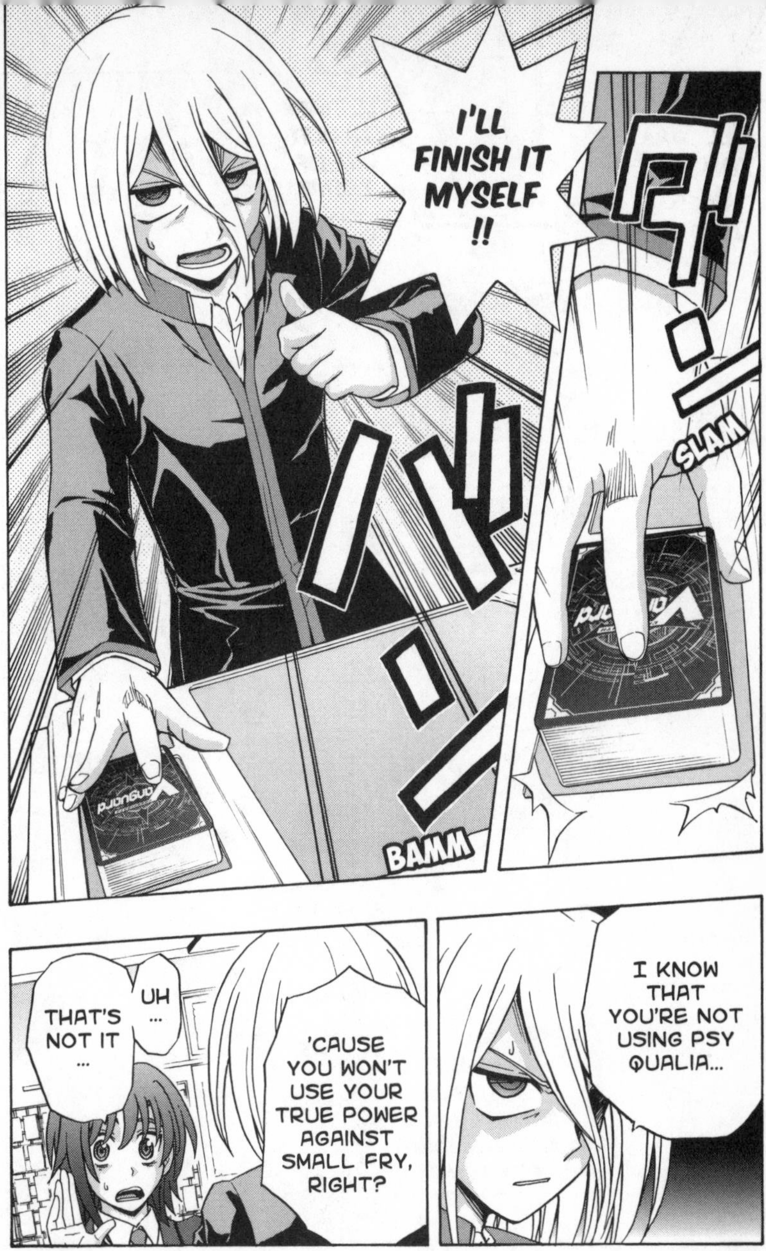
SLAM
I'LL FINISH IT MYSELF !!
BAMM
I KNOW THAT YOU'RE NOT USING PSY QUALIA...
'CAUSE YOU WON'T USE YOUR TRUE POWER AGAINST SMALL FRY, RIGHT?
UH ...
THAT'S NOT IT ...

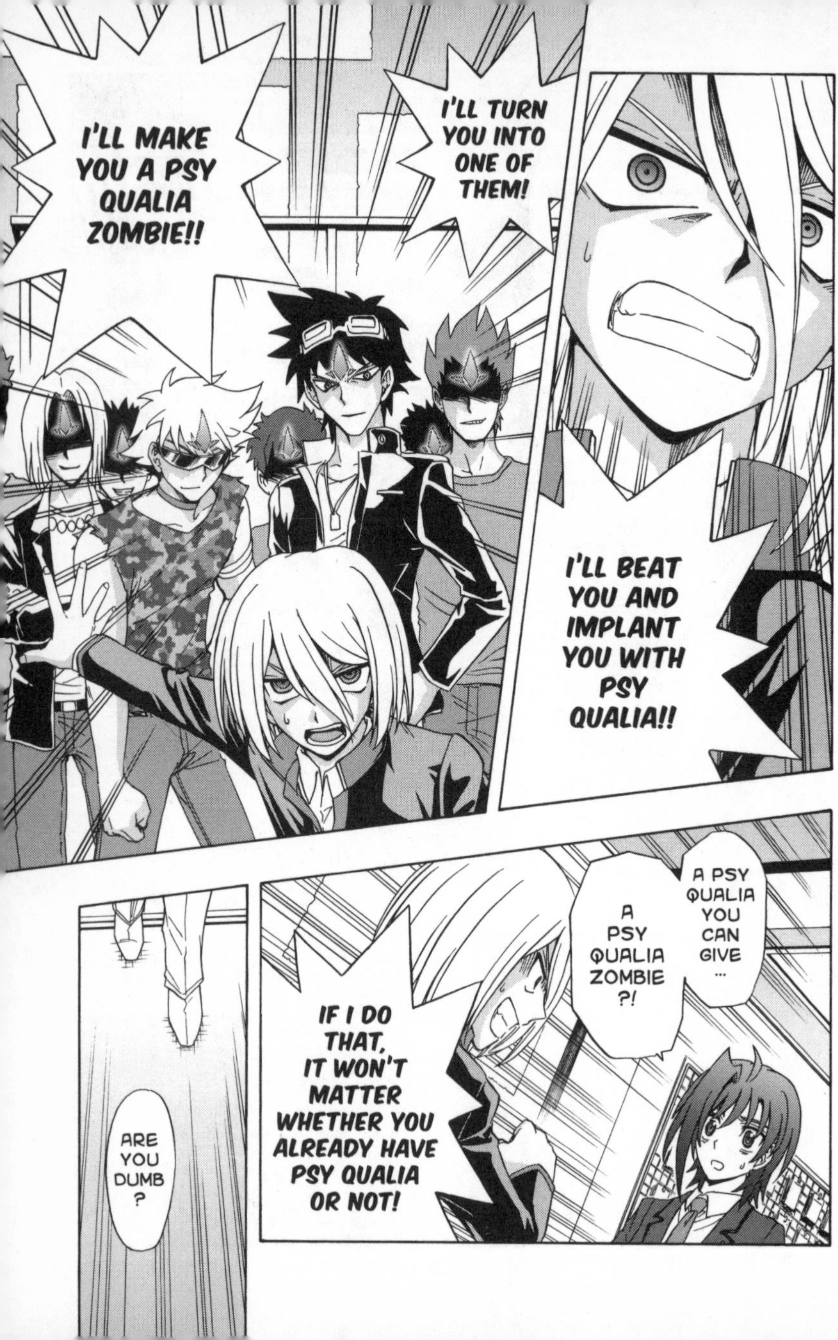
I'LL BEAT YOU AND IMPLANT YOU WITH PSY QUALIA!!
I'LL TURN YOU INTO ONE OF THEM!
I'LL MAKE YOU A PSY QUALIA ZOMBIE!!
A PSY QUALIA YOU CAN GIVE ...
A PSY QUALIA ZOMBIE ?!
IF I DO THAT, IT WON'T MATTER WHETHER YOU ALREADY HAVE PSY QUALIA OR NOT!
ARE YOU DUMB ?

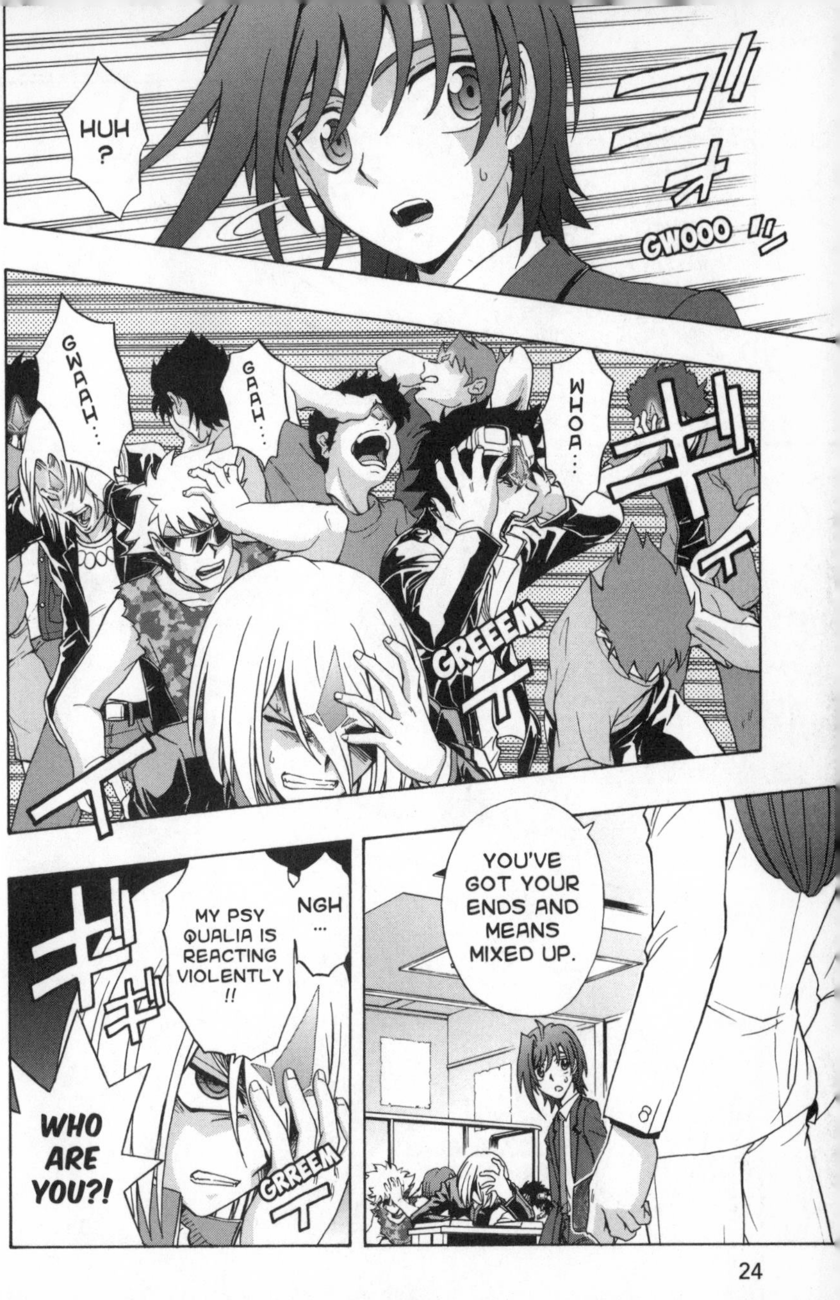
HUH?
GWOOO
WHOA...
GAAH...
GWAAAH...
GREEEM
YOU'VE GOT YOUR ENDS AND MEANS MIXED UP.
NGH...
MY PSY QUALIA IS REACTING VIOLENTLY!!
WHO ARE YOU?!
GRREEM

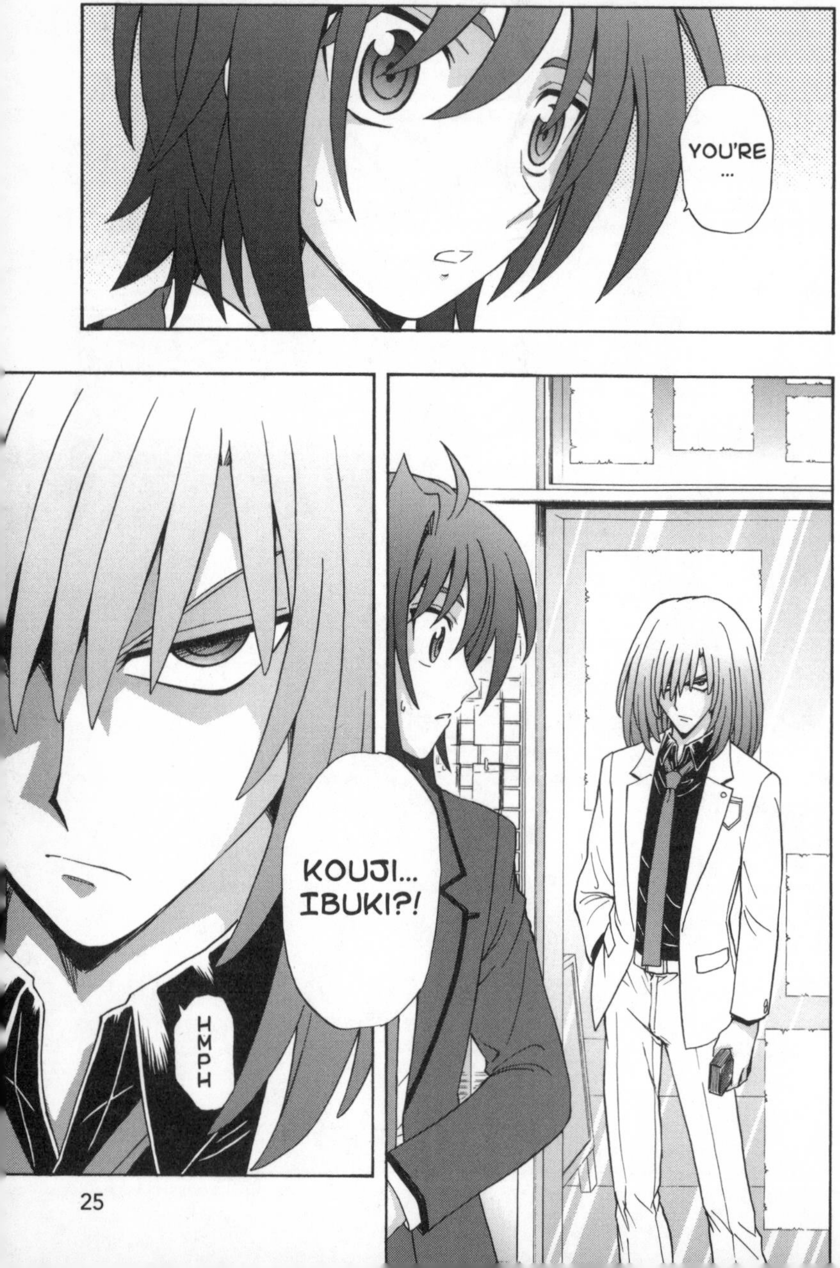
YOU'RE ...
KOUJI... IBUKI?!
HMPH

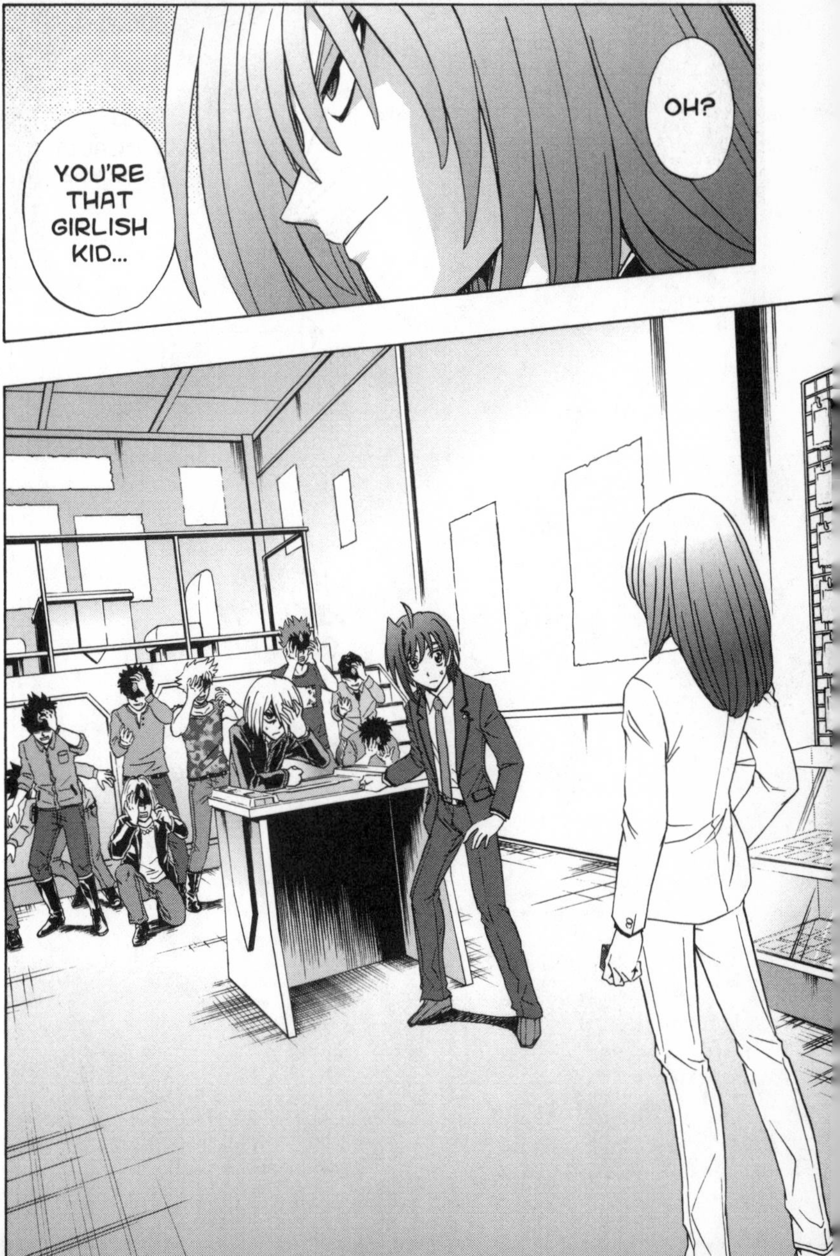
OH?
YOU'RE THAT GIRLISH KID...

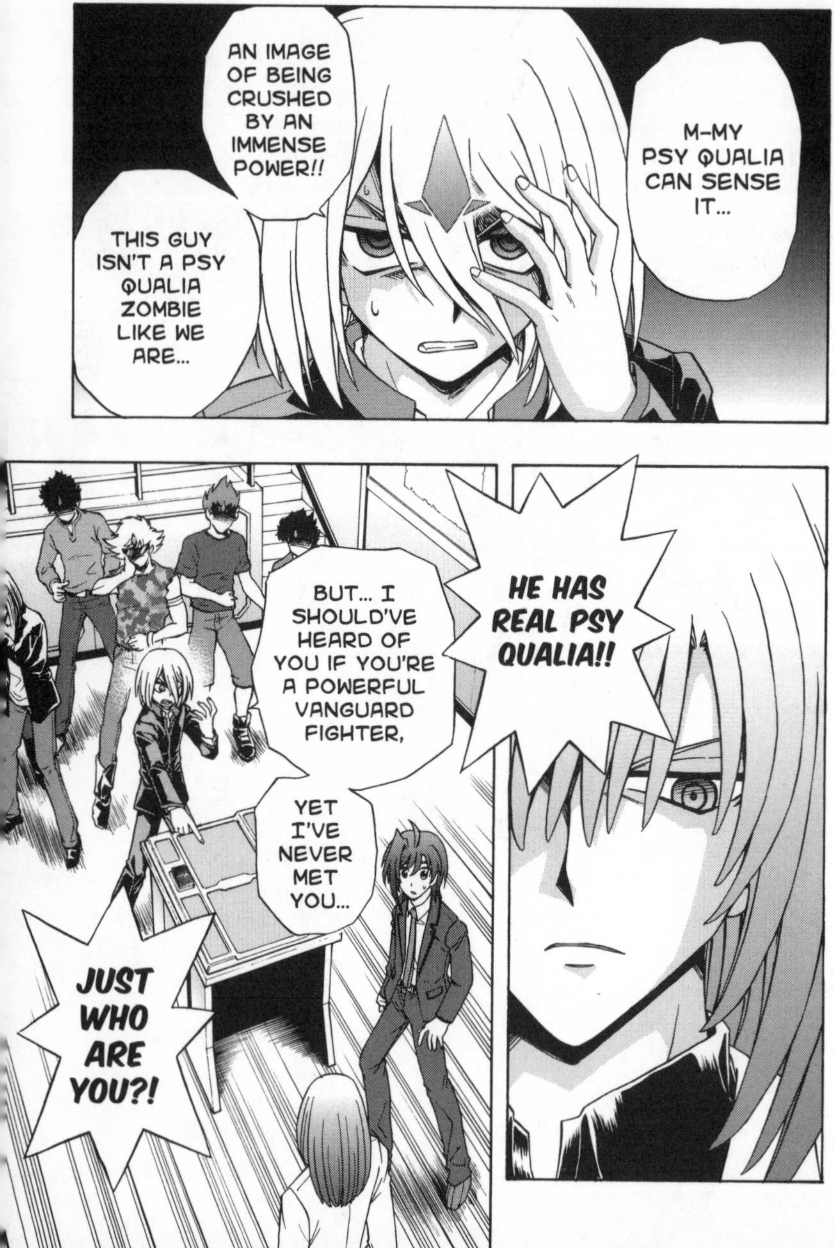
M-MY PSY QUALIA CAN SENSE IT...
AN IMAGE OF BEING CRUSHED BY AN IMMENSE POWER!!
THIS GUY ISN'T A PSY QUALIA ZOMBIE LIKE WE ARE...
HE HAS REAL PSY QUALIA!!
BUT... I SHOULD'VE HEARD OF YOU IF YOU'RE A POWERFUL VANGUARD FIGHTER,
YET I'VE NEVER MET YOU...
JUST WHO ARE YOU?!

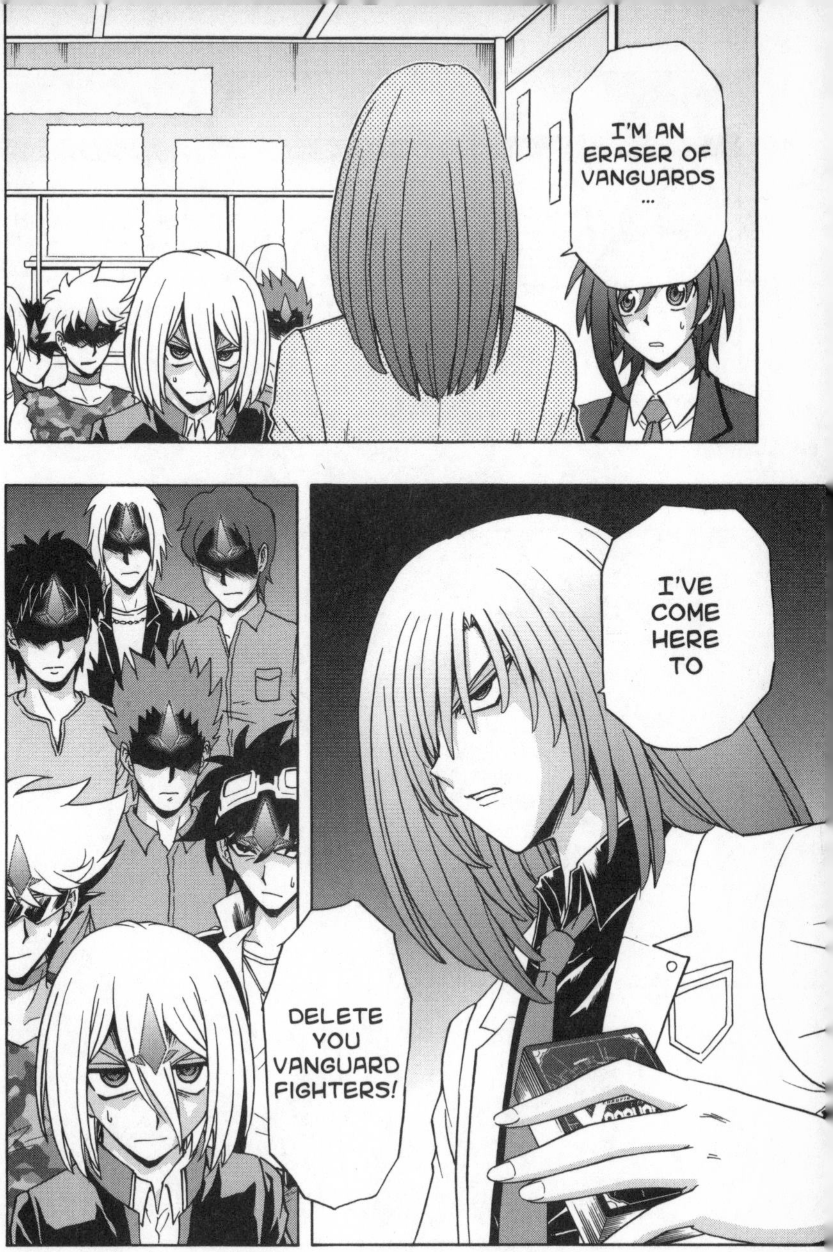
I'M AN ERASER OF VANGUARDS ...
I'VE COME HERE TO
DELETE YOU VANGUARD FIGHTERS!

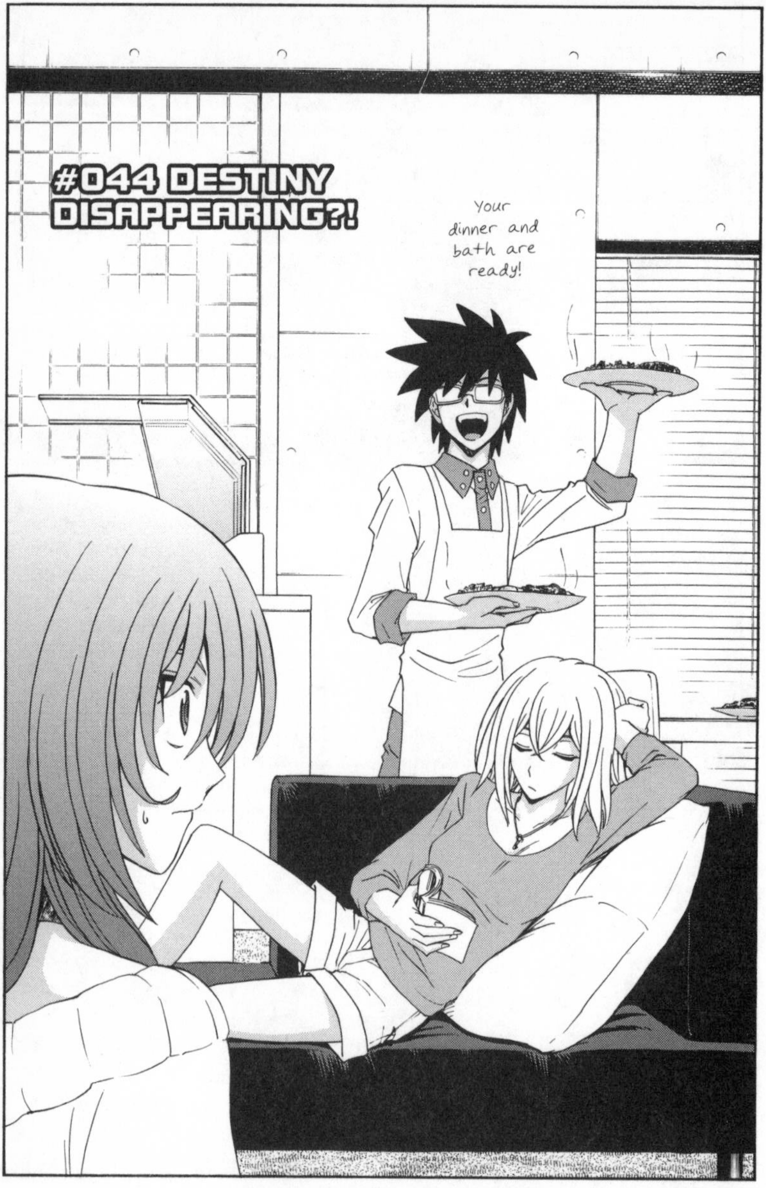
#044 DESTINY DISAPPEARING?!
Your dinner and bath are ready!

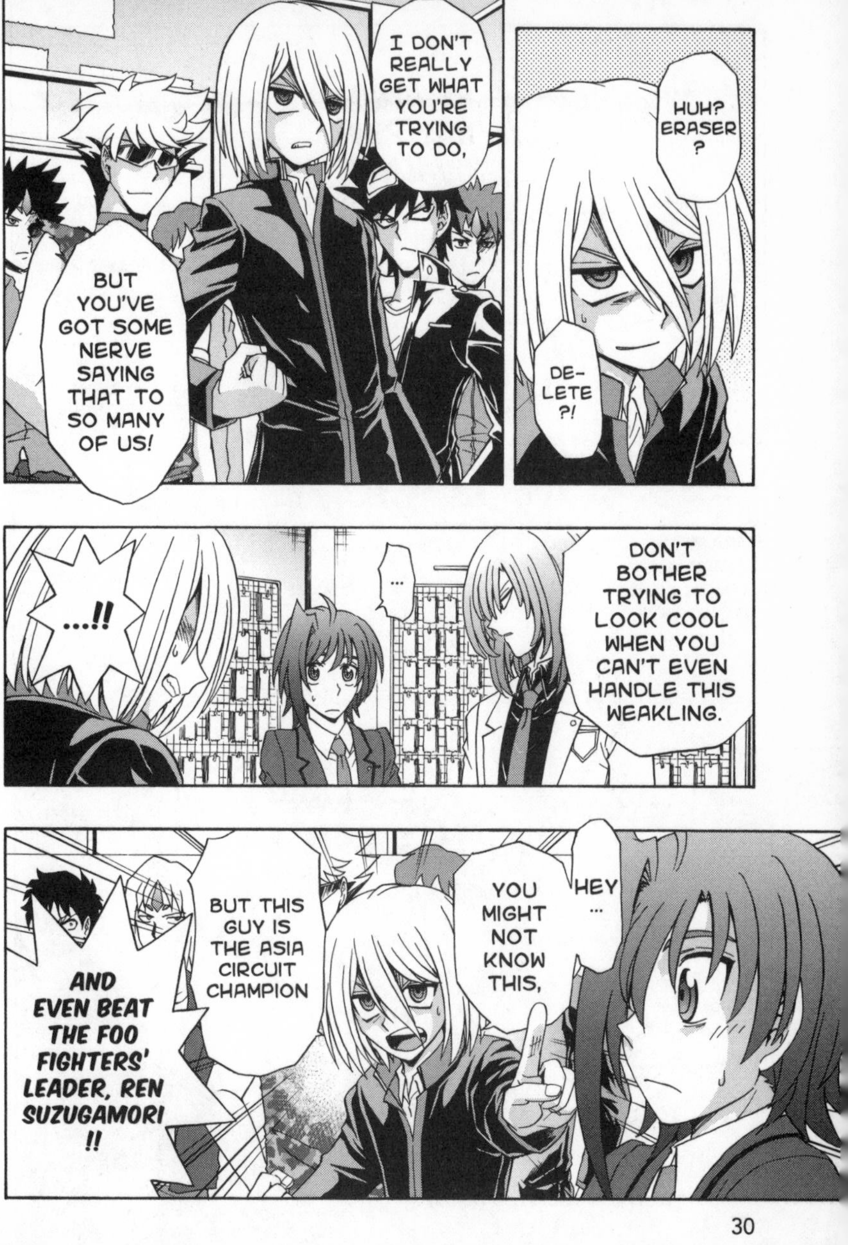
HUH? ERASER ?
DE-LETE ?!
I DON'T REALLY GET WHAT YOU'RE TRYING TO DO,
BUT YOU'VE GOT SOME NERVE SAYING THAT TO SO MANY OF US!
DON'T BOTHER TRYING TO LOOK COOL WHEN YOU CAN'T EVEN HANDLE THIS WEAKLING.
...
...!!
HEY ...
YOU MIGHT NOT KNOW THIS,
BUT THIS GUY IS THE ASIA CIRCUIT CHAMPION
AND EVEN BEAT THE FOO FIGHTERS' LEADER, REN SUZUGAMORI !!

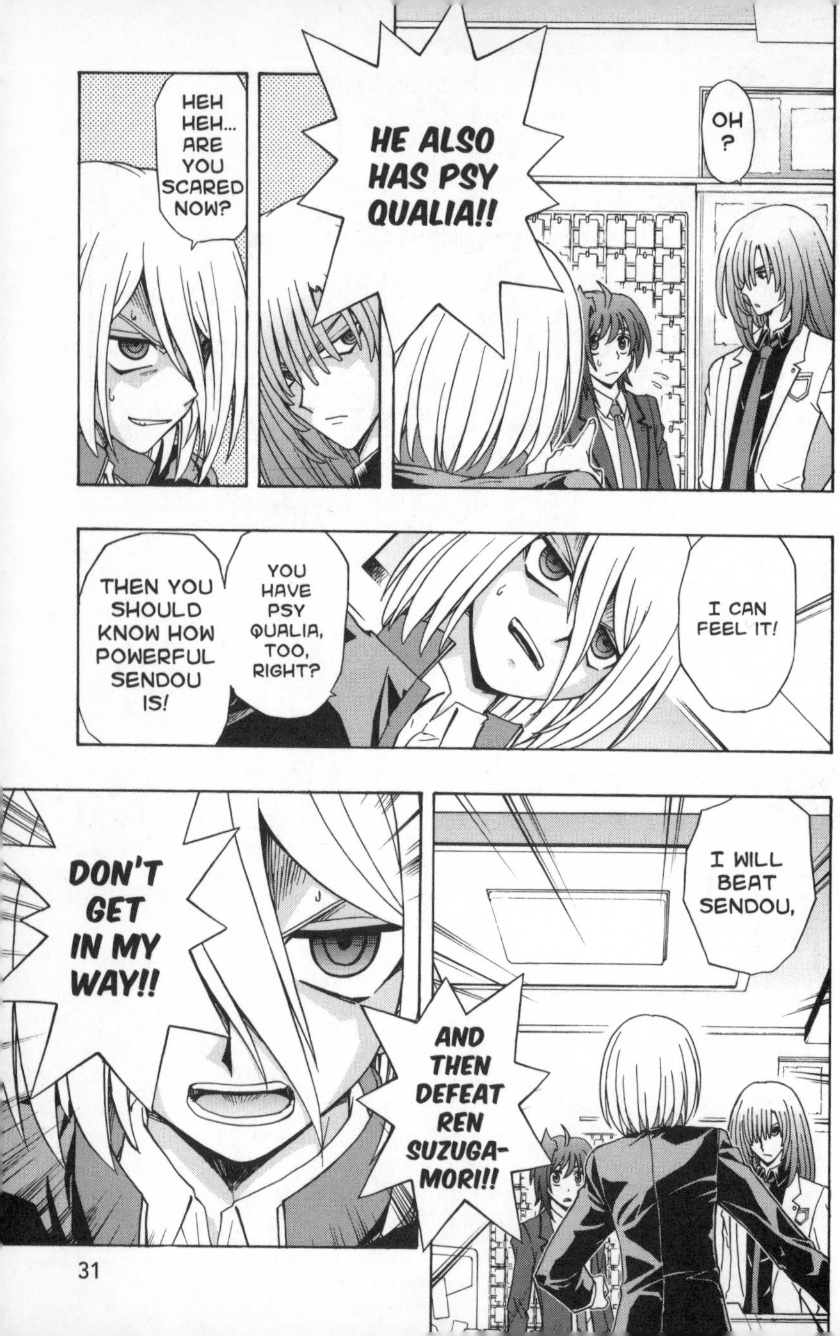
OH?
HE ALSO HAS PSY QUALIA!!
HEH HEH... ARE YOU SCARED NOW?
I CAN FEEL IT!
YOU HAVE PSY QUALIA, TOO, RIGHT?
THEN YOU SHOULD KNOW HOW POWERFUL SENDOU IS!
I WILL BEAT SENDOU,
AND THEN DEFEAT REN SUZUGA-MORI!!
DON'T GET IN MY WAY!!

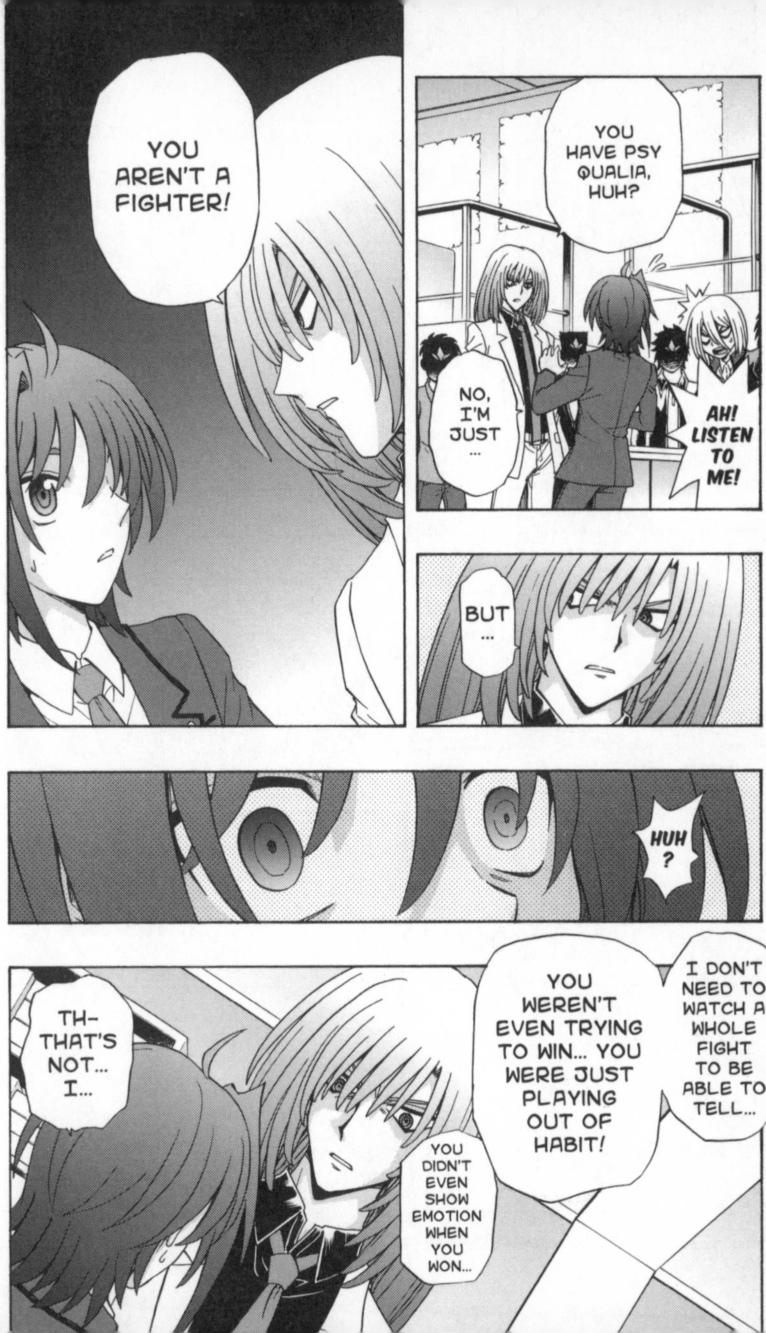
YOU HAVE PSY QUALIA, HUH?
AH! LISTEN TO ME!
NO, I'M JUST ...
BUT ...
YOU AREN'T A FIGHTER!
HUH ?
I DON'T NEED TO WATCH A WHOLE FIGHT TO BE ABLE TO TELL...
YOU WEREN'T EVEN TRYING TO WIN... YOU WERE JUST PLAYING OUT OF HABIT!
YOU DIDN'T EVEN SHOW EMOTION WHEN YOU WON...
TH-THAT'S NOT... I...

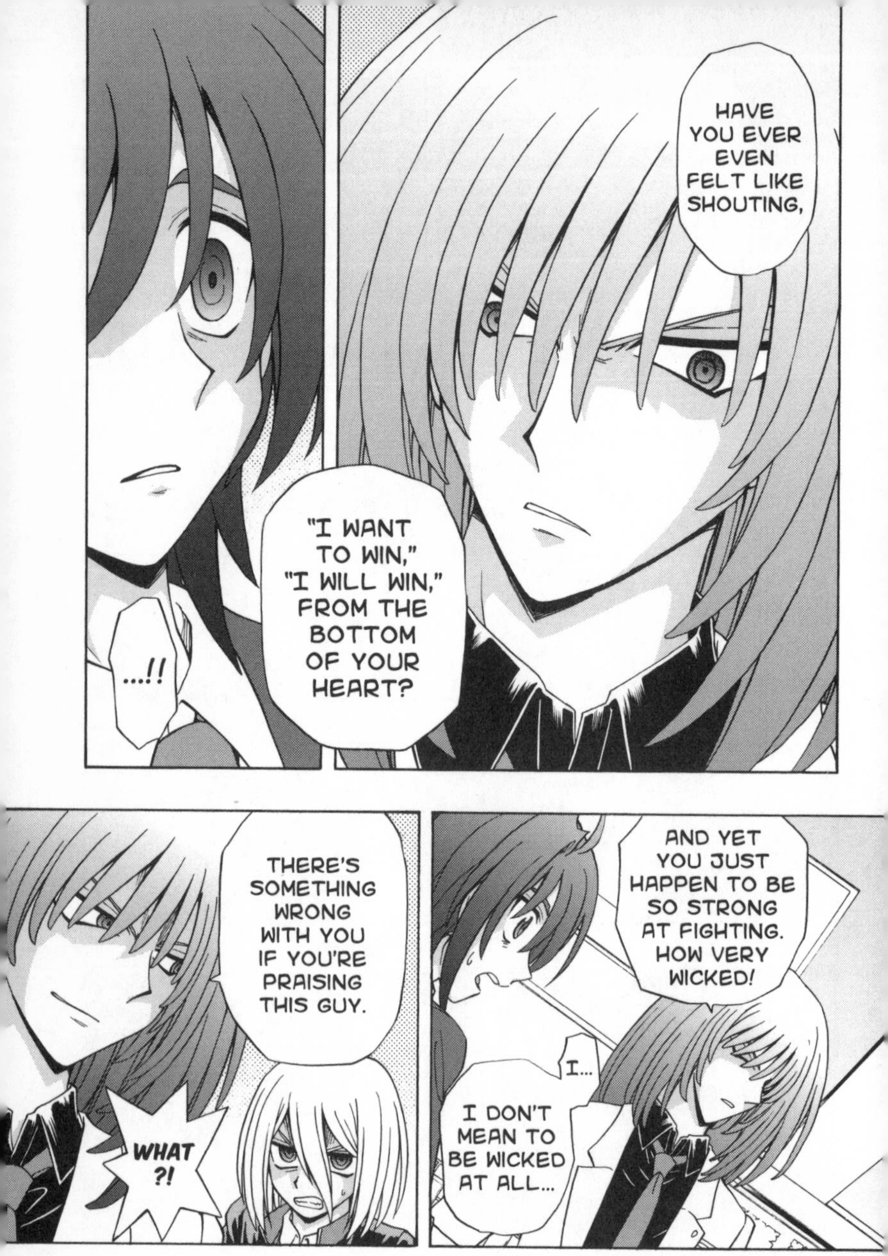
HAVE YOU EVER EVEN FELT LIKE SHOUTING,
"I WANT TO WIN," "I WILL WIN," FROM THE BOTTOM OF YOUR HEART?
...!!
AND YET YOU JUST HAPPEN TO BE SO STRONG AT FIGHTING. HOW VERY WICKED!
I...
I DON'T MEAN TO BE WICKED AT ALL...
THERE'S SOMETHING WRONG WITH YOU IF YOU'RE PRAISING THIS GUY.
WHAT?!

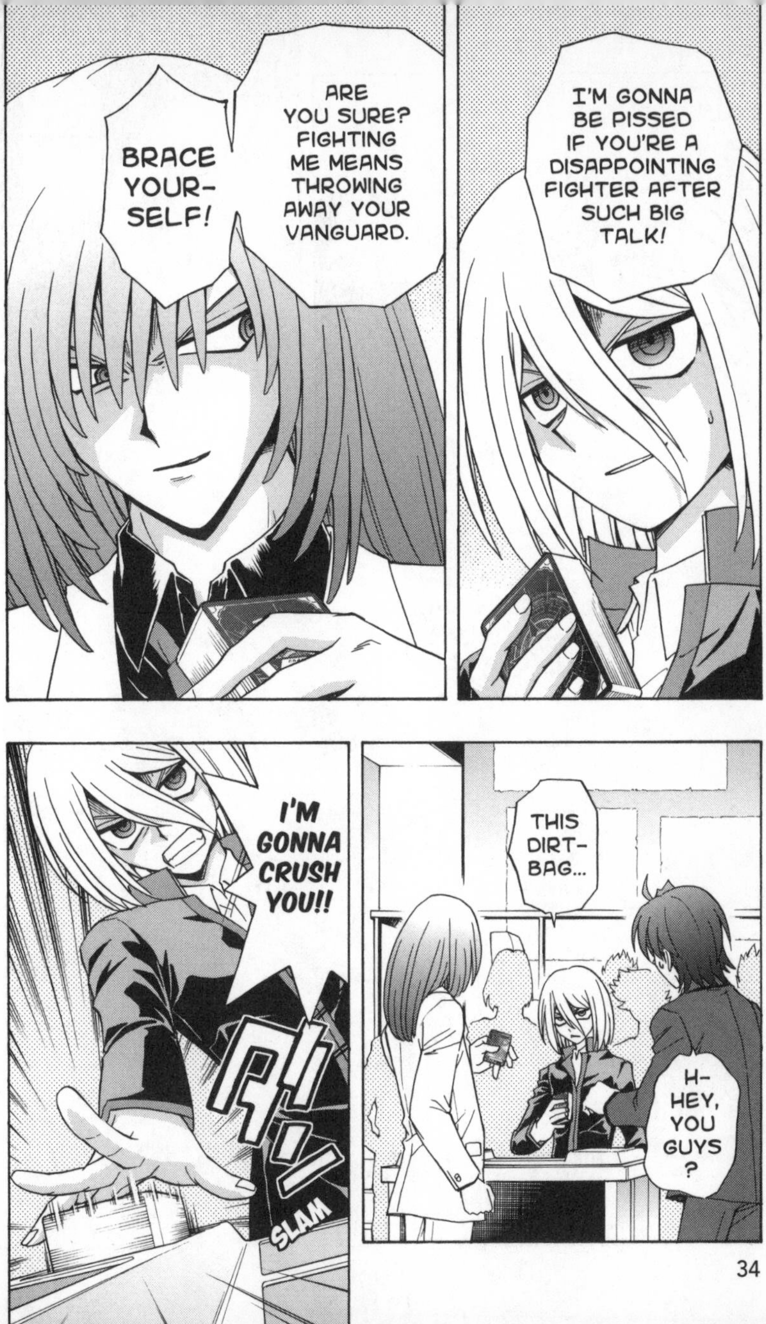

I'M GONNA BE PISSED IF YOU'RE A DISAPPOINTING FIGHTER AFTER SUCH BIG TALK!
ARE YOU SURE? FIGHTING ME MEANS THROWING AWAY YOUR VANGUARD.
BRACE YOUR-SELF!
THIS DIRT-BAG...
H-HEY, YOU GUYS?
I'M GONNA CRUSH YOU!!
SLAM

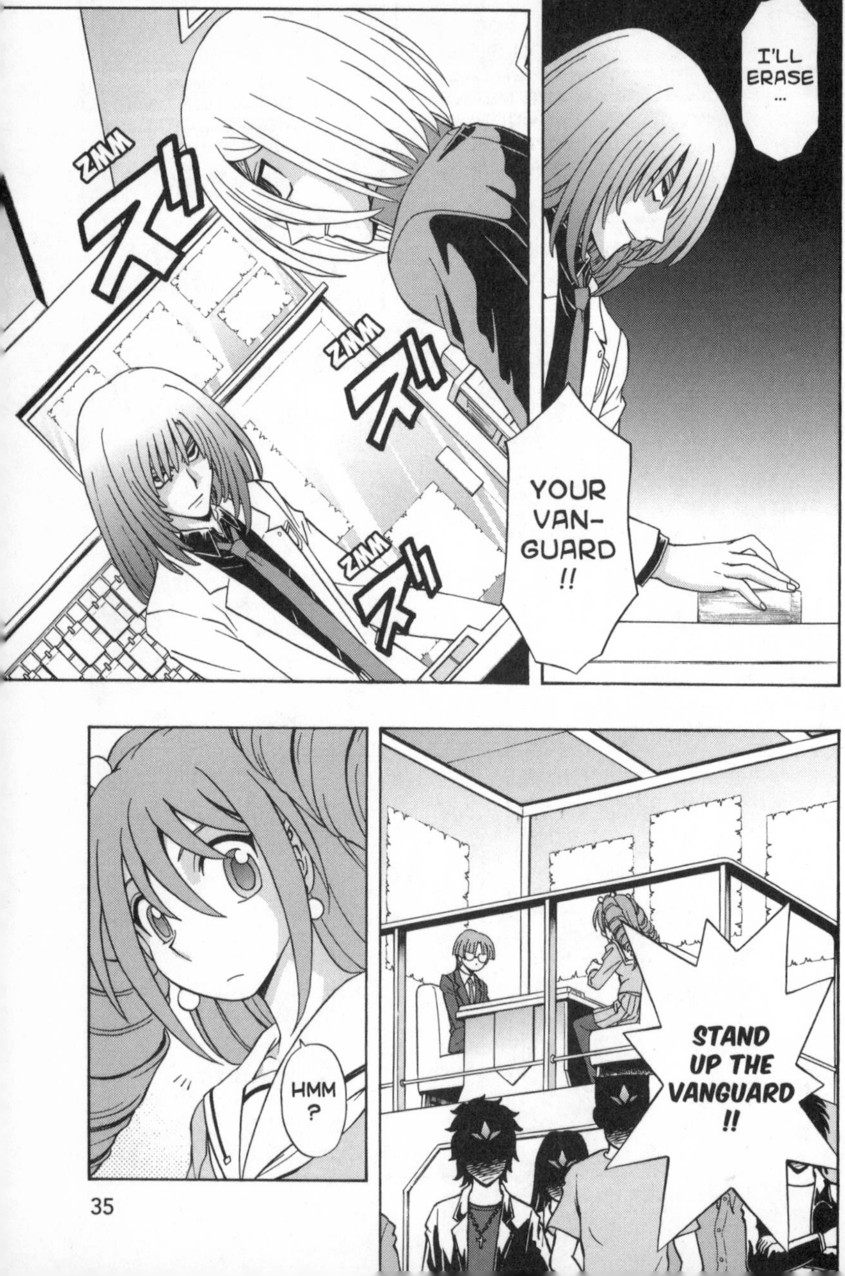
I'LL ERASE ...
YOUR VAN-GUARD !!
ZMM
ZMM
ZMM
STAND UP THE VANGUARD !!
HMM ?

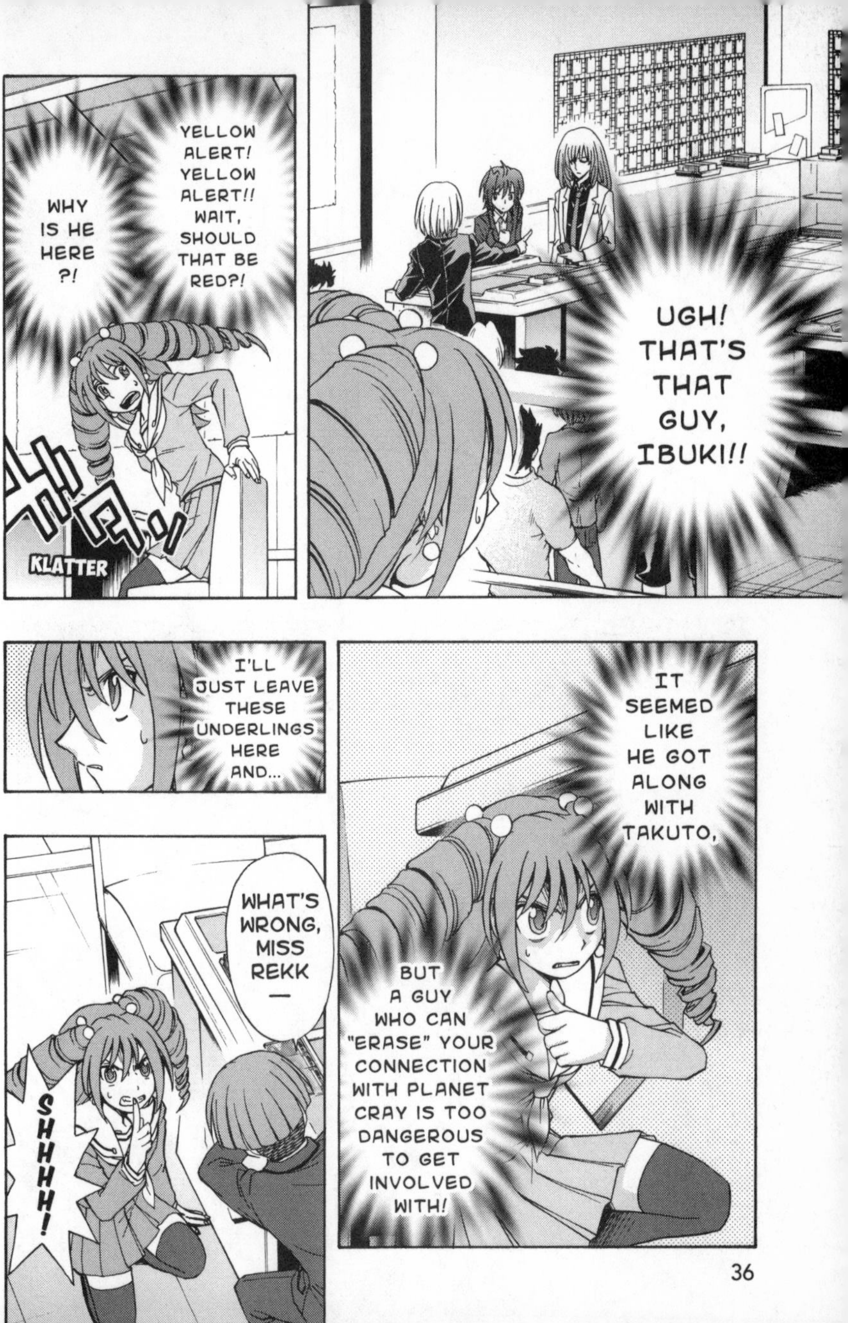
UGH! THAT'S THAT GUY, IBUKI!!
YELLOW ALERT! YELLOW ALERT!! WAIT, SHOULD THAT BE RED?!
WHY IS HE HERE ?!
KLATTER
IT SEEMED LIKE HE GOT ALONG WITH TAKUTO,
BUT A GUY WHO CAN "ERASE" YOUR CONNECTION WITH PLANET CRAY IS TOO DANGEROUS TO GET INVOLVED WITH!
I'LL JUST LEAVE THESE UNDERLINGS HERE AND...
WHAT'S WRONG, MISS REKK —
SHHHH!

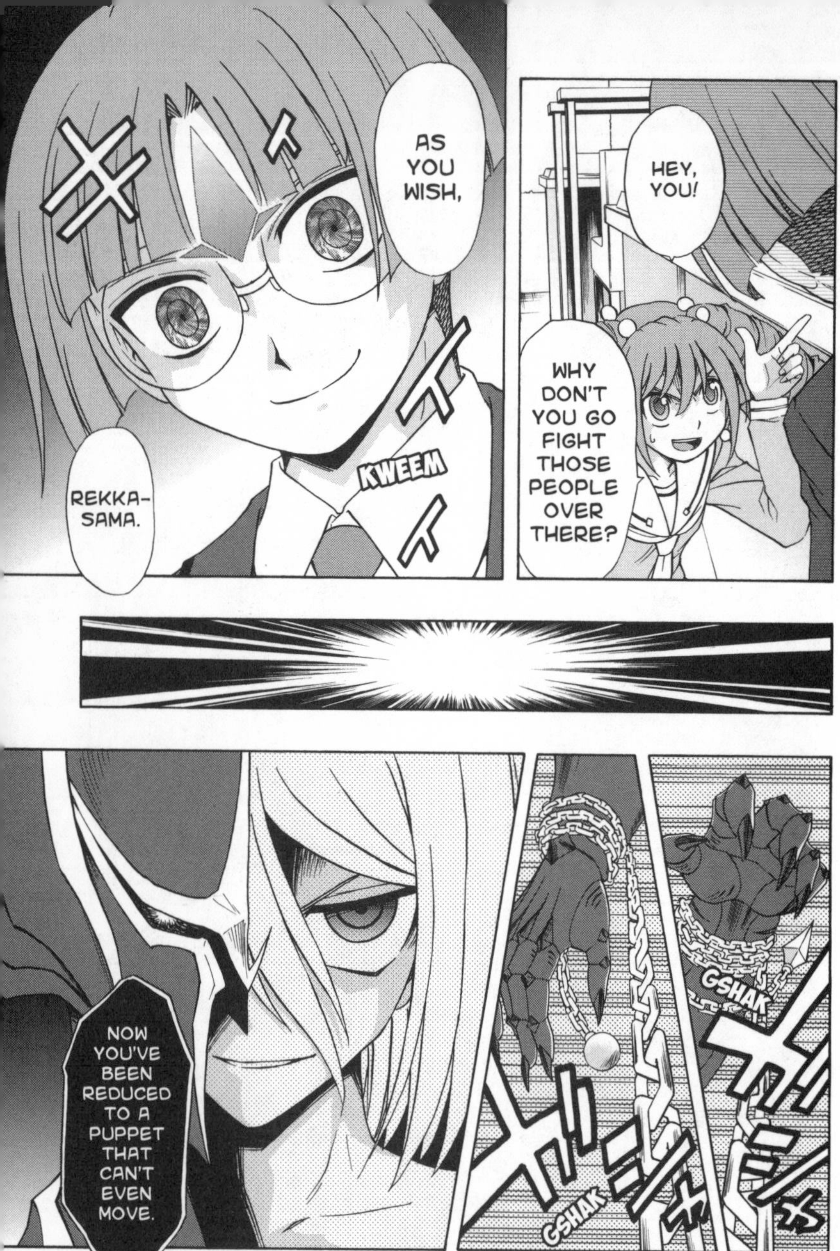
HEY, YOU!
WHY DON'T YOU GO FIGHT THOSE PEOPLE OVER THERE?
AS YOU WISH,
KWEEM
REKKA-SAMA.
GSHAK
GSHAK
NOW YOU'VE BEEN REDUCED TO A PUPPET THAT CAN'T EVEN MOVE.

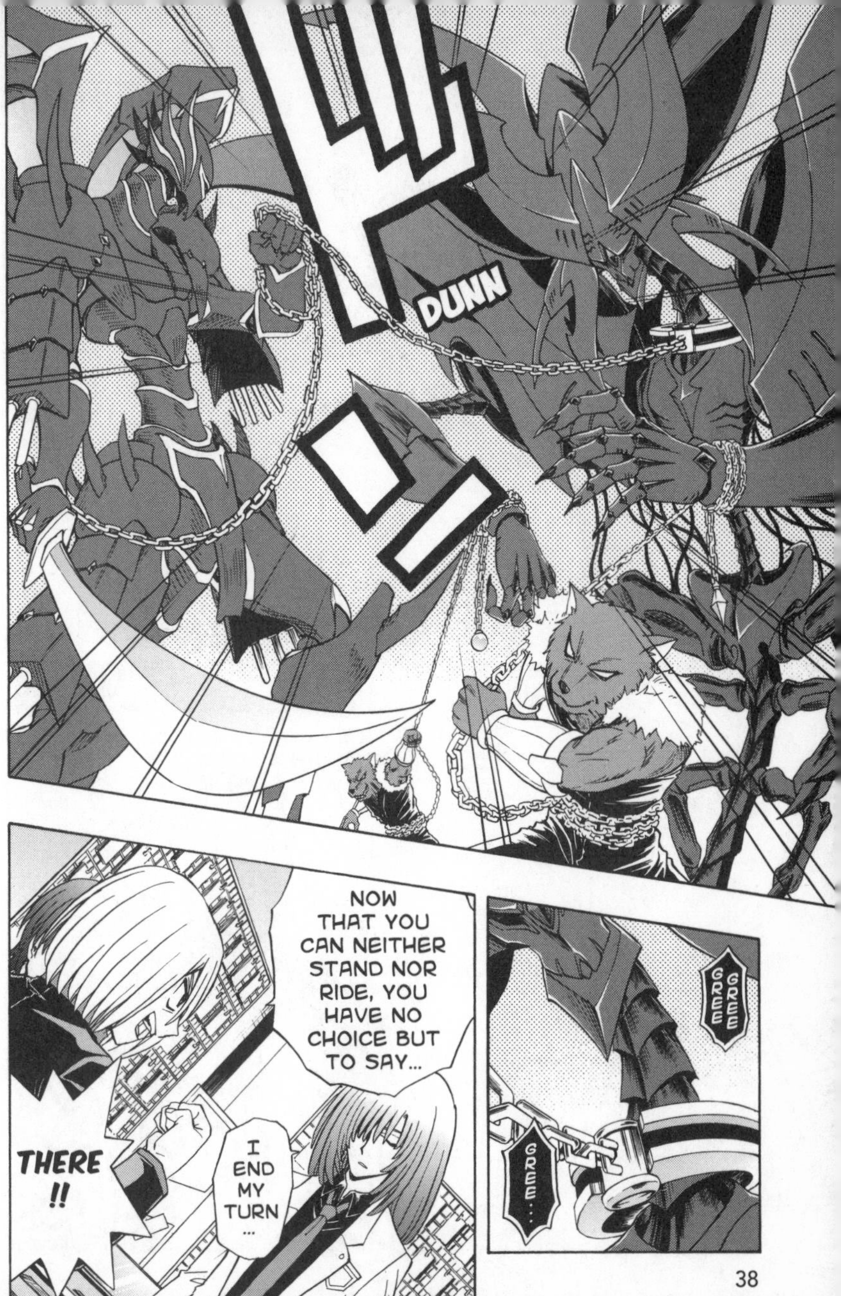
DUNN
GREE GREE
GREE...
NOW THAT YOU CAN NEITHER STAND NOR RIDE, YOU HAVE NO CHOICE BUT TO SAY...
I END MY TURN...
THERE!!

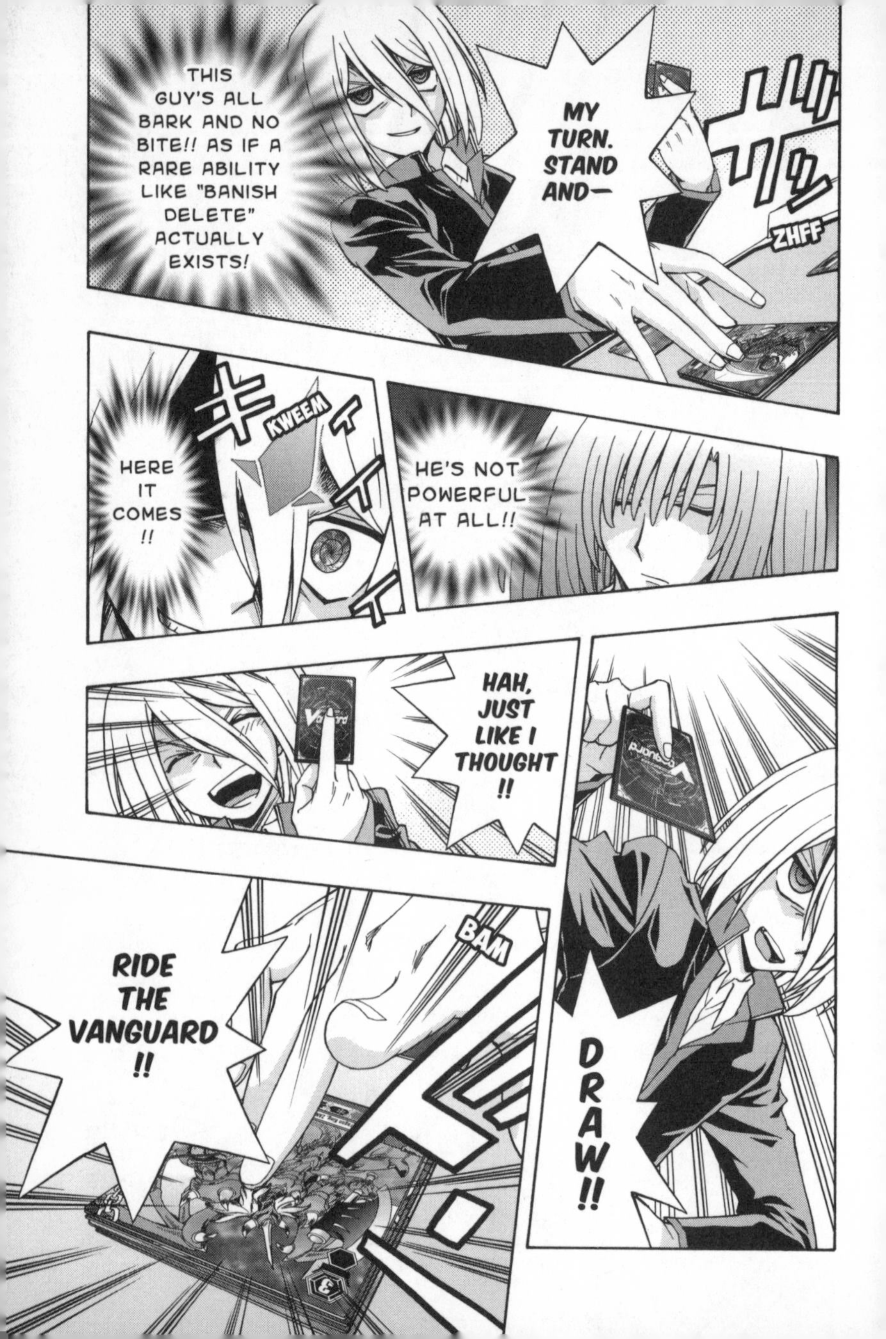
MY TURN. STAND AND—
ZHFF
THIS GUY'S ALL BARK AND NO BITE!! AS IF A RARE ABILITY LIKE "BANISH DELETE" ACTUALLY EXISTS!
HE'S NOT POWERFUL AT ALL!!
KWEEM
HERE IT COMES !!
DRAW!!
HAH, JUST LIKE I THOUGHT !!
BAM
RIDE THE VANGUARD !!

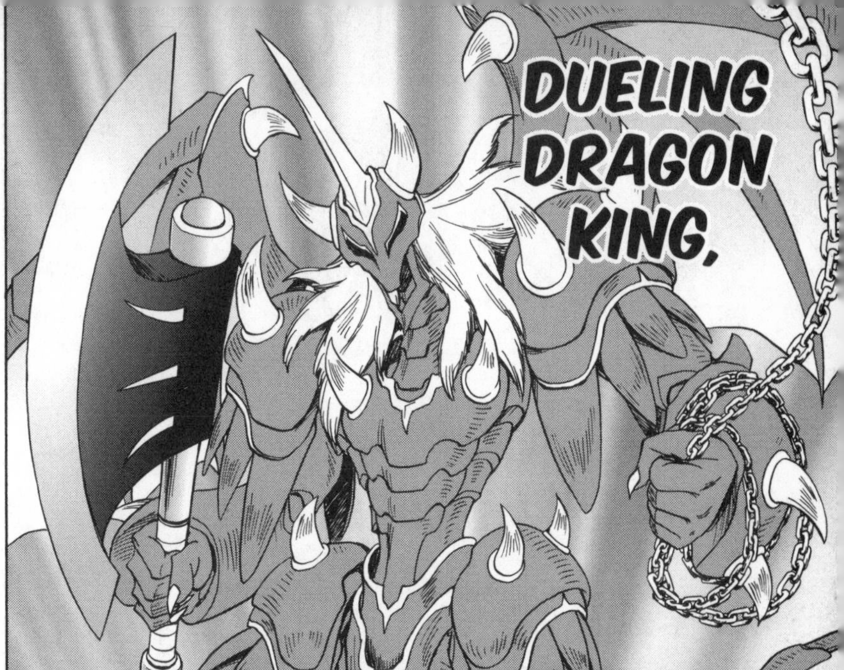
DUELING DRAGON KING,
ZANGEKI !!!

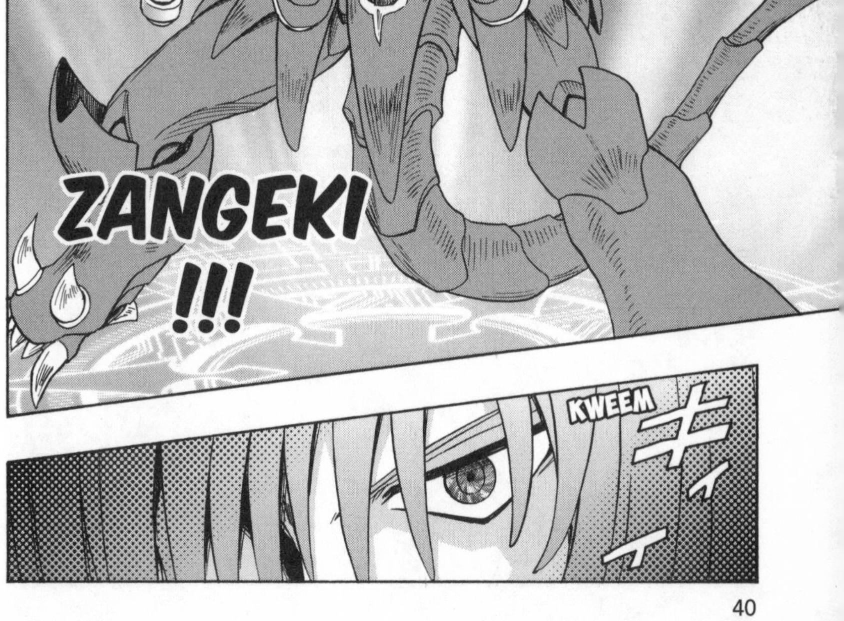
KWEEM
キィィ

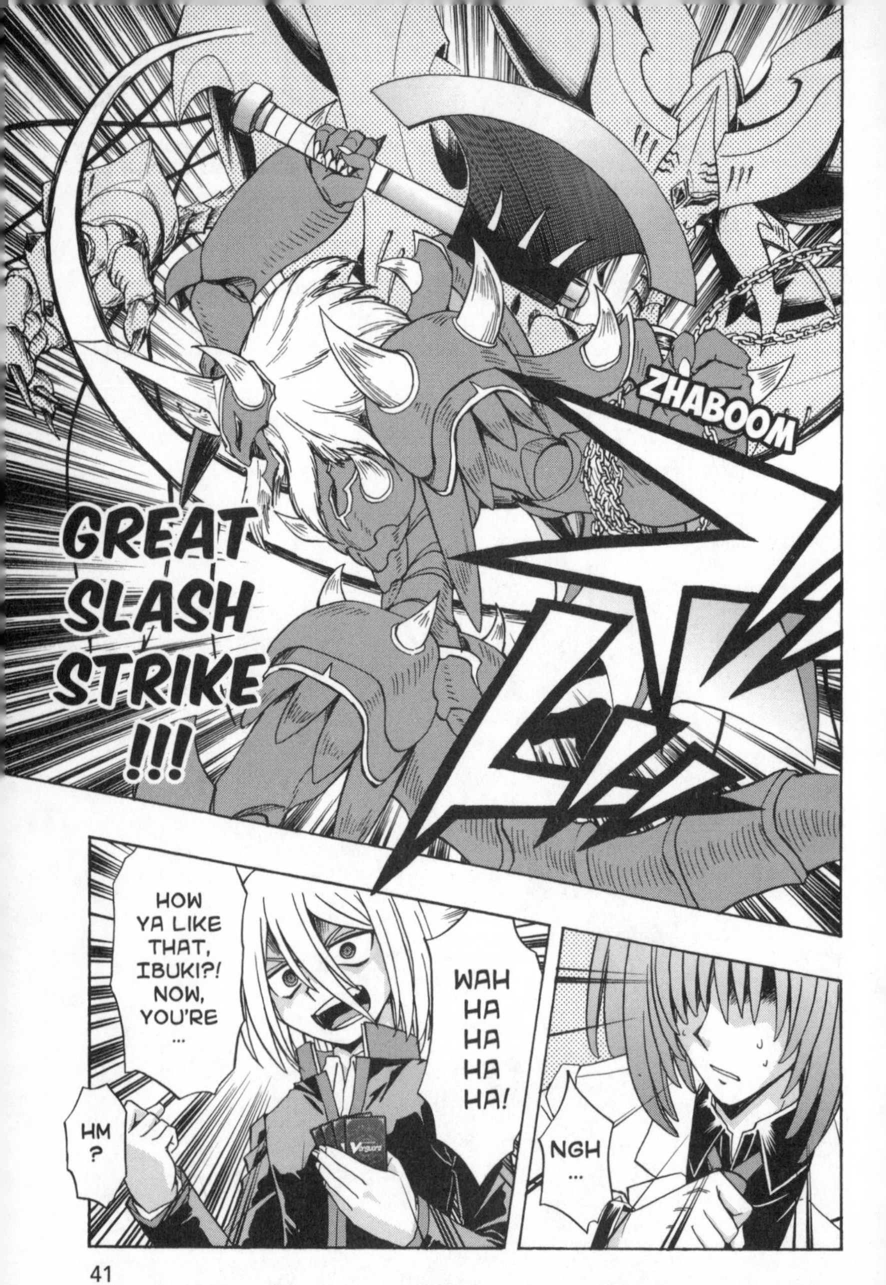
ZHABOOM
GREAT SLASH STRIKE!!!
NGH ...
HOW YA LIKE THAT, IBUKI?! NOW, YOU'RE ...
WAH HA HA HA HA HA!
HM?

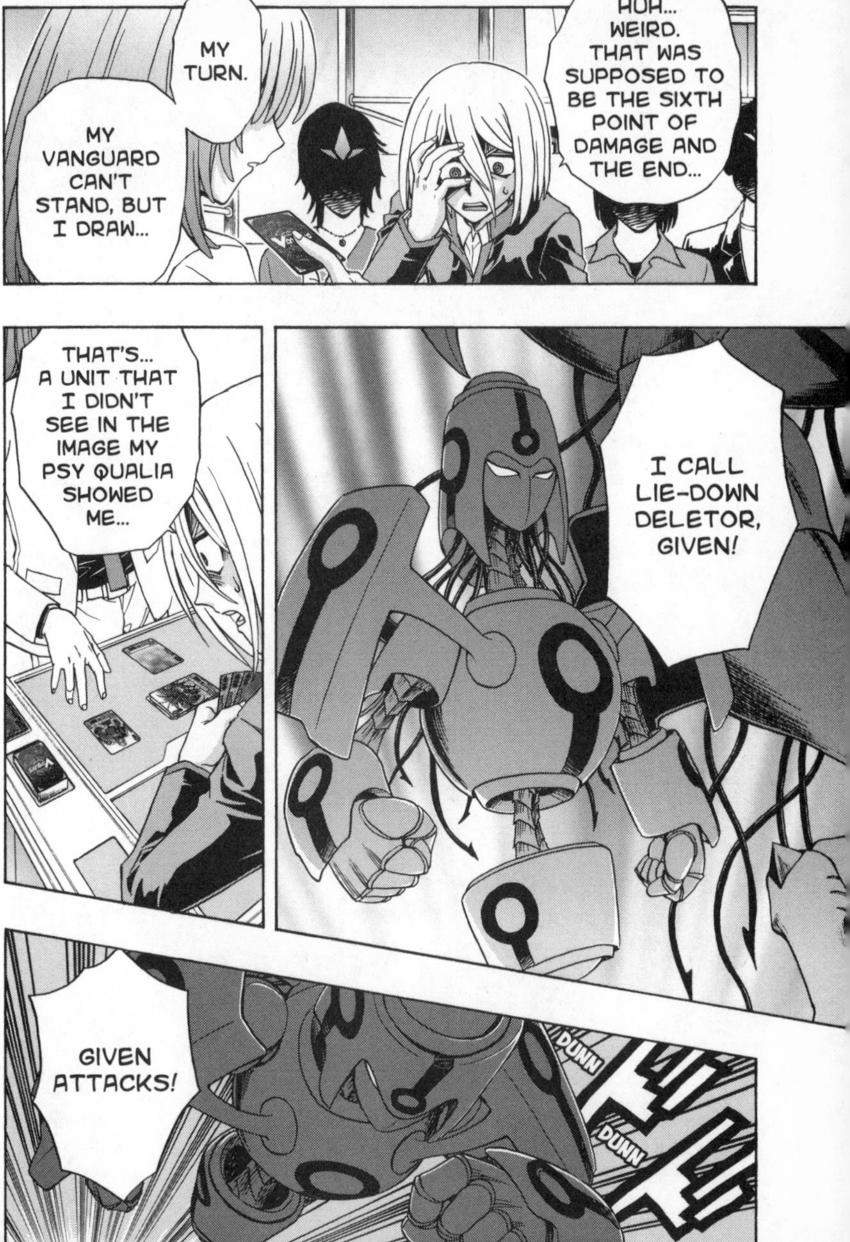
HUH... WEIRD. THAT WAS SUPPOSED TO BE THE SIXTH POINT OF DAMAGE AND THE END...
MY TURN.
MY VANGUARD CAN'T STAND, BUT I DRAW...
I CALL LIE-DOWN DELETOR, GIVEN!
THAT'S... A UNIT THAT I DIDN'T SEE IN THE IMAGE MY PSY QUALIA SHOWED ME...
DUNN
DUNN
GIVEN ATTACKS!

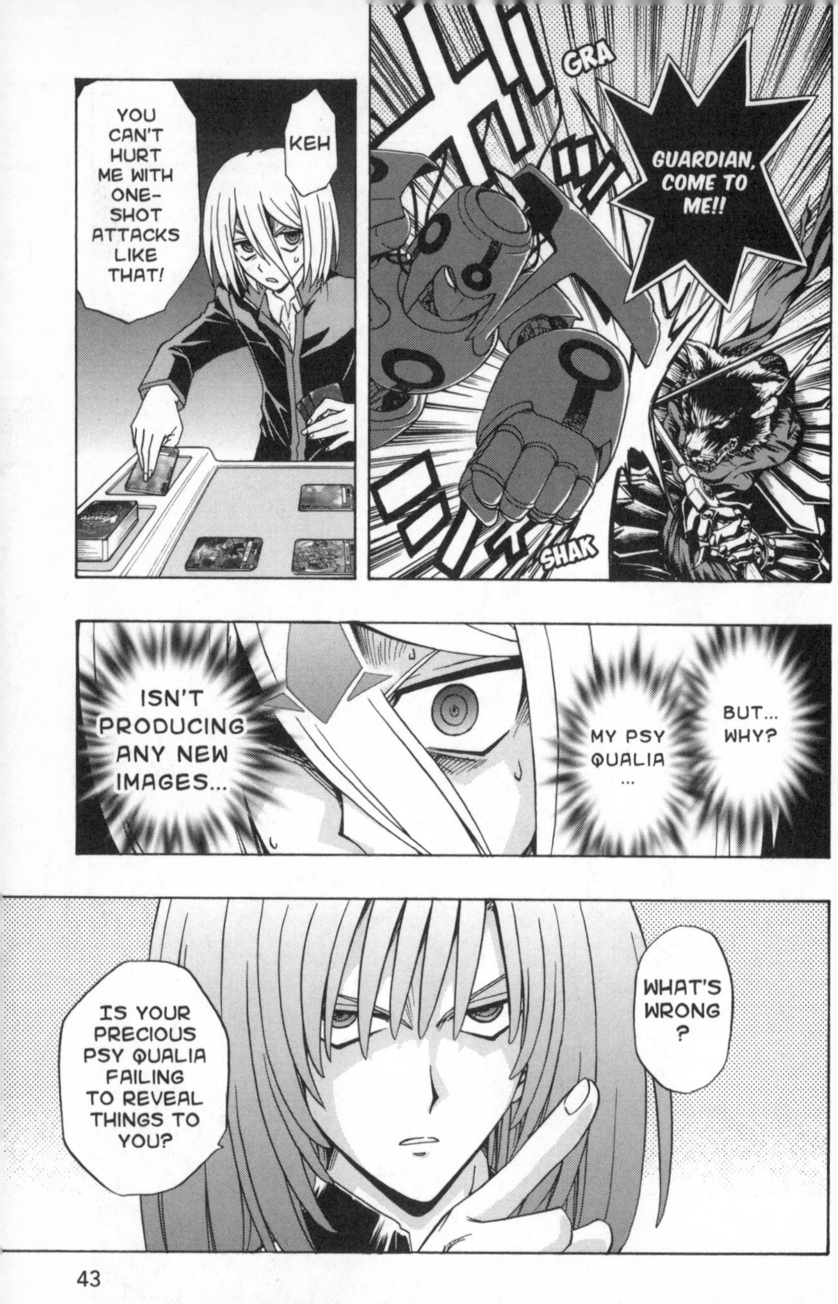
GRA
GUARDIAN, COME TO ME!!
SHAK
KEH
YOU CAN'T HURT ME WITH ONE-SHOT ATTACKS LIKE THAT!
BUT... WHY?
MY PSY QUALIA ...
ISN'T PRODUCING ANY NEW IMAGES...
WHAT'S WRONG?
IS YOUR PRECIOUS PSY QUALIA FAILING TO REVEAL THINGS TO YOU?

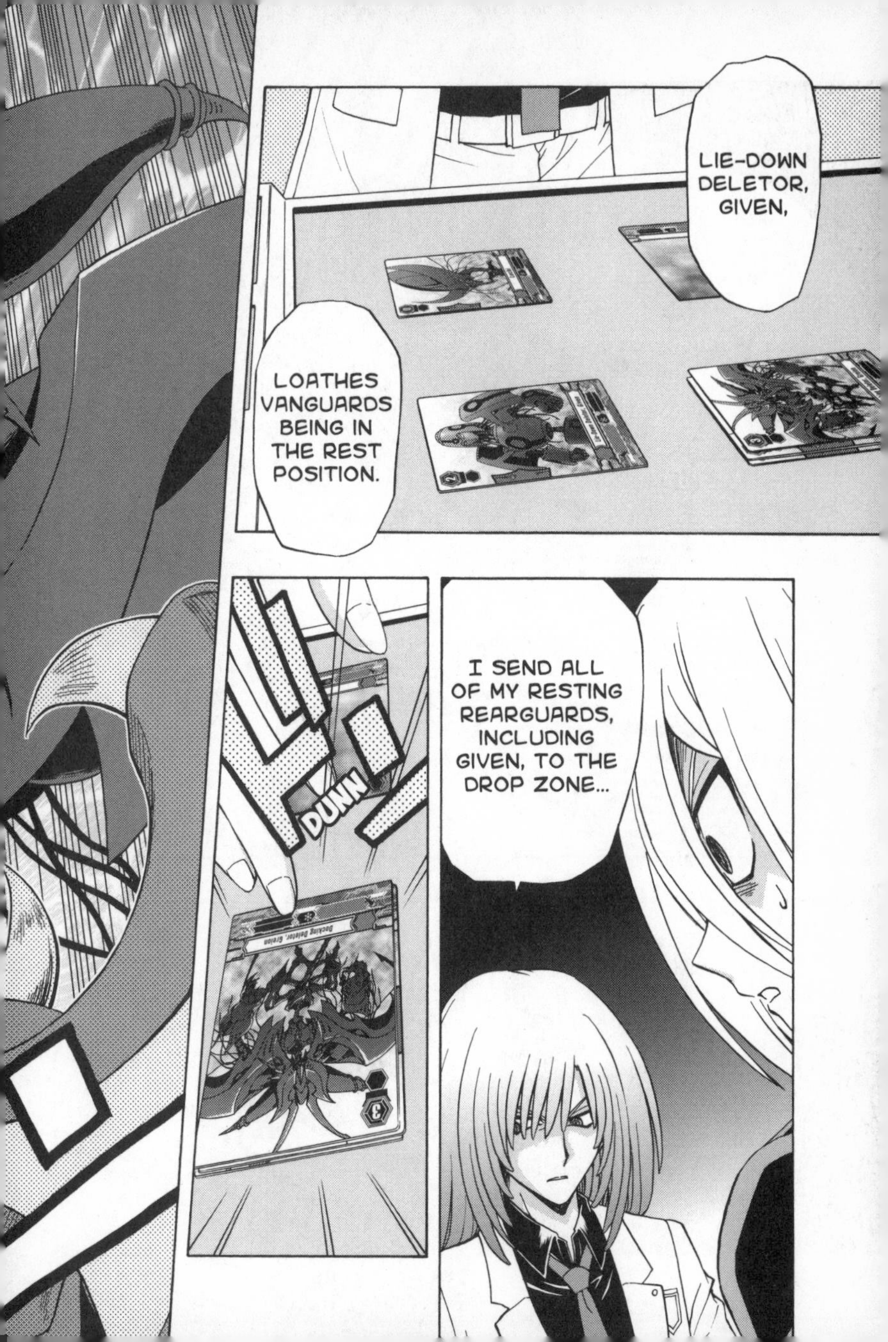
LIE-DOWN DELETOR, GIVEN,
LOATHES VANGUARDS BEING IN THE REST POSITION.
I SEND ALL OF MY RESTING REARGUARDS, INCLUDING GIVEN, TO THE DROP ZONE...
DUNN

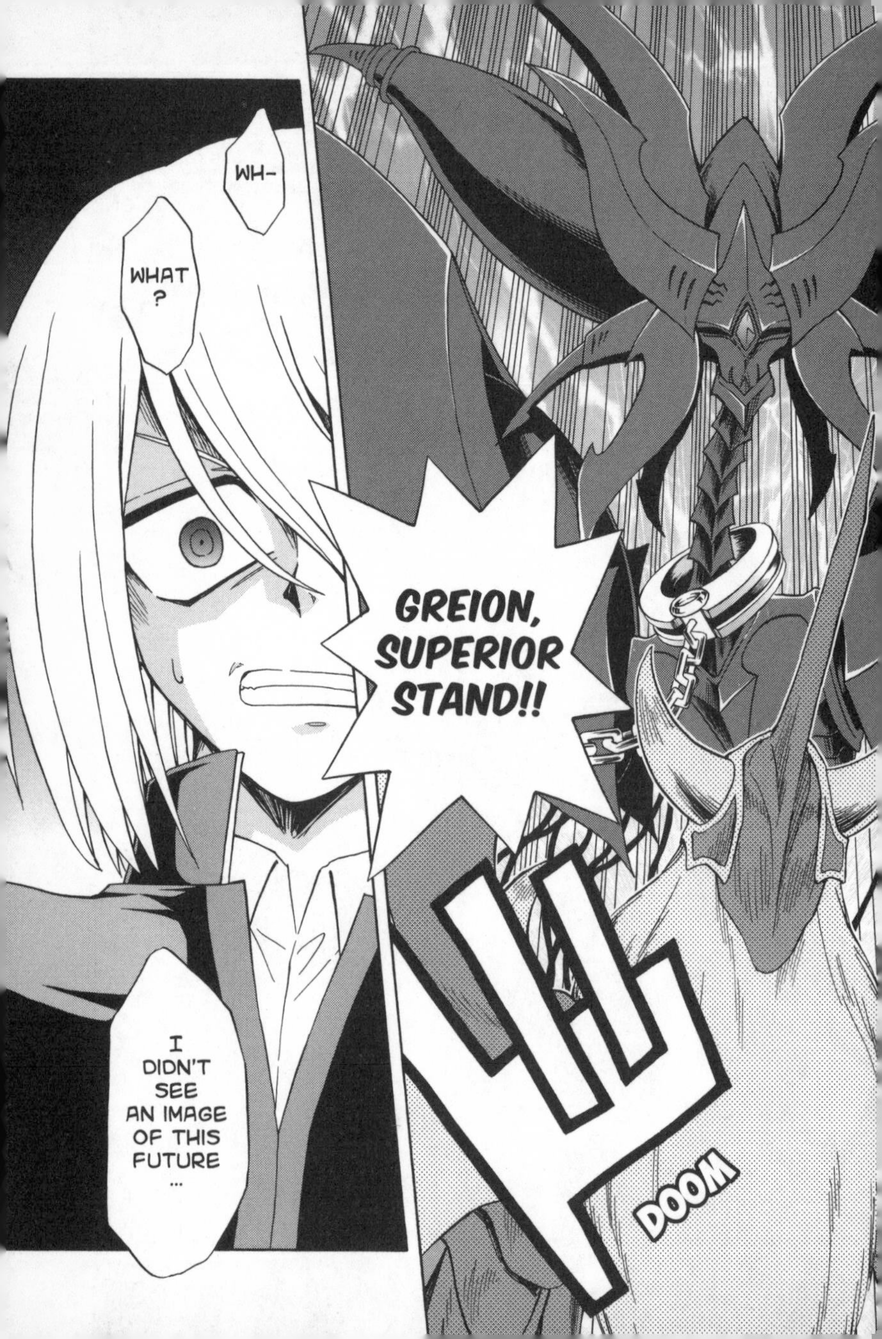
GREION, SUPERIOR STAND!!
DOOM
WH-
WHAT?
I DIDN'T SEE AN IMAGE OF THIS FUTURE...

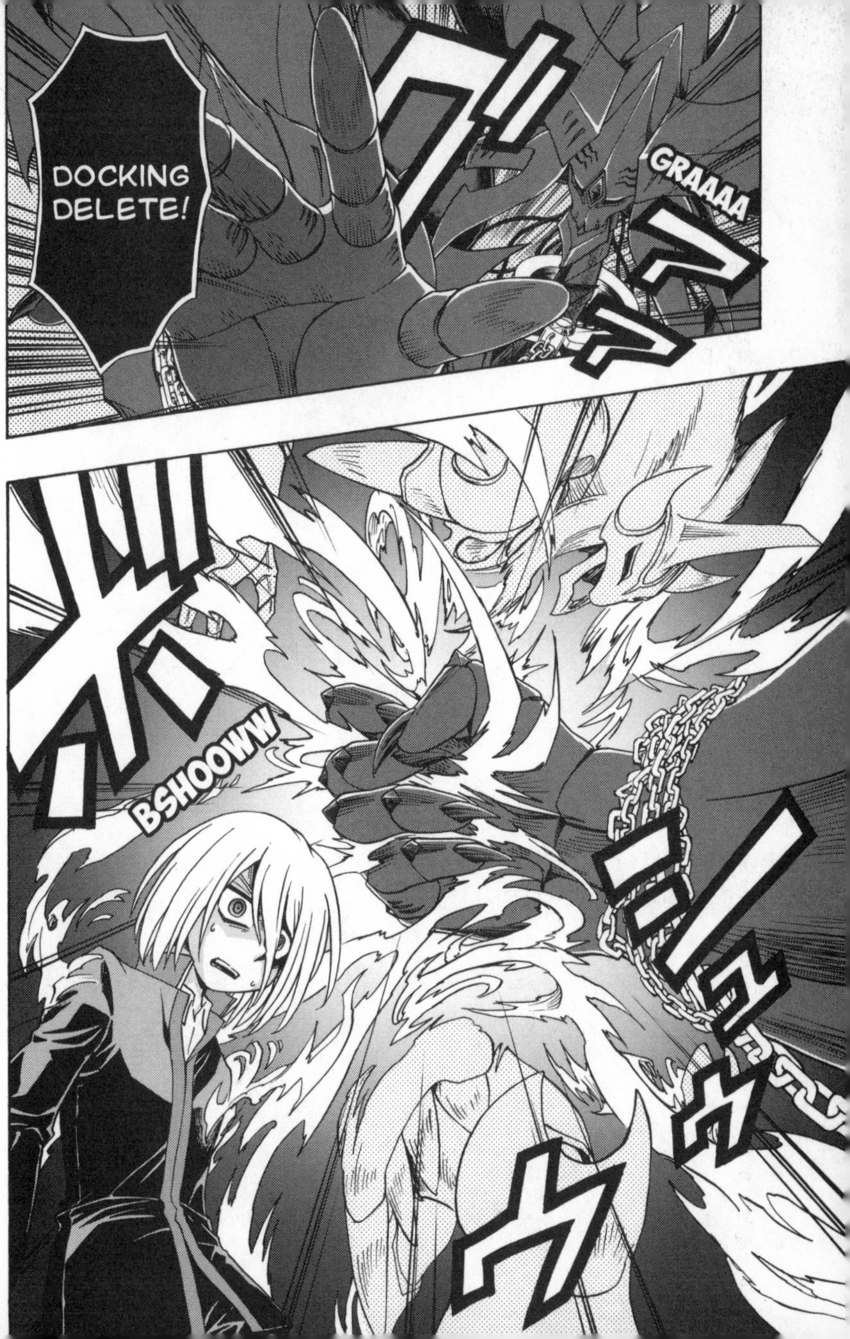
DOCKING DELETE!
GRAAAA
BSHOOWW

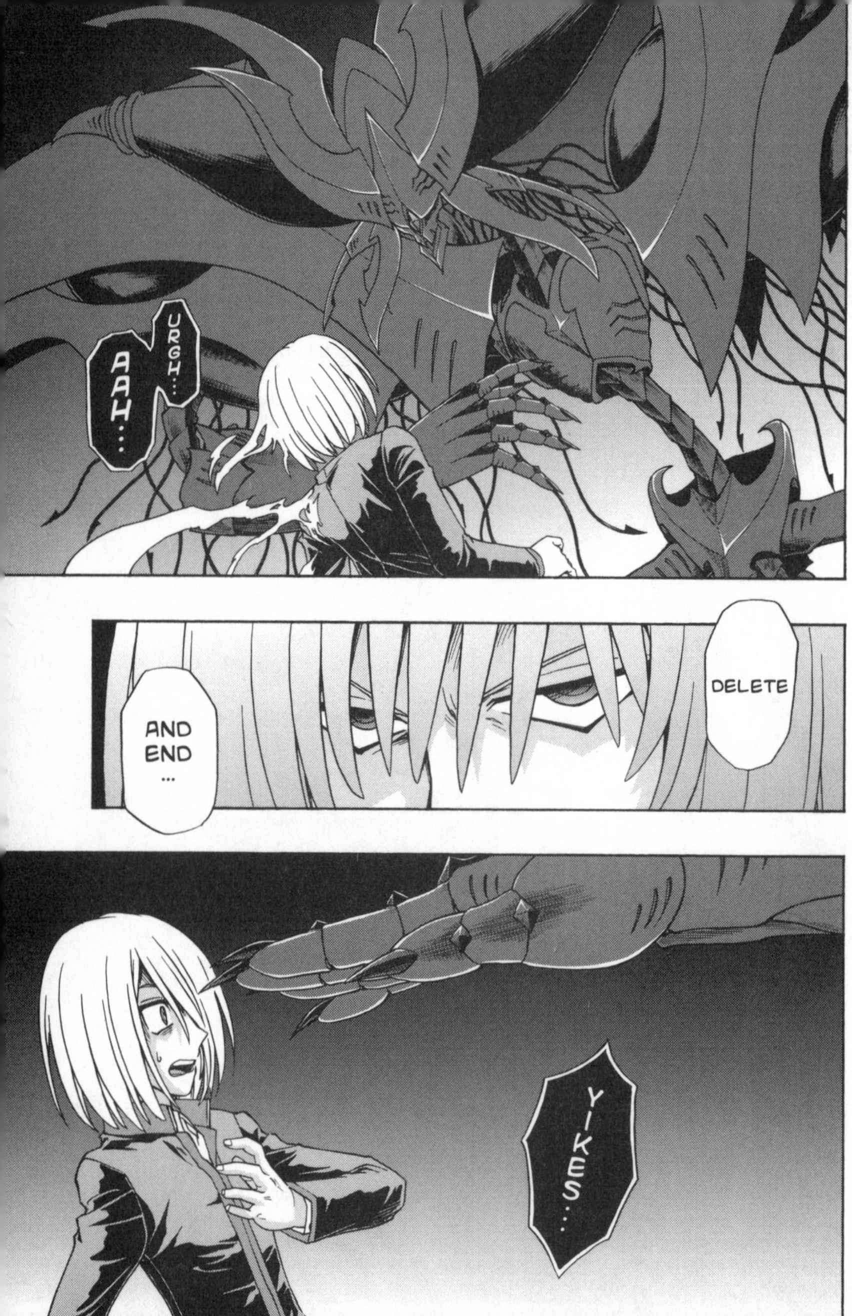
URGH...
AAH...
DELETE
AND END ...
YIKES...

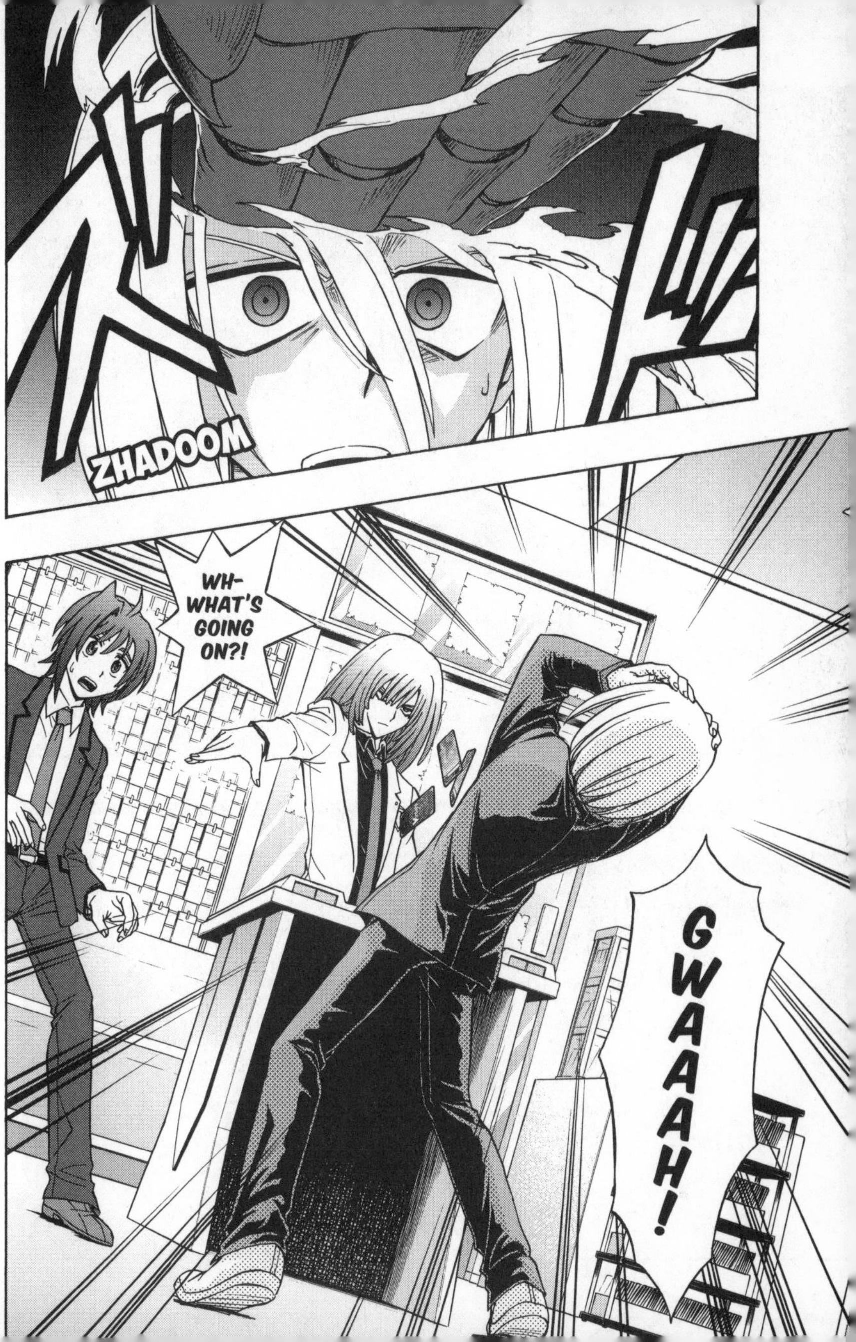
ZHADOOM
WH-WHAT'S GOING ON?!
GWAAAAH!

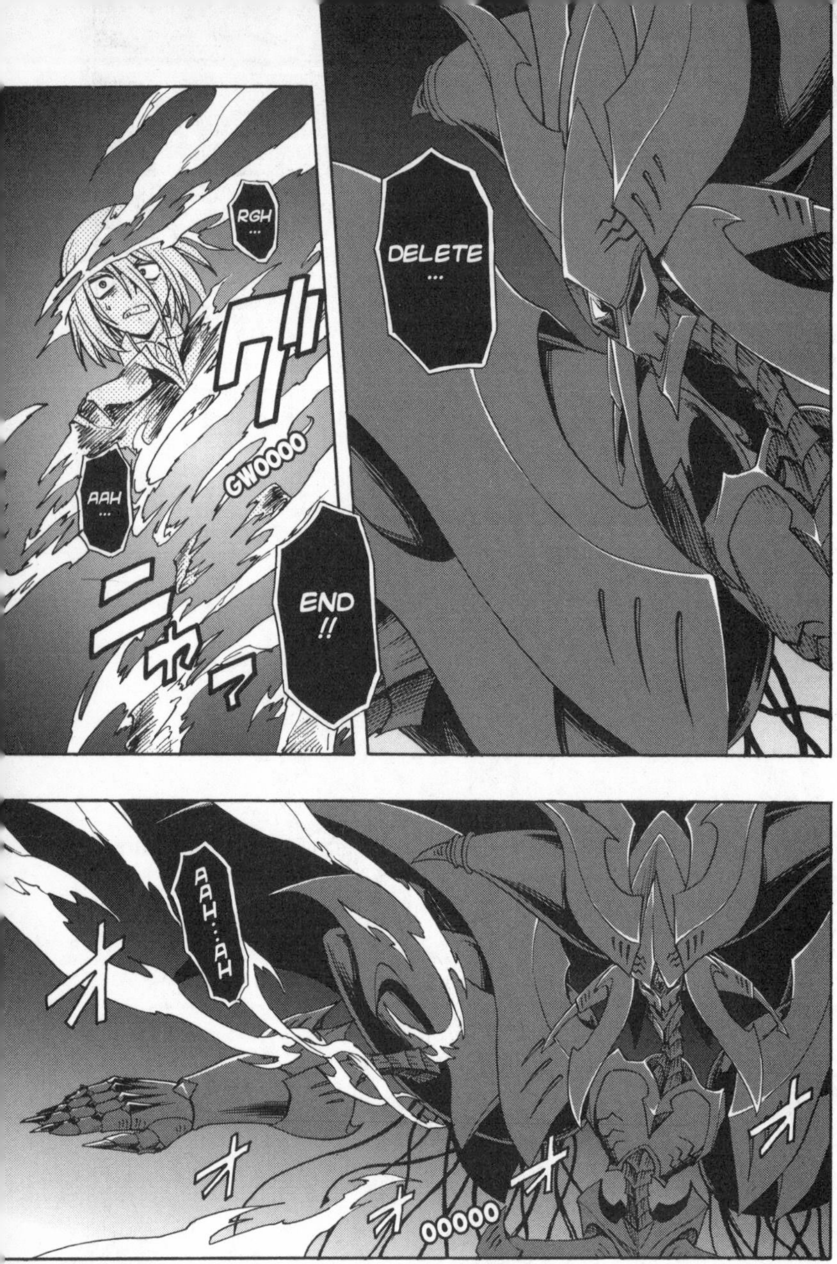
DELETE ...
END !!
RGH ...
GWOOOO
AAH ...
AAH...AH
オ
オ
オ
OOOOO

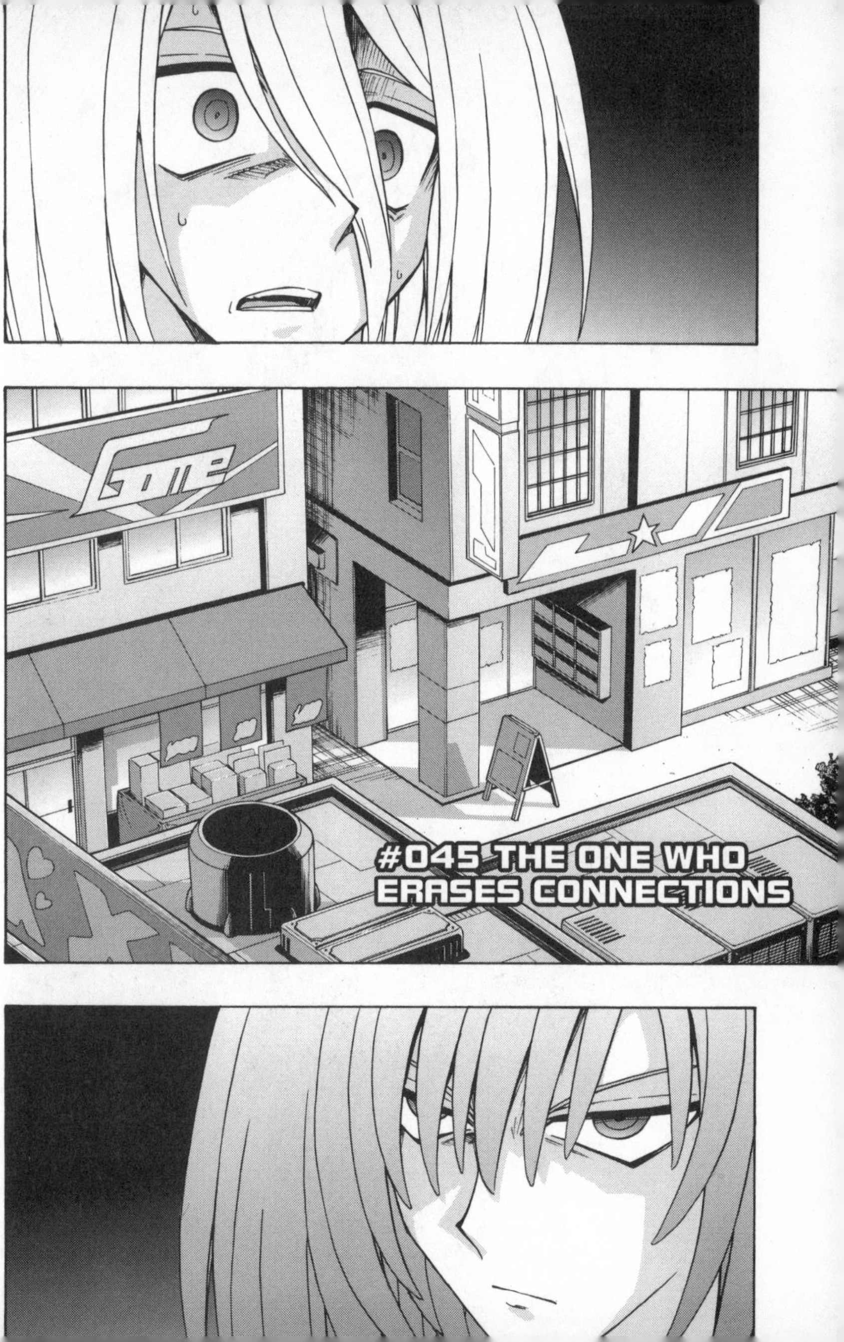
#045 THE ONE WHO ERASES CONNECTIONS

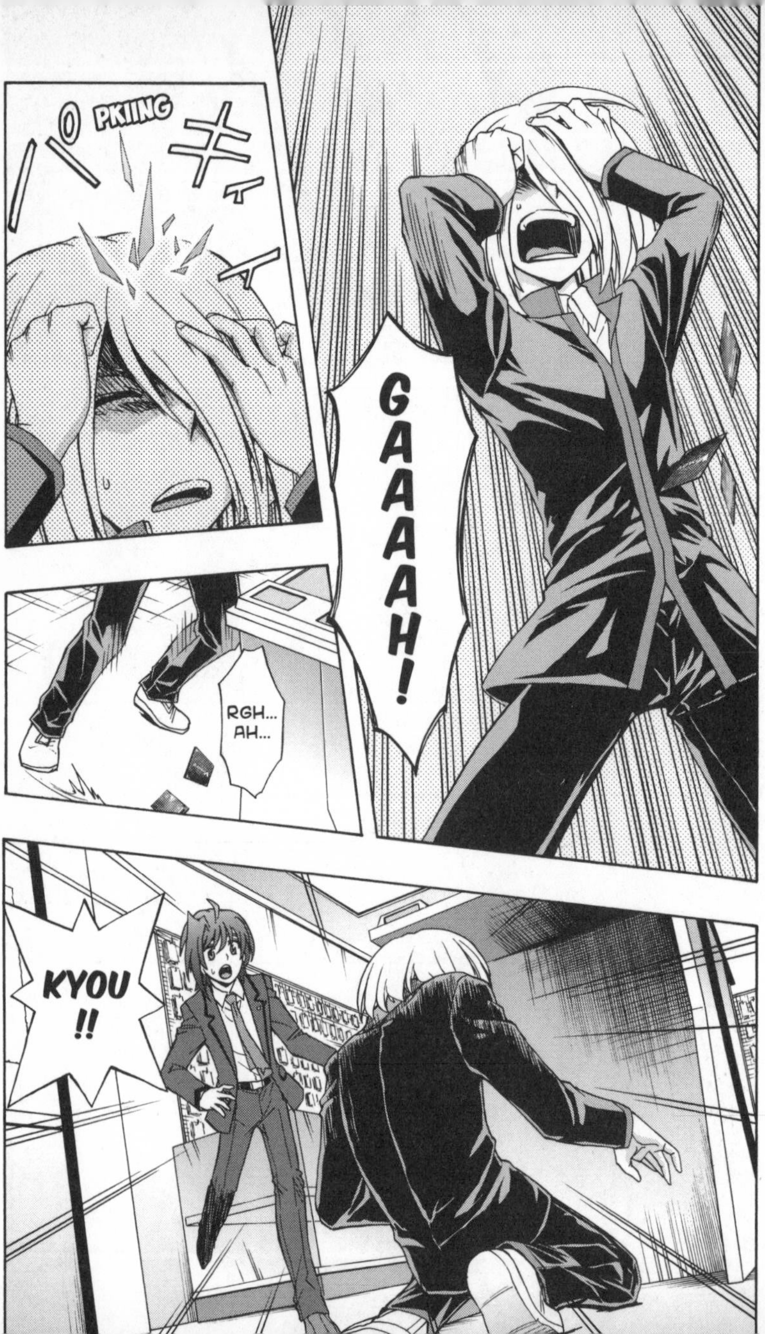
GAAAAAH!
パキィ
PKIING
RGH... AH...
KYOU !!

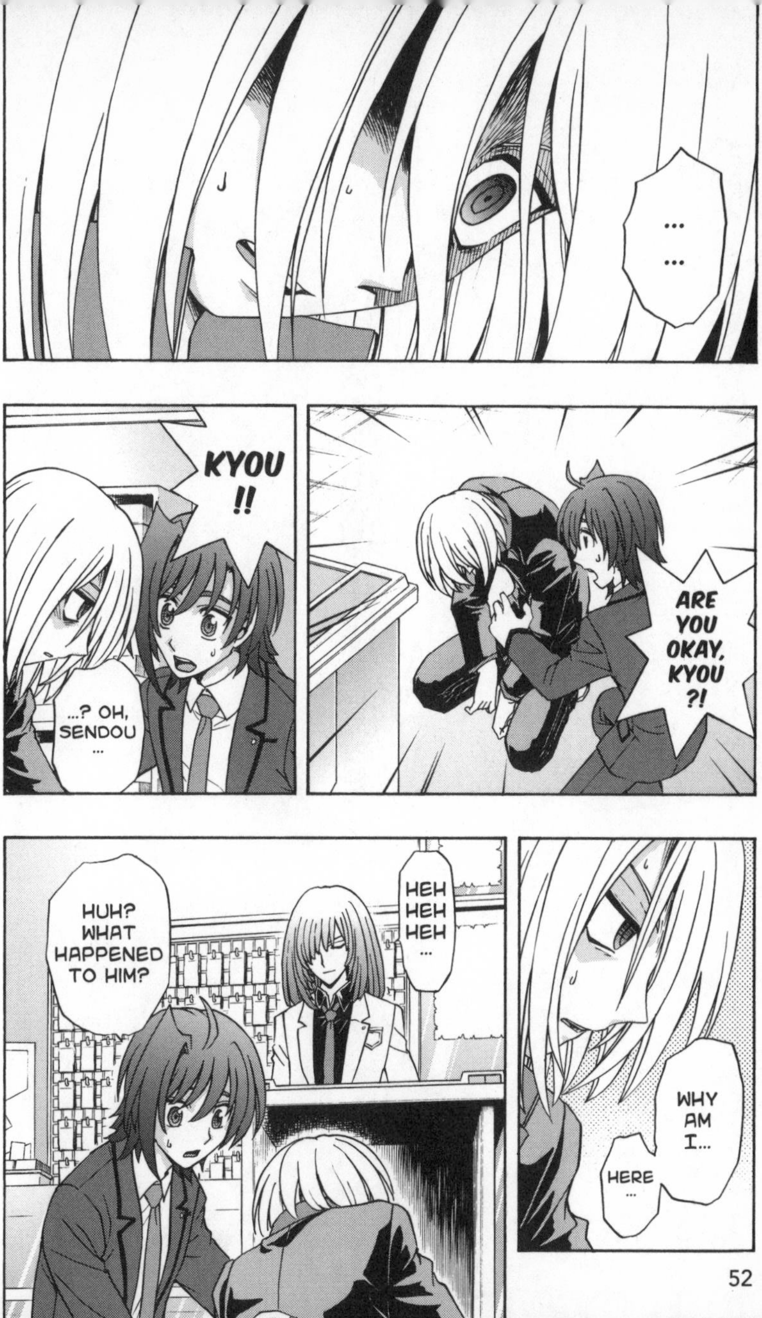

... ...
ARE YOU OKAY, KYOU?!
KYOU !!
...? OH, SENDOU ...
WHY AM I...
HERE ...
HEH HEH HEH ...
HUH? WHAT HAPPENED TO HIM?

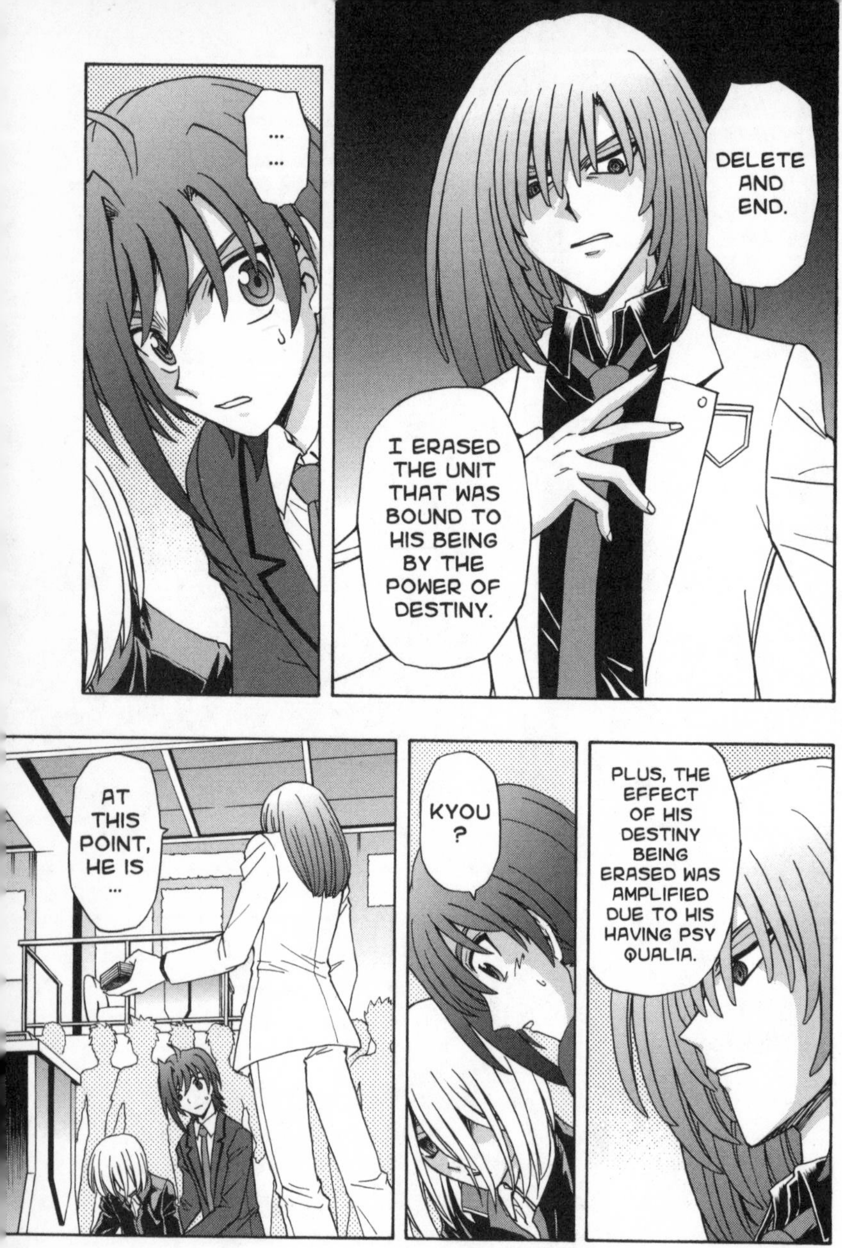
DELETE AND END.
I ERASED THE UNIT THAT WAS BOUND TO HIS BEING BY THE POWER OF DESTINY.
... ...
PLUS, THE EFFECT OF HIS DESTINY BEING ERASED WAS AMPLIFIED DUE TO HIS HAVING PSY QUALIA.
KYOU?
AT THIS POINT, HE IS ...

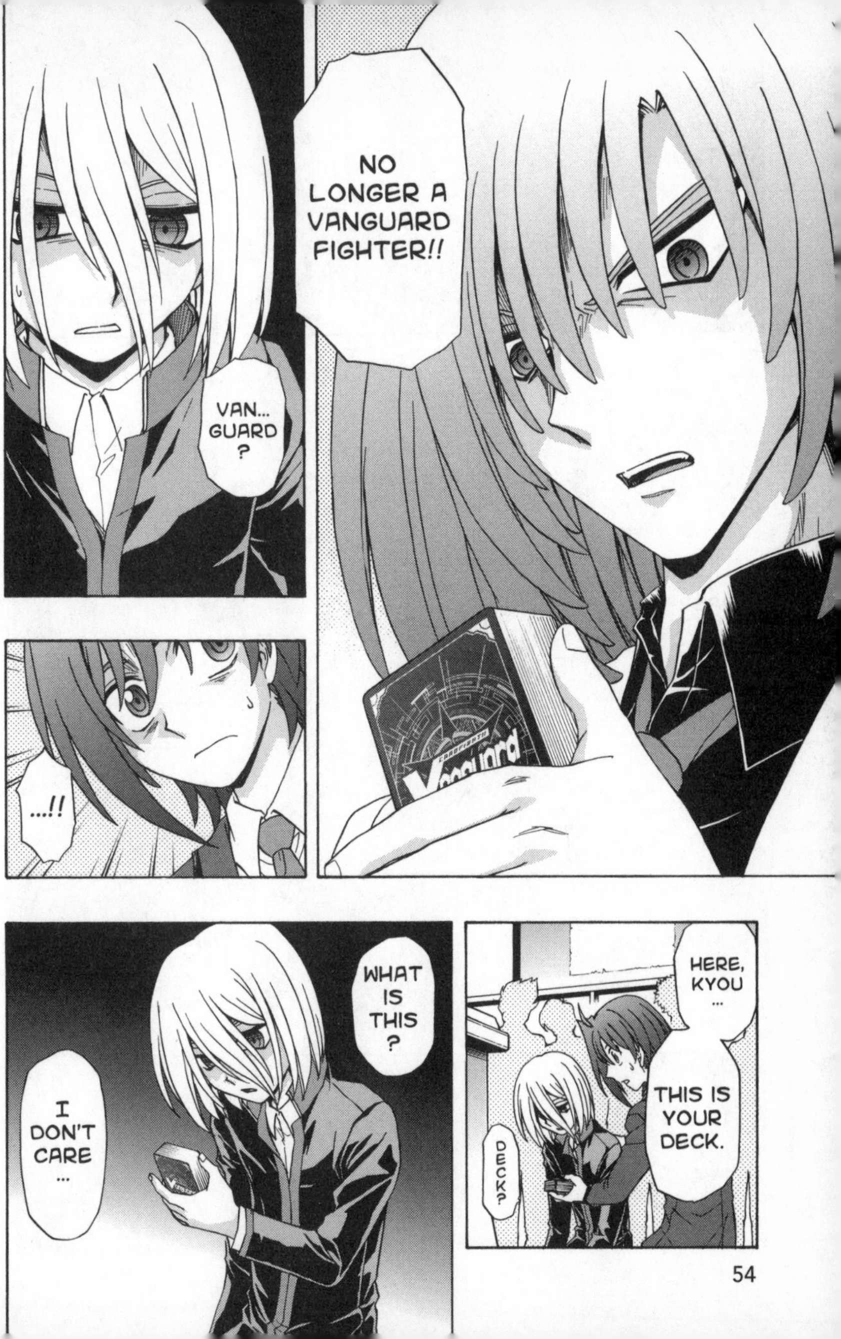
NO LONGER A VANGUARD FIGHTER!!
VAN... GUARD ?
...!!
HERE, KYOU ...
THIS IS YOUR DECK.
DECK?
WHAT IS THIS ?
I DON'T CARE ...

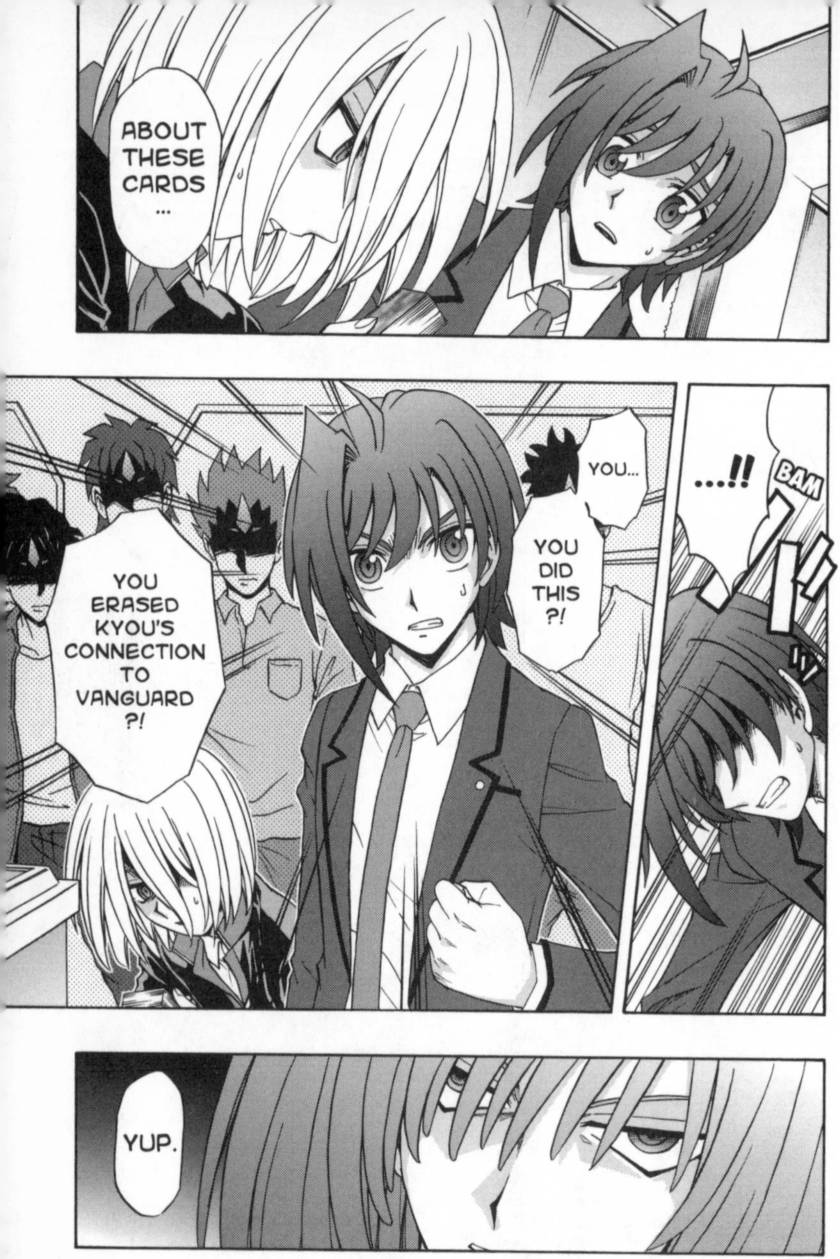
ABOUT THESE CARDS...
...!!
BAM
YOU...
YOU DID THIS?!
YOU ERASED KYOU'S CONNECTION TO VANGUARD?!
YUP.

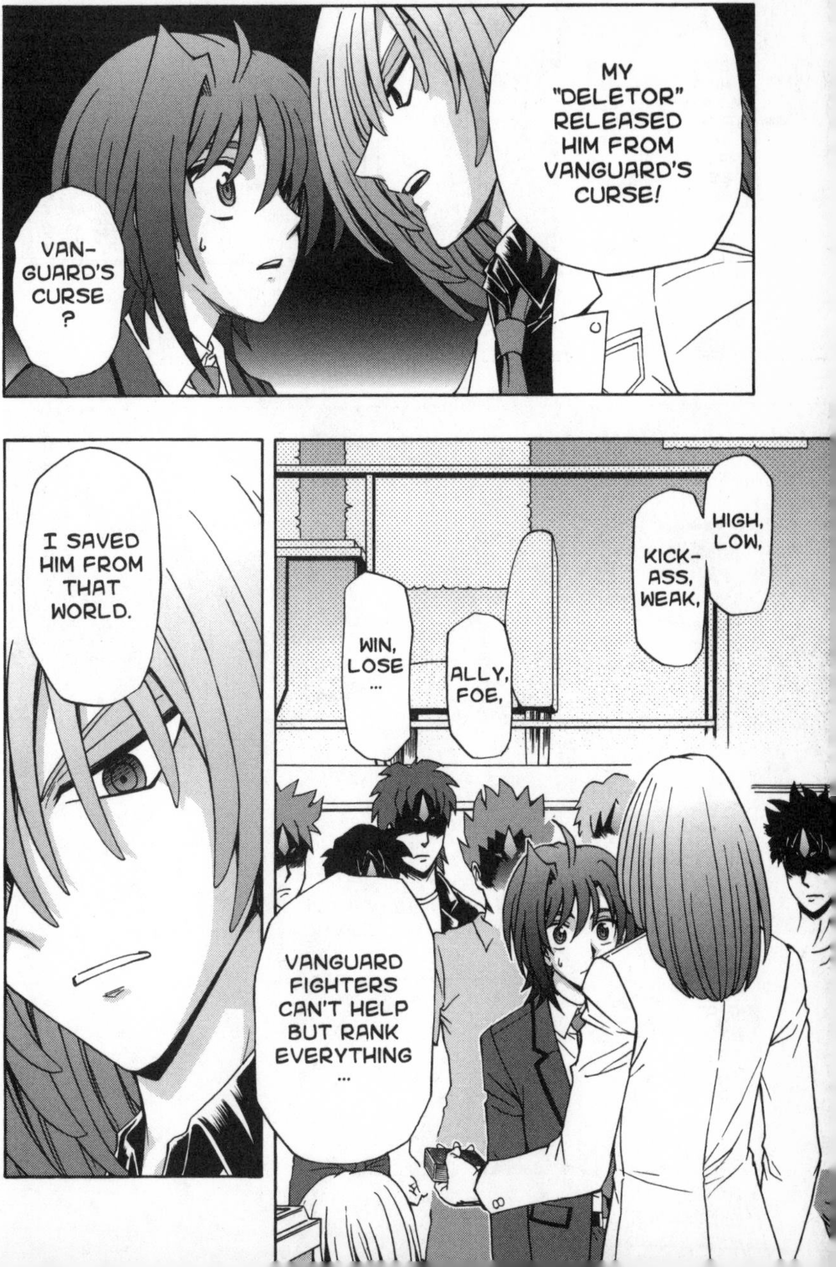
MY "DELETOR" RELEASED HIM FROM VANGUARD'S CURSE!
VAN-GUARD'S CURSE ?
HIGH, LOW,
KICK-ASS, WEAK,
ALLY, FOE,
WIN, LOSE ...
VANGUARD FIGHTERS CAN'T HELP BUT RANK EVERYTHING ...
I SAVED HIM FROM THAT WORLD.

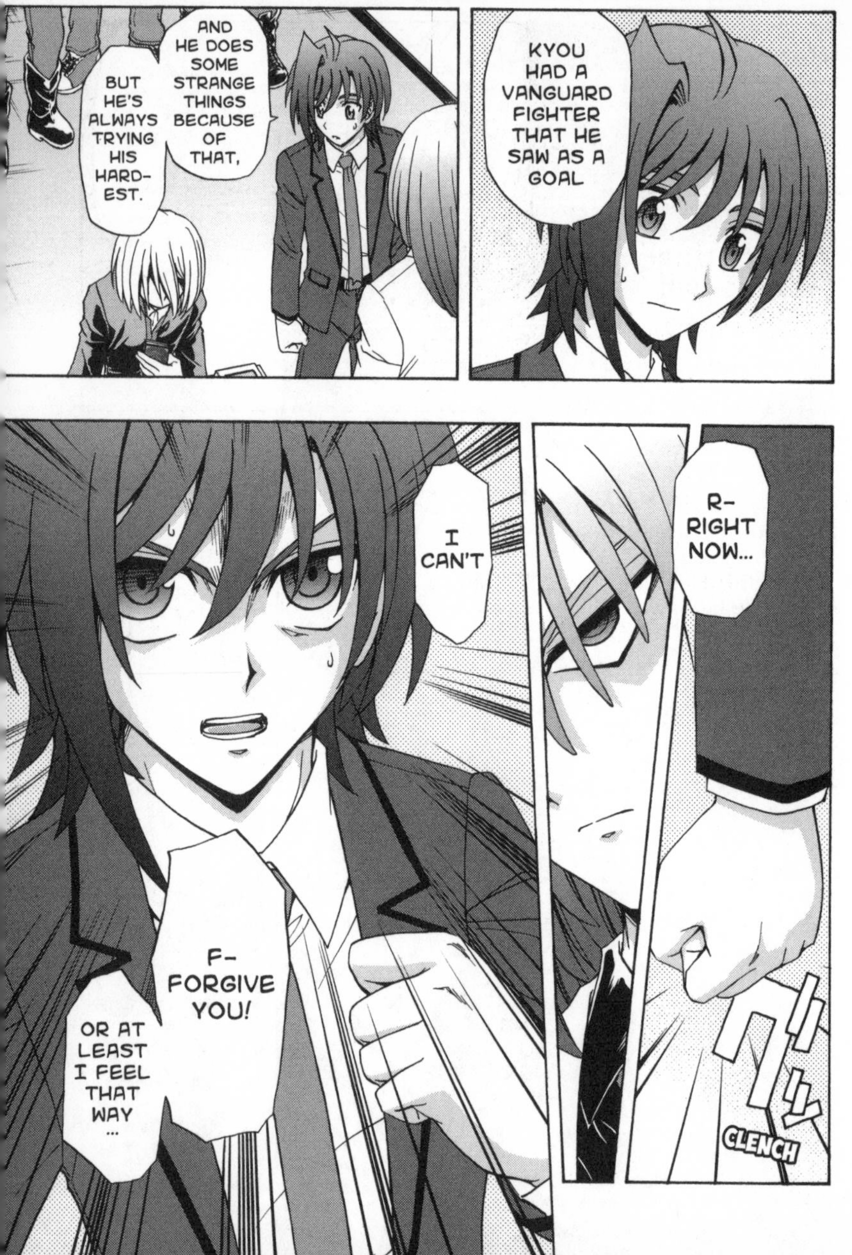
KYOU HAD A VANGUARD FIGHTER THAT HE SAW AS A GOAL
AND HE DOES SOME STRANGE THINGS BECAUSE OF THAT,
BUT HE'S ALWAYS TRYING HIS HARDEST.
R-RIGHT NOW...
CLENCH
I CAN'T
F-FORGIVE YOU!
OR AT LEAST I FEEL THAT WAY ...

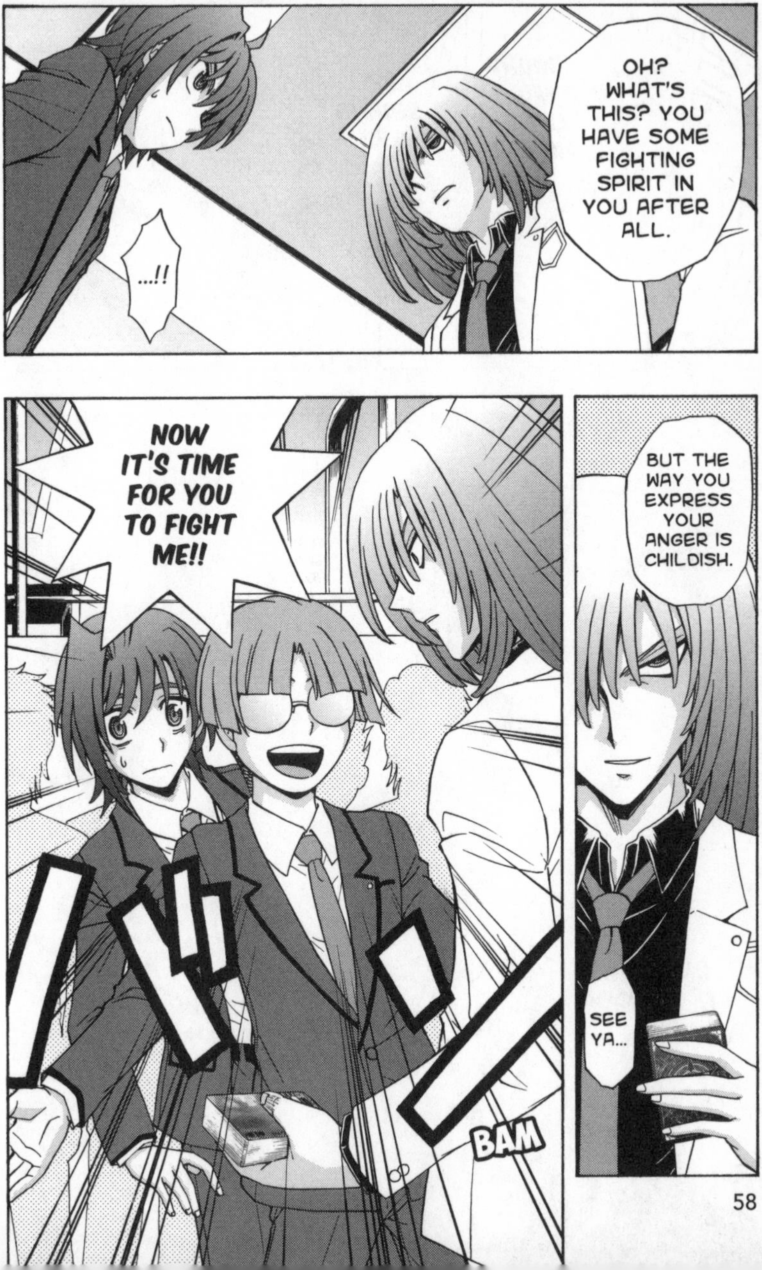
OH? WHAT'S THIS? YOU HAVE SOME FIGHTING SPIRIT IN YOU AFTER ALL.
...!!
BUT THE WAY YOU EXPRESS YOUR ANGER IS CHILDISH.
SEE YA...
NOW IT'S TIME FOR YOU TO FIGHT ME!!
BAM

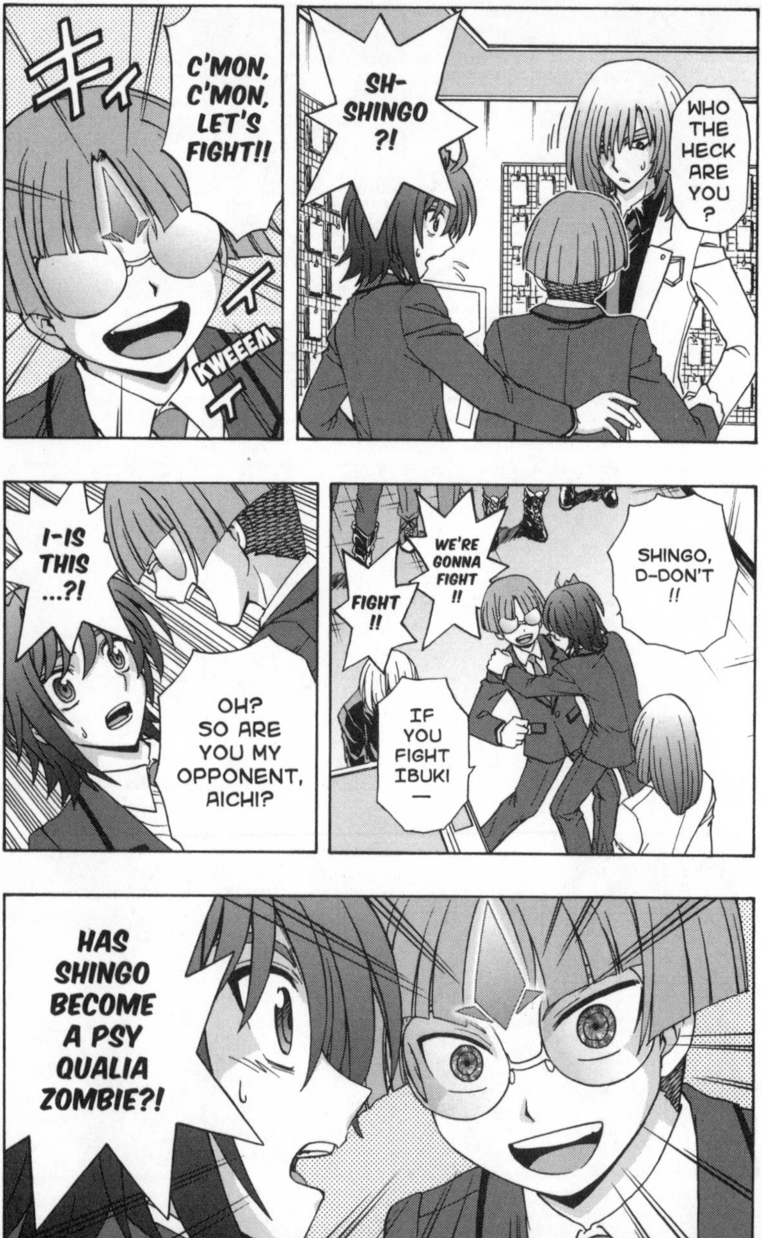
SH-SHINGO?!
WHO THE HECK ARE YOU?
C'MON, C'MON, LET'S FIGHT!!
KWEEEM
SHINGO, D-DON'T!!
WE'RE GONNA FIGHT!!
FIGHT!!
IF YOU FIGHT IBUKI—
I-IS THIS...?!
OH? SO ARE YOU MY OPPONENT, AICHI?
HAS SHINGO BECOME A PSY QUALIA ZOMBIE?!

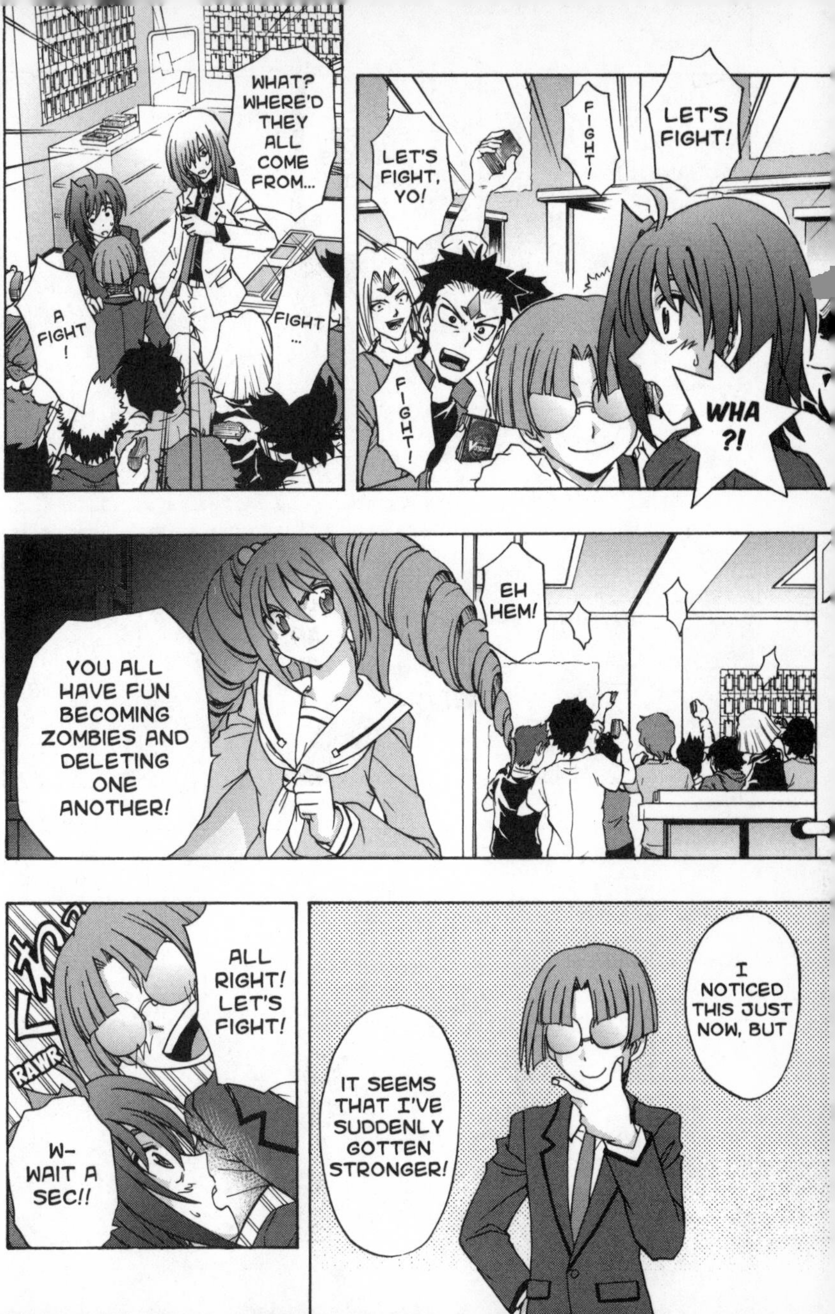
LET'S FIGHT!
FIGHT!
LET'S FIGHT, YO!
FIGHT!
WHA?!
WHAT? WHERE'D THEY ALL COME FROM...
FIGHT...
A FIGHT!
EH HEM!
YOU ALL HAVE FUN BECOMING ZOMBIES AND DELETING ONE ANOTHER!
I NOTICED THIS JUST NOW, BUT
IT SEEMS THAT I'VE SUDDENLY GOTTEN STRONGER!
ALL RIGHT! LET'S FIGHT!
RAWR
W-WAIT A SEC!!

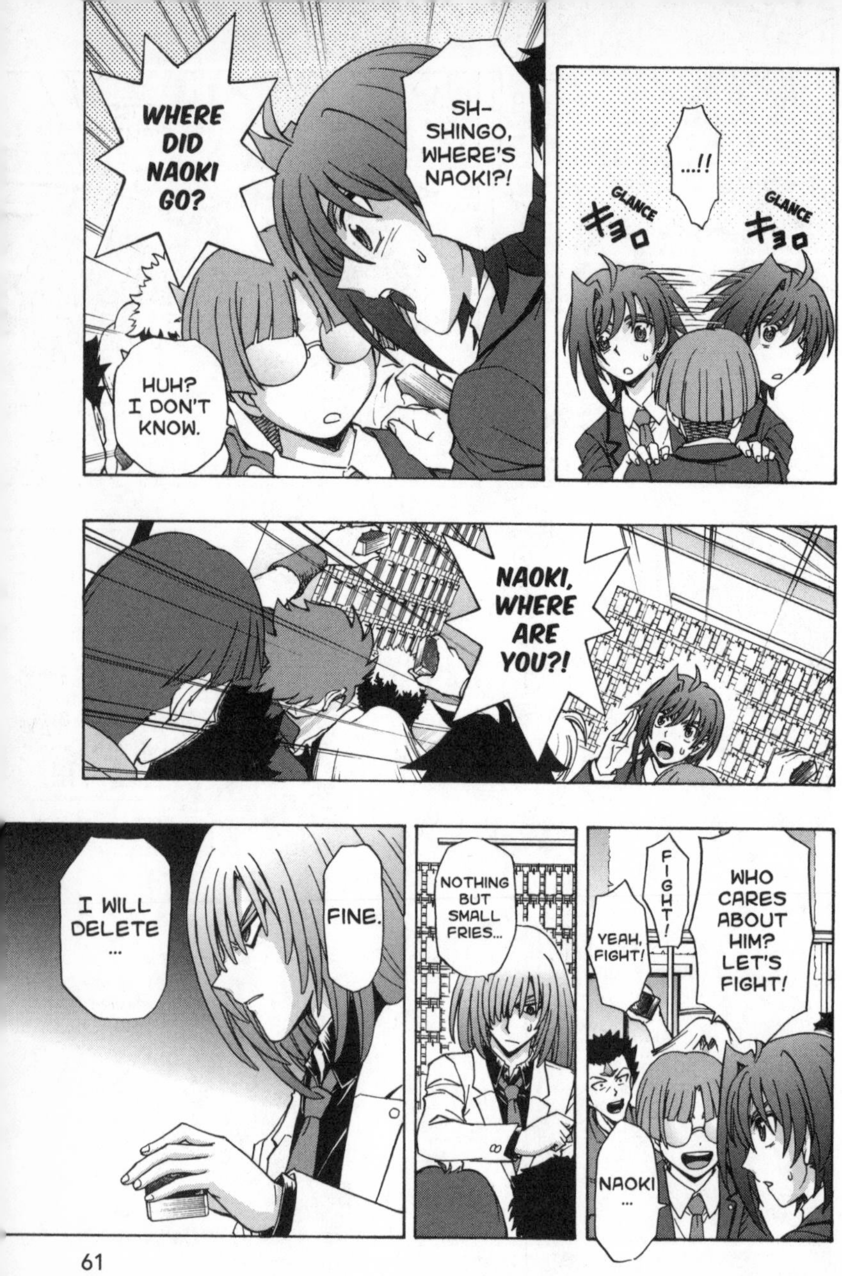
...!!
GLANCE
ギョロ
GLANCE
ギョロ
SH-SHINGO, WHERE'S NAOKI?!
WHERE DID NAOKI GO?
HUH? I DON'T KNOW.
NAOKI, WHERE ARE YOU?!
WHO CARES ABOUT HIM? LET'S FIGHT!
FIGHT!
YEAH, FIGHT!
NAOKI ...
NOTHING BUT SMALL FRIES...
FINE.
I WILL DELETE ...

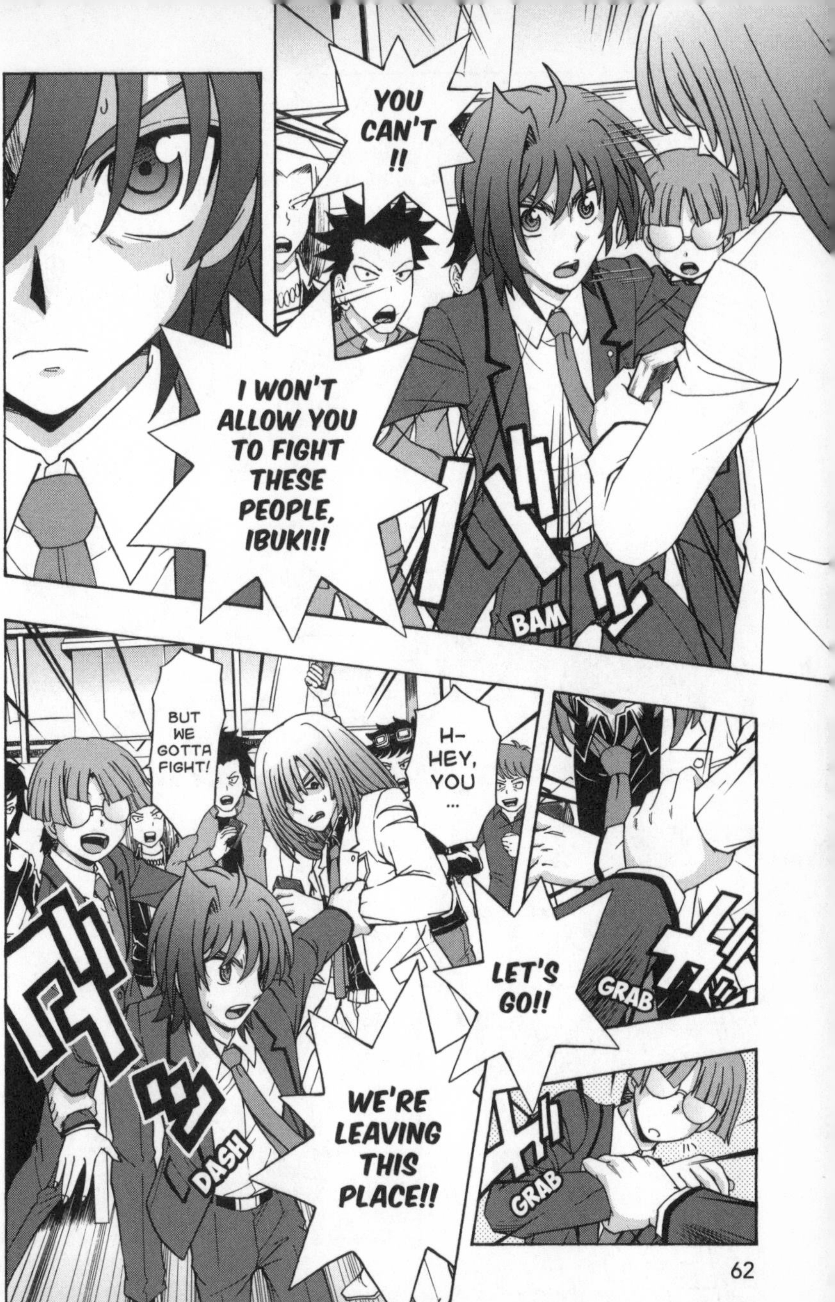
YOU CAN'T !!
I WON'T ALLOW YOU TO FIGHT THESE PEOPLE, IBUKI!!
BAM
GRAB
LET'S GO!!
GRAB
H-HEY, YOU ...
BUT WE GOTTA FIGHT!
WE'RE LEAVING THIS PLACE!!
DASH

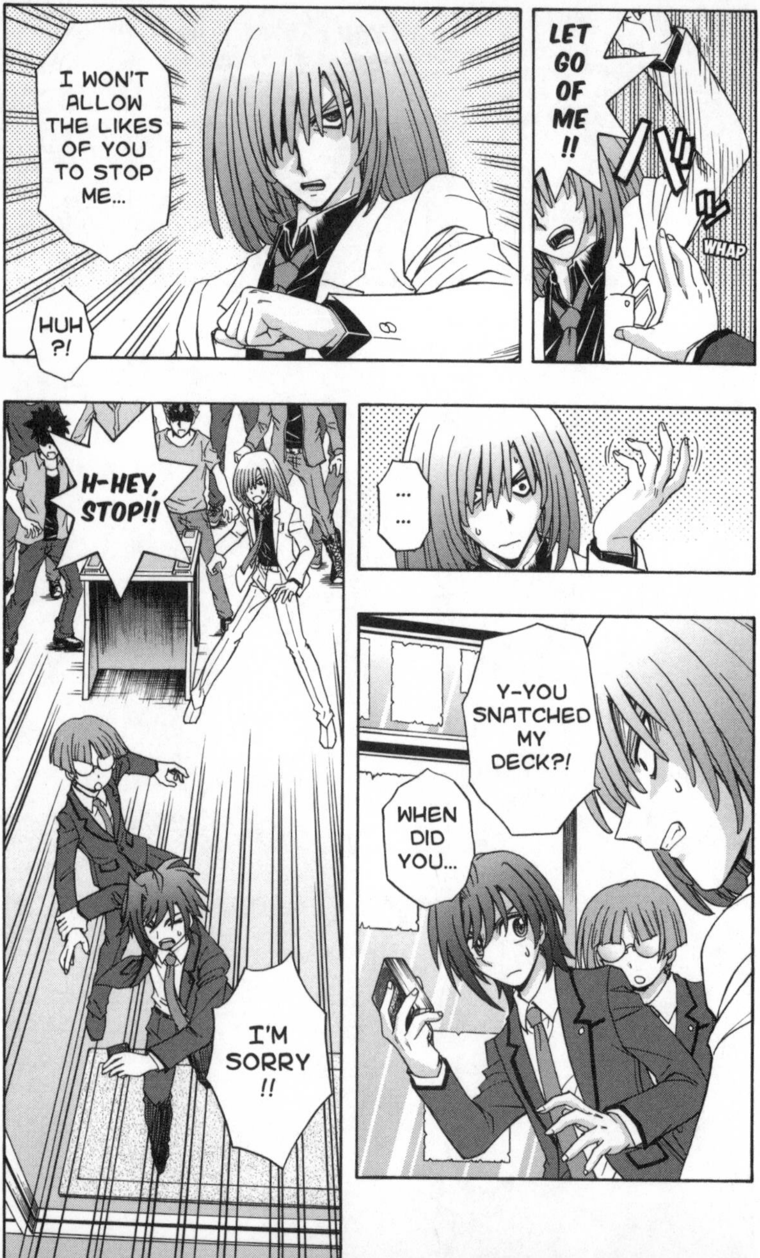
LET GO OF ME!!
WHAP
I WON'T ALLOW THE LIKES OF YOU TO STOP ME...
HUH?!
......
Y-YOU SNATCHED MY DECK?!
WHEN DID YOU...
H-HEY, STOP!!
I'M SORRY!!

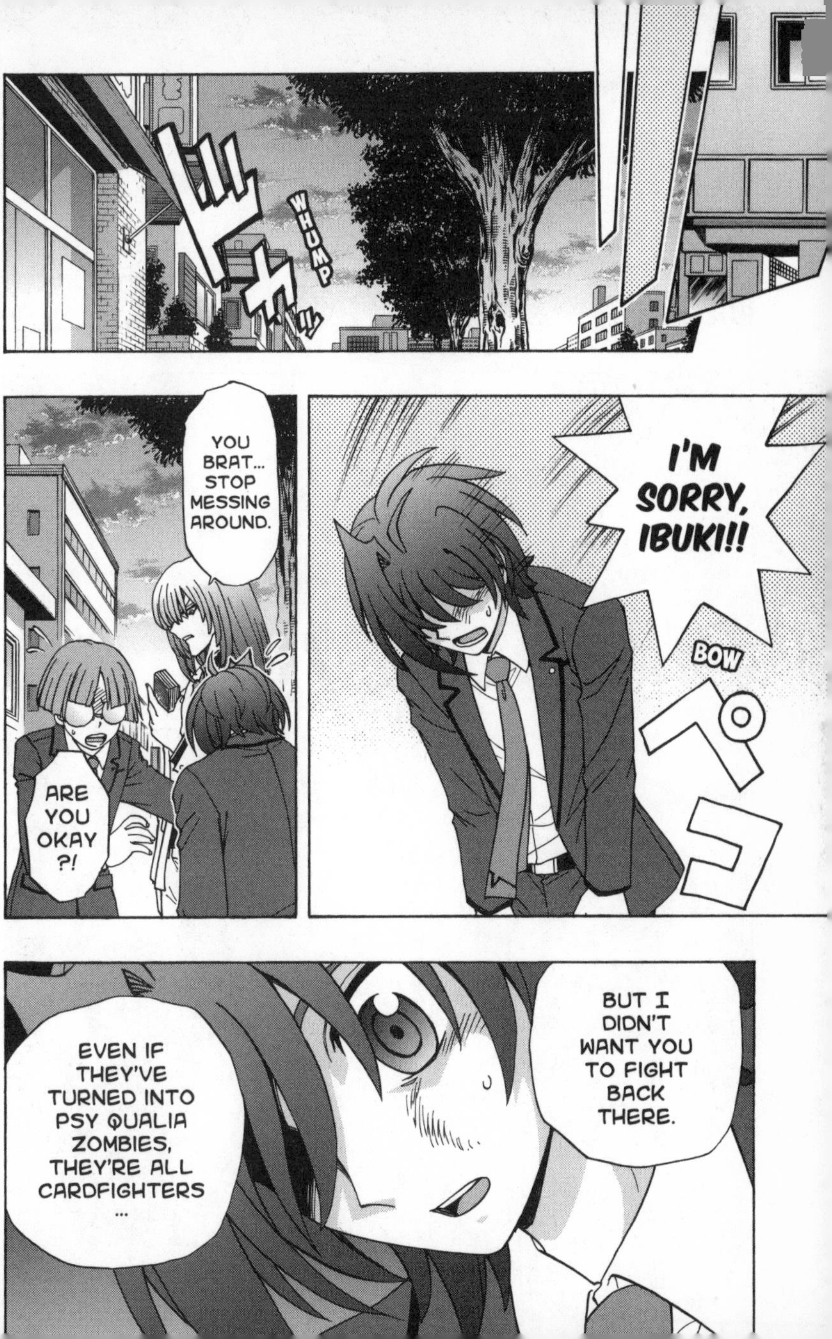
WHUMP
I'M SORRY, IBUKI!!
BOW
YOU BRAT... STOP MESSING AROUND.
ARE YOU OKAY?!
BUT I DIDN'T WANT YOU TO FIGHT BACK THERE.
EVEN IF THEY'VE TURNED INTO PSY QUALIA ZOMBIES, THEY'RE ALL CARDFIGHTERS...

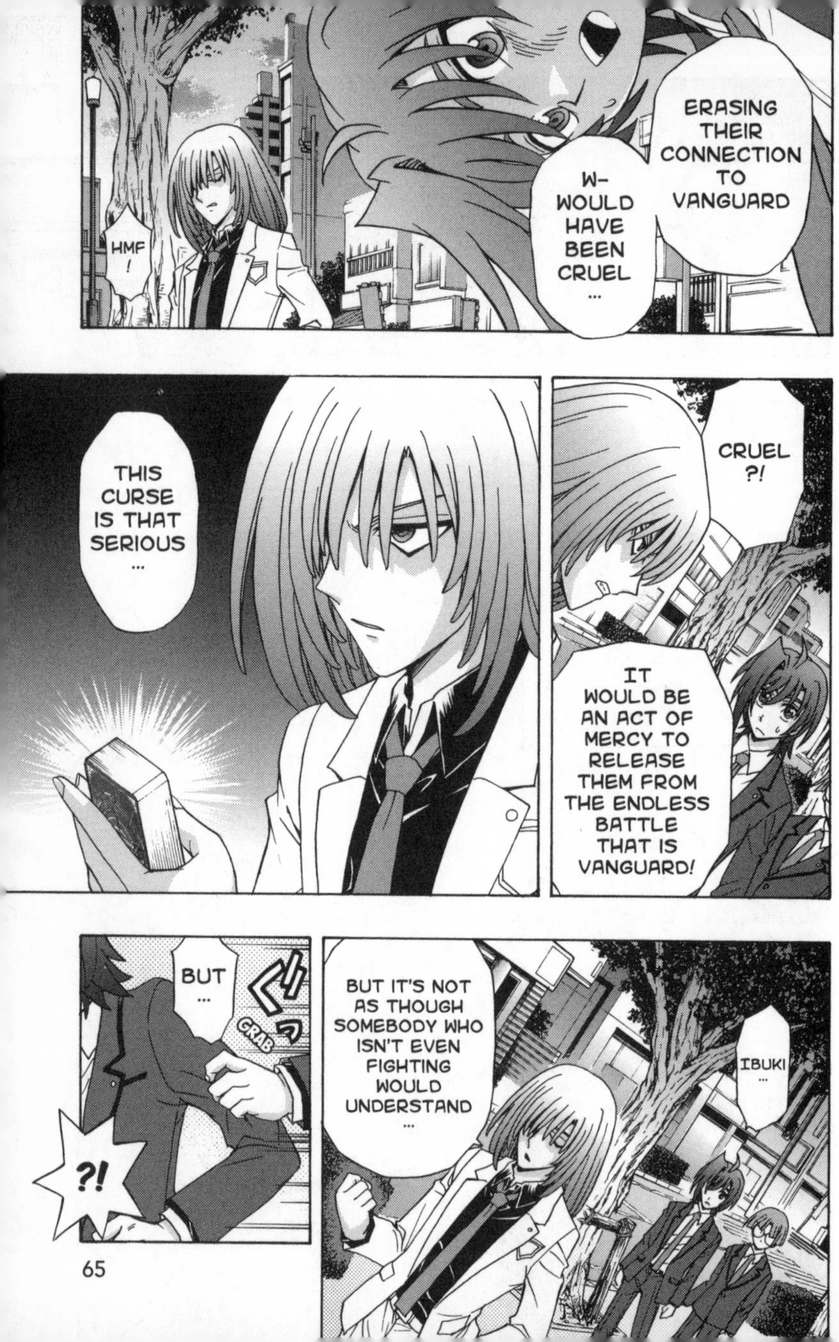
ERASING THEIR CONNECTION TO VANGUARD
W-WOULD HAVE BEEN CRUEL ...
HMF!
CRUEL?!
IT WOULD BE AN ACT OF MERCY TO RELEASE THEM FROM THE ENDLESS BATTLE THAT IS VANGUARD!
THIS CURSE IS THAT SERIOUS ...
IBUKI ...
BUT IT'S NOT AS THOUGH SOMEBODY WHO ISN'T EVEN FIGHTING WOULD UNDERSTAND ...
BUT ...
GRAB
?!

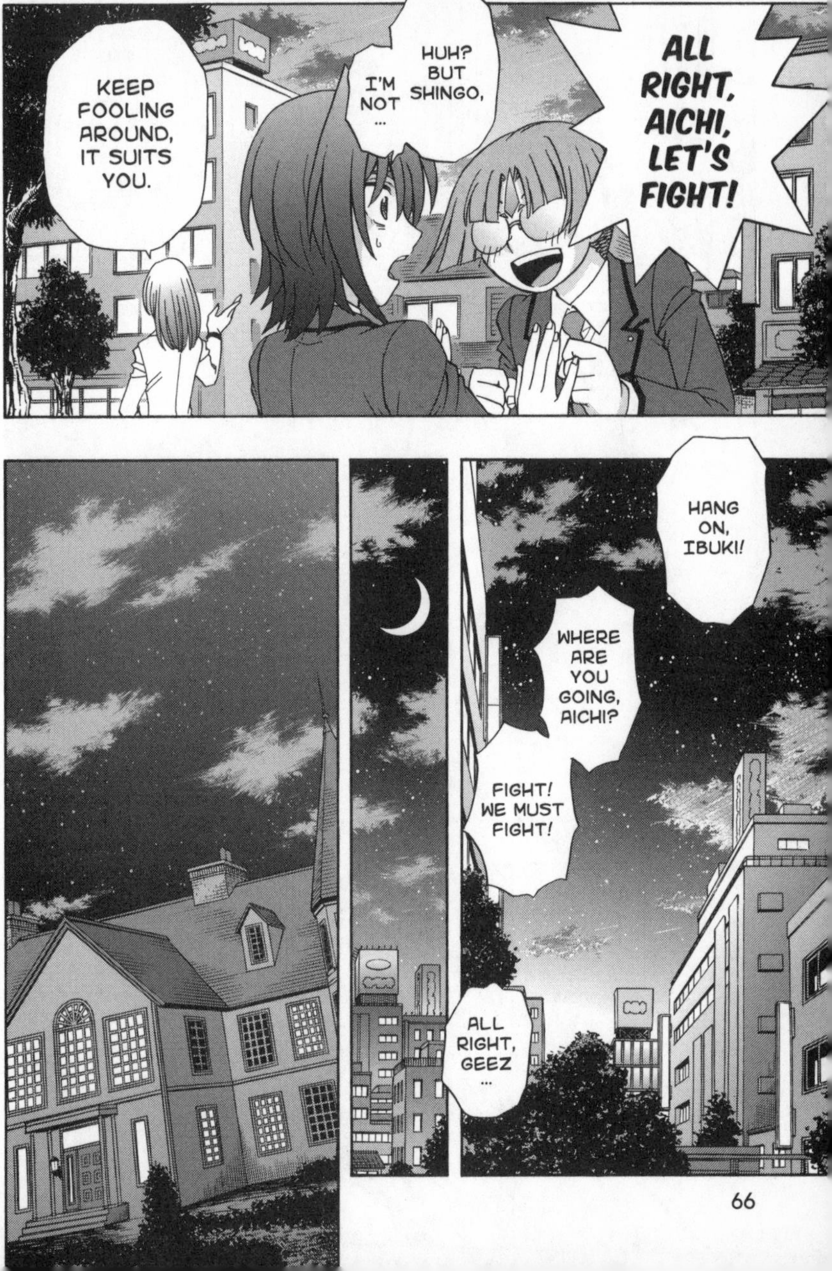
ALL RIGHT, AICHI, LET'S FIGHT!
HUH? BUT SHINGO,
I'M NOT ...
KEEP FOOLING AROUND, IT SUITS YOU.
HANG ON, IBUKI!
WHERE ARE YOU GOING, AICHI?
FIGHT! WE MUST FIGHT!
ALL RIGHT, GEEZ ...

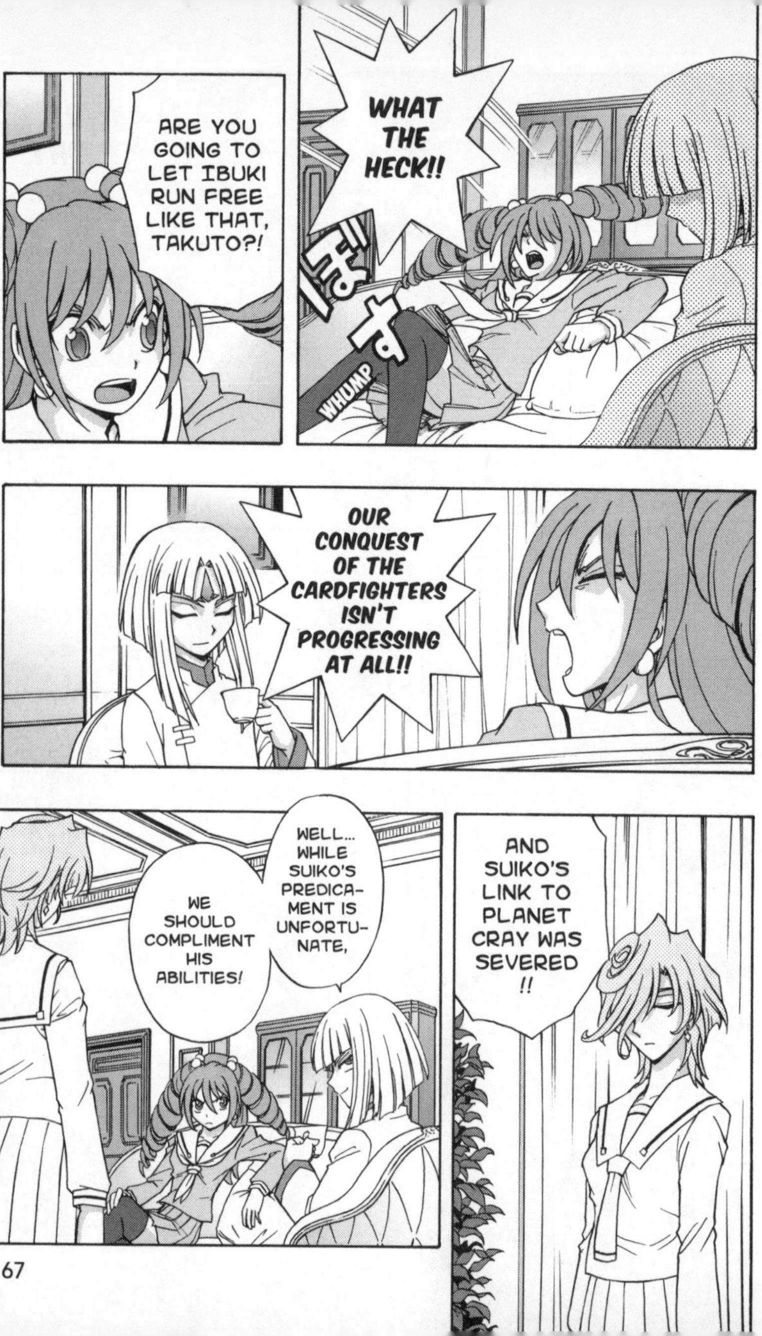
WHAT THE HECK!!
WHUMP
ARE YOU GOING TO LET IBUKI RUN FREE LIKE THAT, TAKUTO?!
OUR CONQUEST OF THE CARDFIGHTERS ISN'T PROGRESSING AT ALL!!
AND SUIKO'S LINK TO PLANET CRAY WAS SEVERED !!
WELL... WHILE SUIKO'S PREDICA-MENT IS UNFORTU-NATE,
WE SHOULD COMPLIMENT HIS ABILITIES!

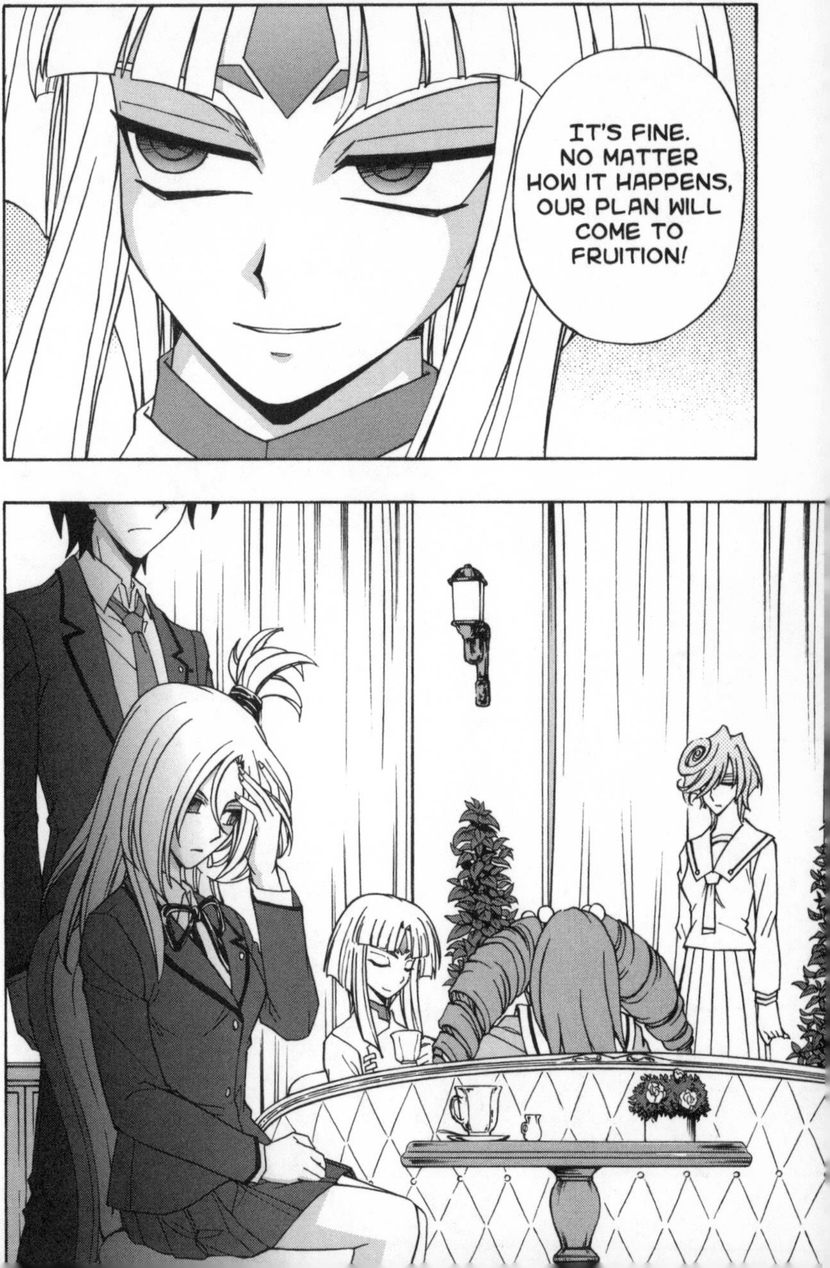
IT'S FINE. NO MATTER HOW IT HAPPENS, OUR PLAN WILL COME TO FRUITION!

CARDFIGHT!! Vanguard

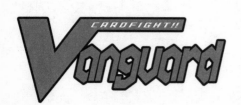

BONUS! CARDFIGHT!! Vanguard

NEVER-BEFORE-SEEN IMAGE BOARDS

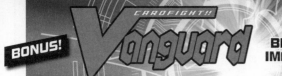

We're revealing the super-secret character references for the units for the new anime series "Cardfight!! Vanguard G"

Blaster Blade

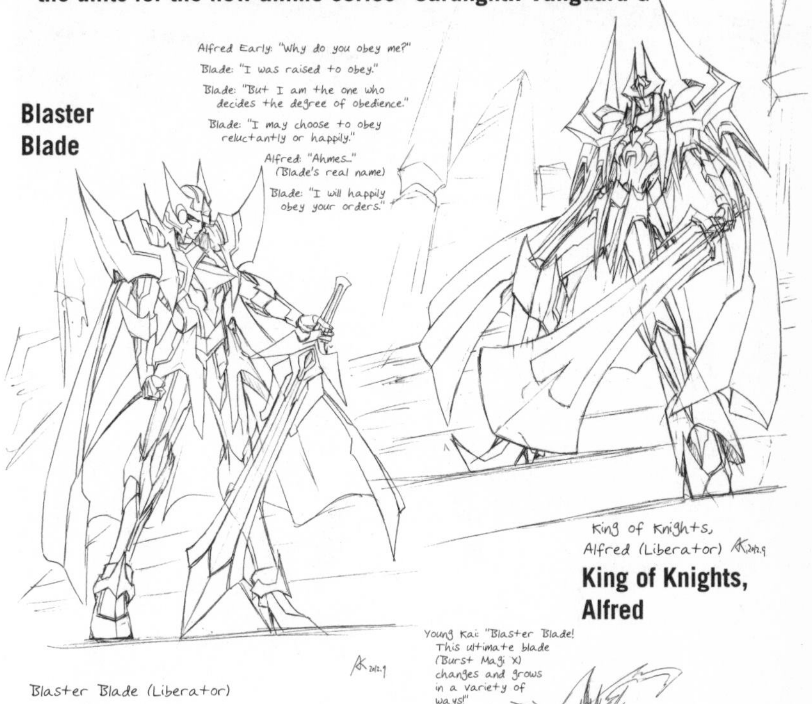

Alfred Early: "Why do you obey me?"
Blade: "I was raised to obey."
Blade: "But I am the one who decides the degree of obedience."
Blade: "I may choose to obey reluctantly or happily."
Alfred: "Ahmes..." (Blade's real name)
Blade: "I will happily obey your orders."
King of Knights, Alfred (Liberator) AK 2012.9
AK 2012.9
Blaster Blade (Liberator)

King of Knights, Alfred

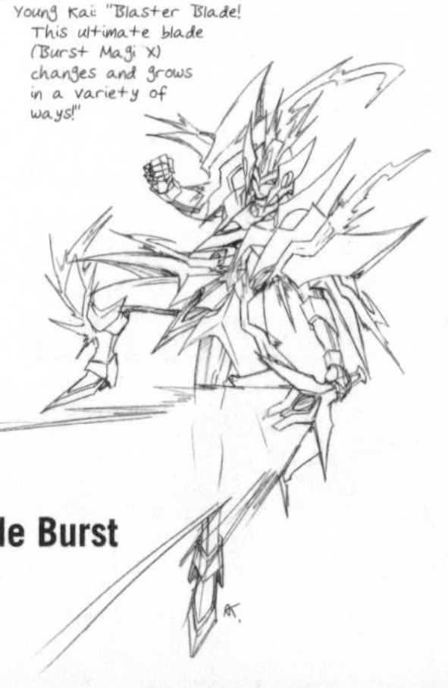

Young Kai: "Blaster Blade! This ultimate blade (Burst Magi X) changes and grows in a variety of ways!"
AK.

G3-Blaster Blade Burst

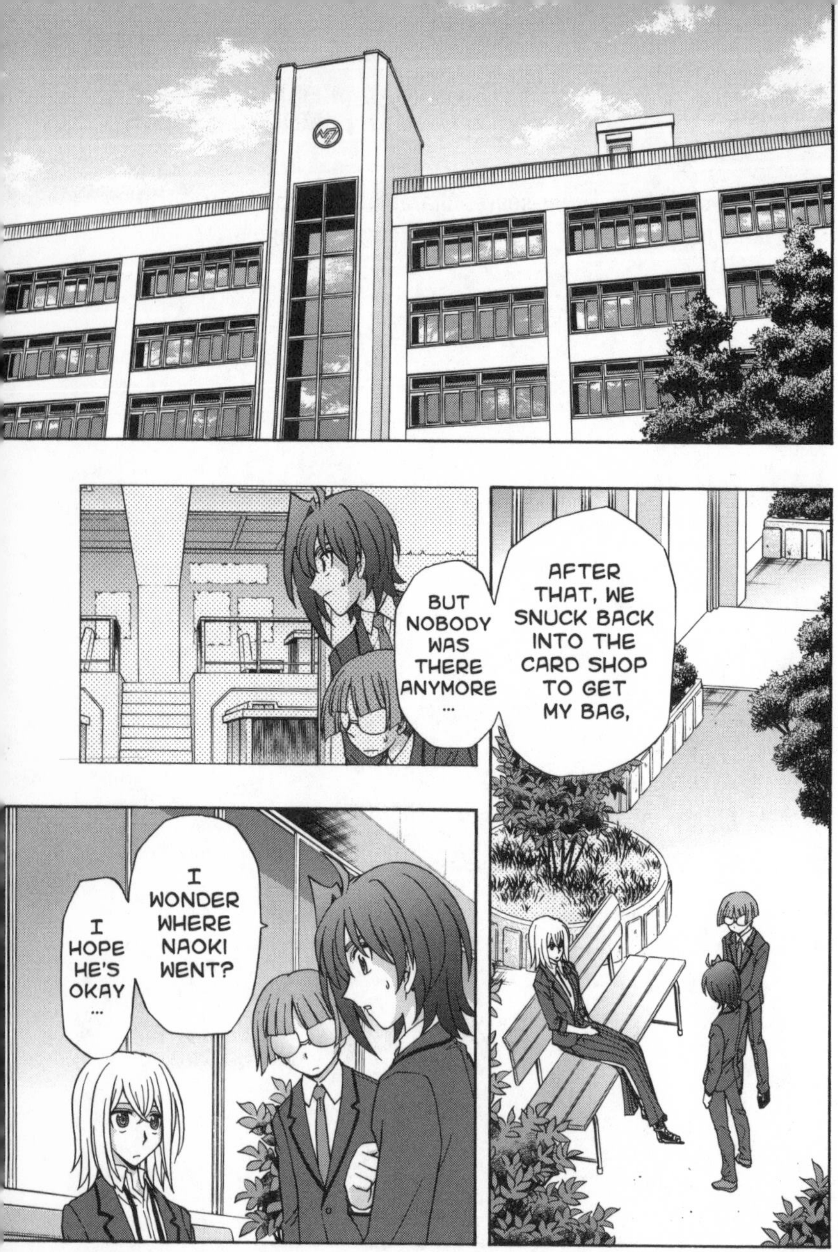
AFTER THAT, WE SNUCK BACK INTO THE CARD SHOP TO GET MY BAG,
BUT NOBODY WAS THERE ANYMORE...
I WONDER WHERE NAOKI WENT?
I HOPE HE'S OKAY...

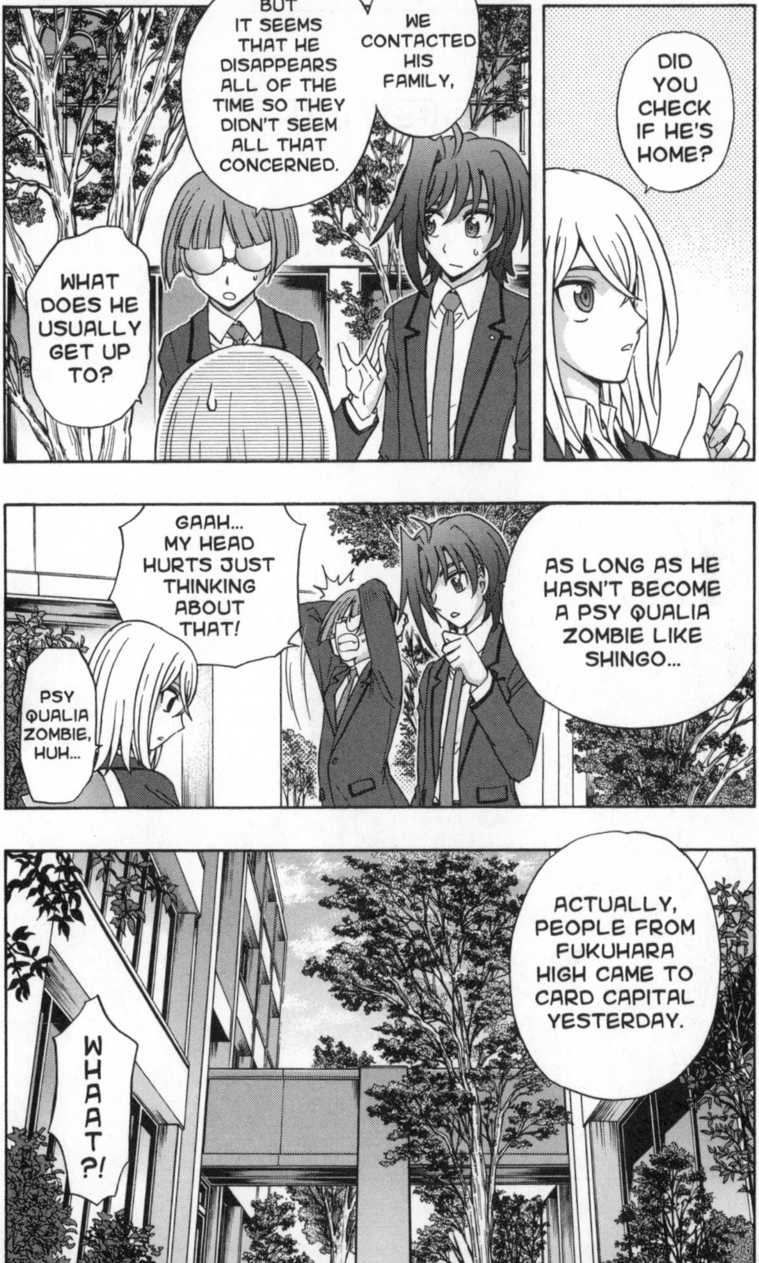
DID YOU CHECK IF HE'S HOME?
WE CONTACTED HIS FAMILY,
BUT IT SEEMS THAT HE DISAPPEARS ALL OF THE TIME SO THEY DIDN'T SEEM ALL THAT CONCERNED.
WHAT DOES HE USUALLY GET UP TO?
AS LONG AS HE HASN'T BECOME A PSY QUALIA ZOMBIE LIKE SHINGO...
GAAH... MY HEAD HURTS JUST THINKING ABOUT THAT!
PSY QUALIA ZOMBIE, HUH...
ACTUALLY, PEOPLE FROM FUKUHARA HIGH CAME TO CARD CAPITAL YESTERDAY.
WHAAAT?!

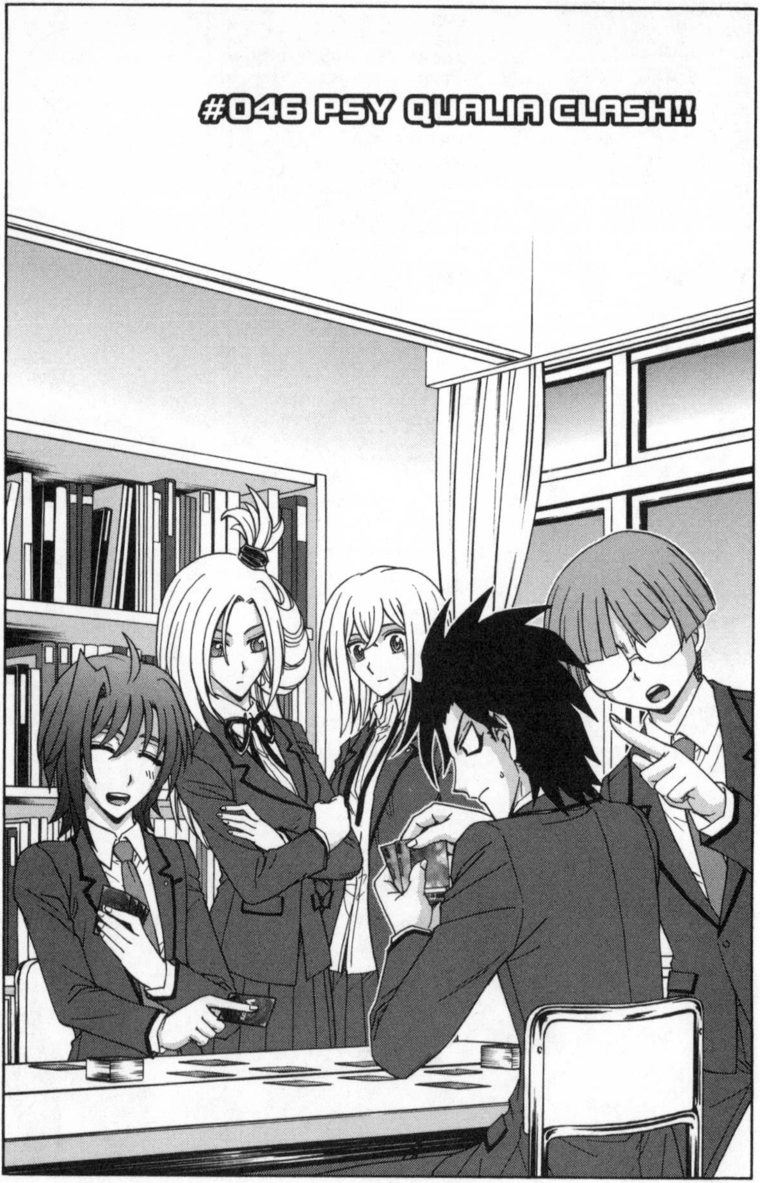
#046 PSY QUALIA CLASH!!

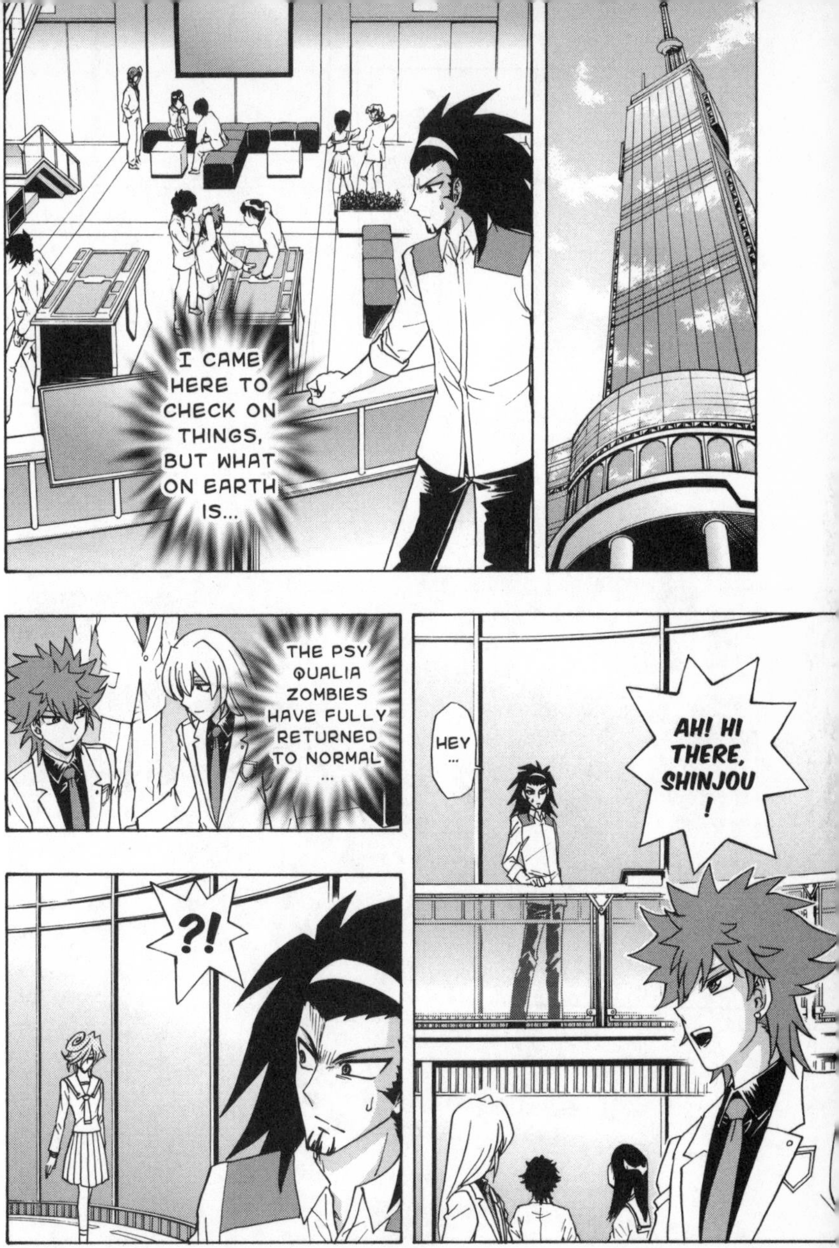
I CAME HERE TO CHECK ON THINGS, BUT WHAT ON EARTH IS...
AH! HI THERE, SHINJOU!
HEY...
THE PSY QUALIA ZOMBIES HAVE FULLY RETURNED TO NORMAL...
?!

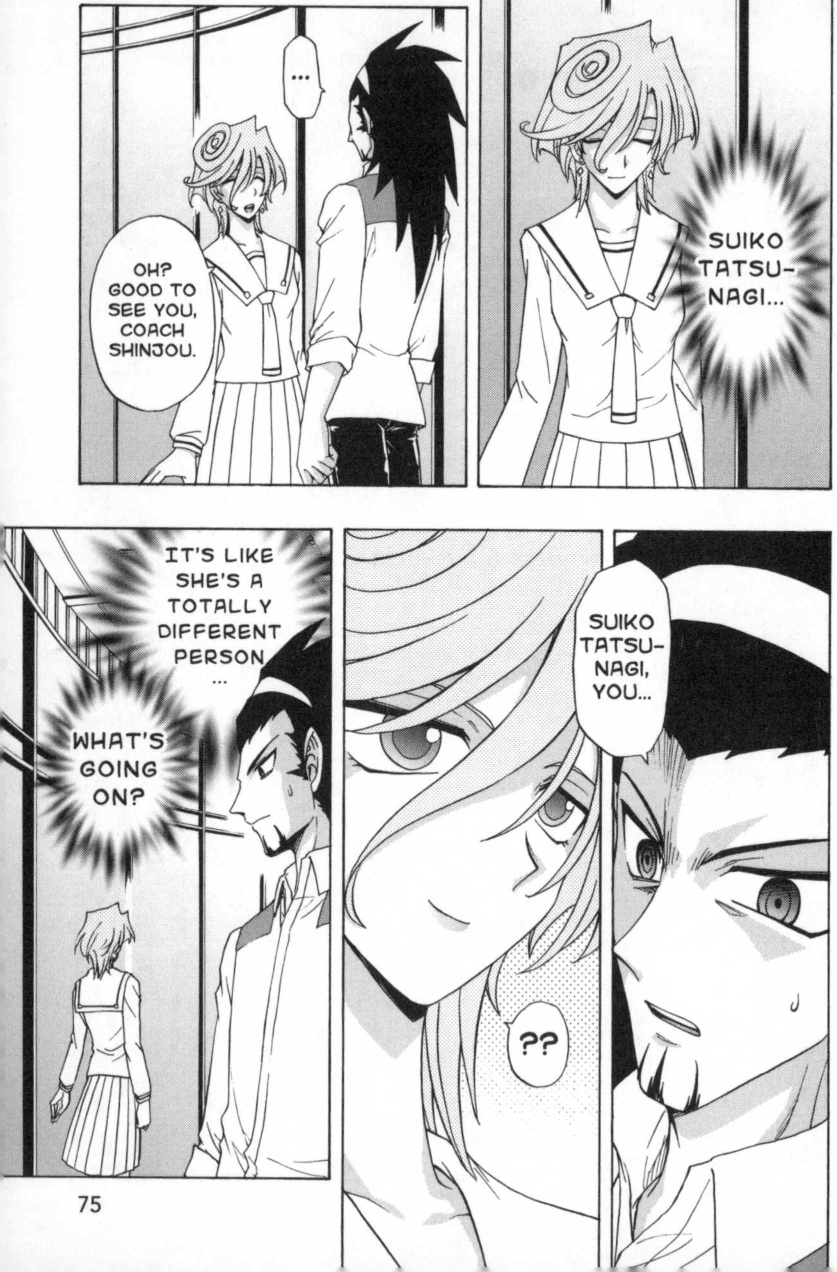
SUIKO TATSU-NAGI...
...
OH? GOOD TO SEE YOU, COACH SHINJOU.
SUIKO TATSU-NAGI, YOU...
??
IT'S LIKE SHE'S A TOTALLY DIFFERENT PERSON ...
WHAT'S GOING ON?

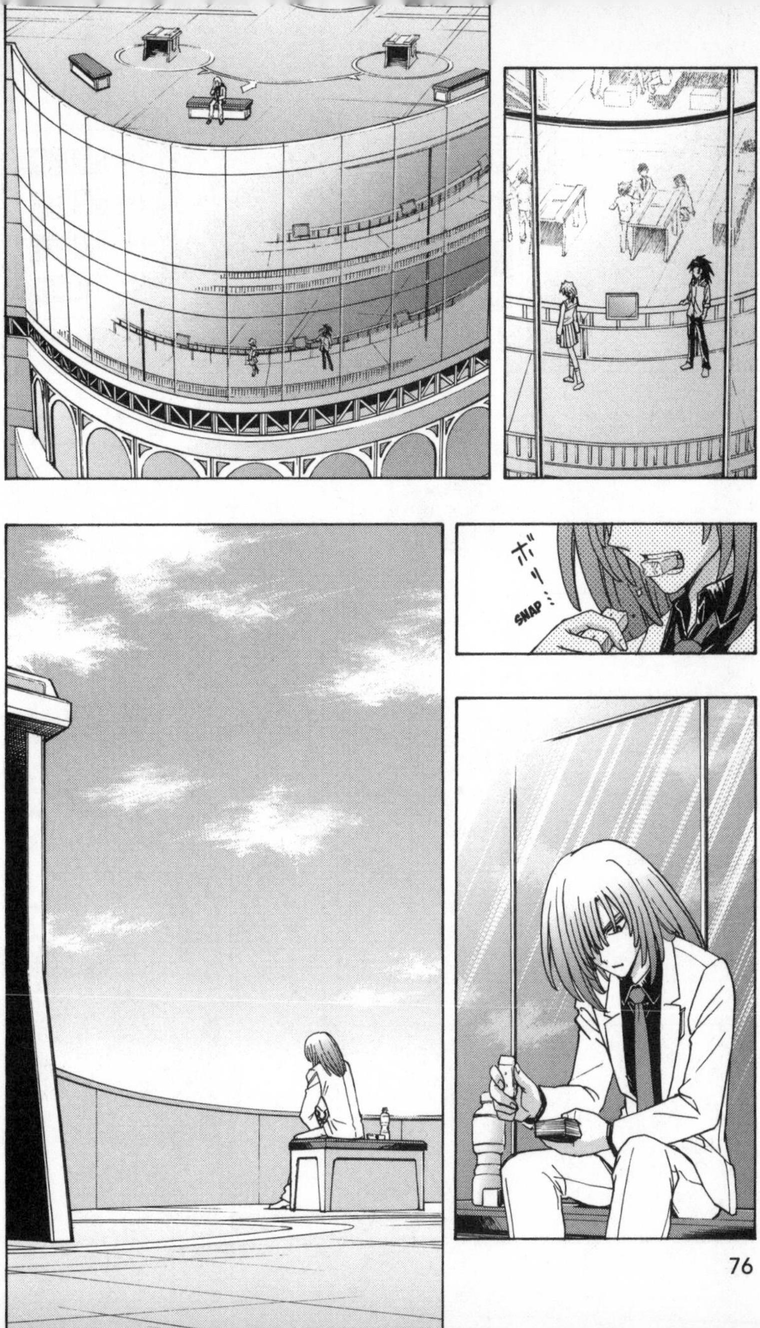
ボリ…
SNAP

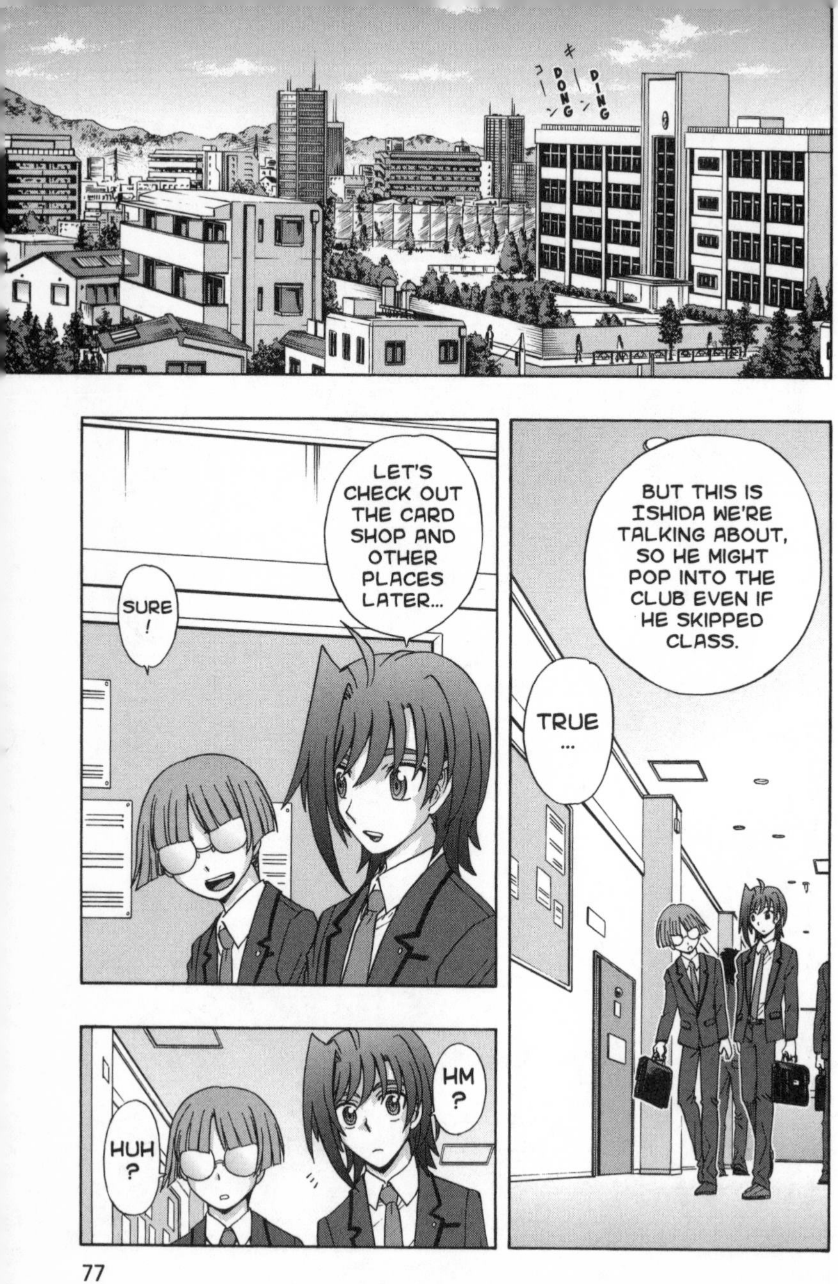
キーン DING
コーン DONG
BUT THIS IS ISHIDA WE'RE TALKING ABOUT, SO HE MIGHT POP INTO THE CLUB EVEN IF HE SKIPPED CLASS.
TRUE...
LET'S CHECK OUT THE CARD SHOP AND OTHER PLACES LATER...
SURE!
HM?
HUH?

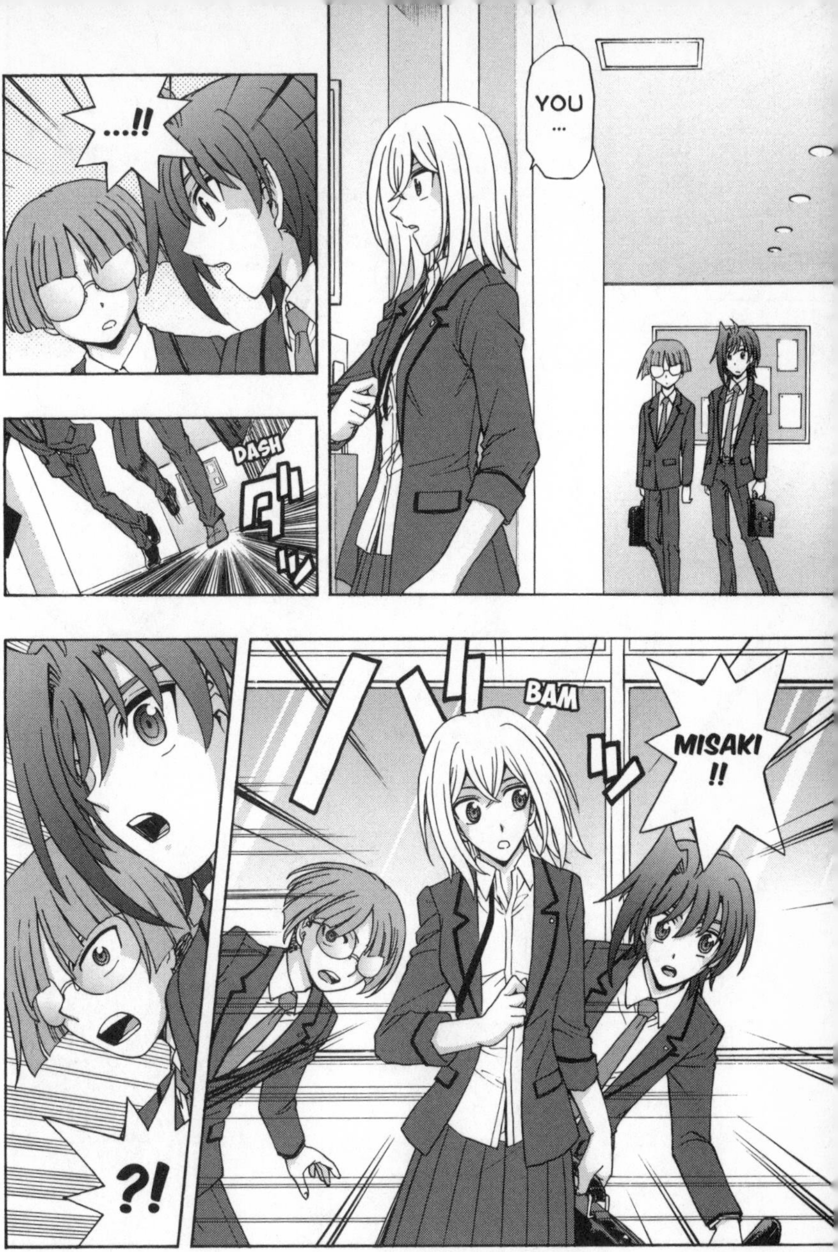
YOU ...
...!!
DASH
BAM
MISAKI !!
?!

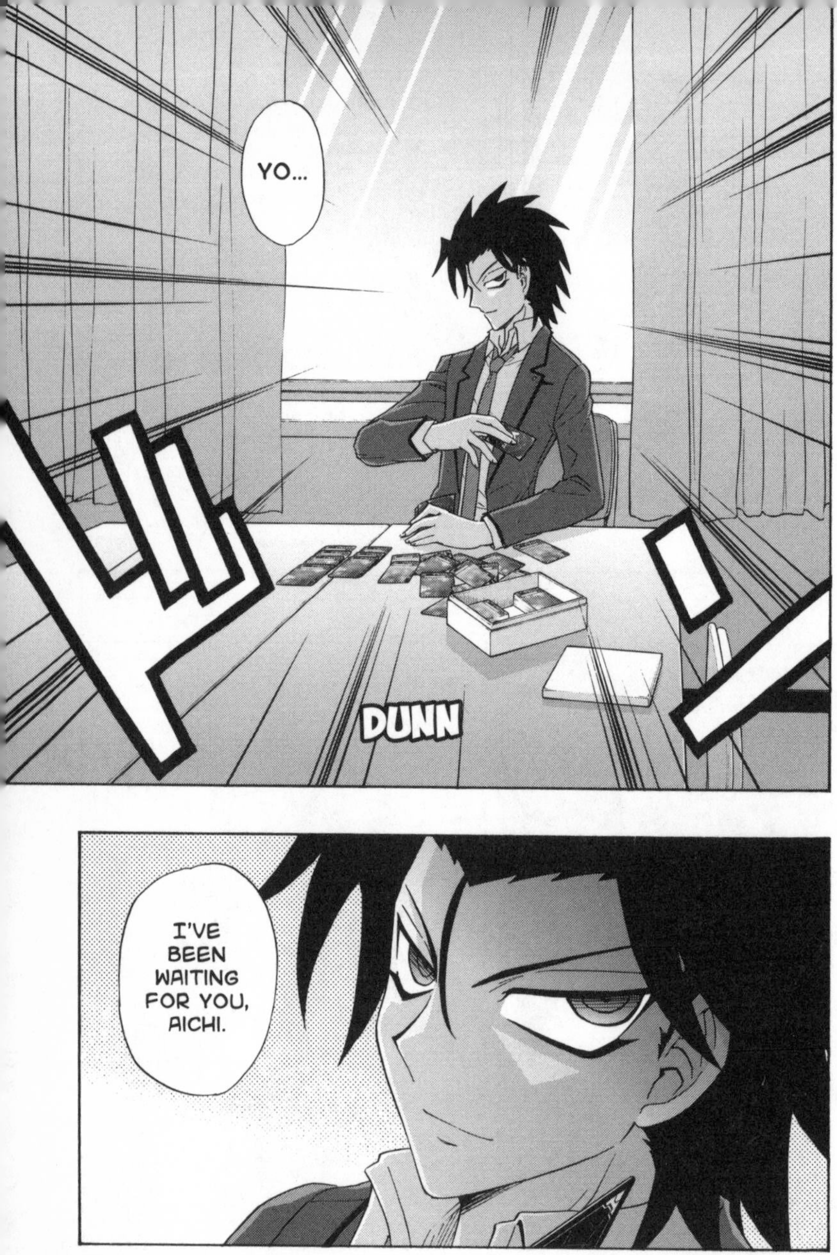
YO...
DUNN
I'VE BEEN WAITING FOR YOU, AICHI.

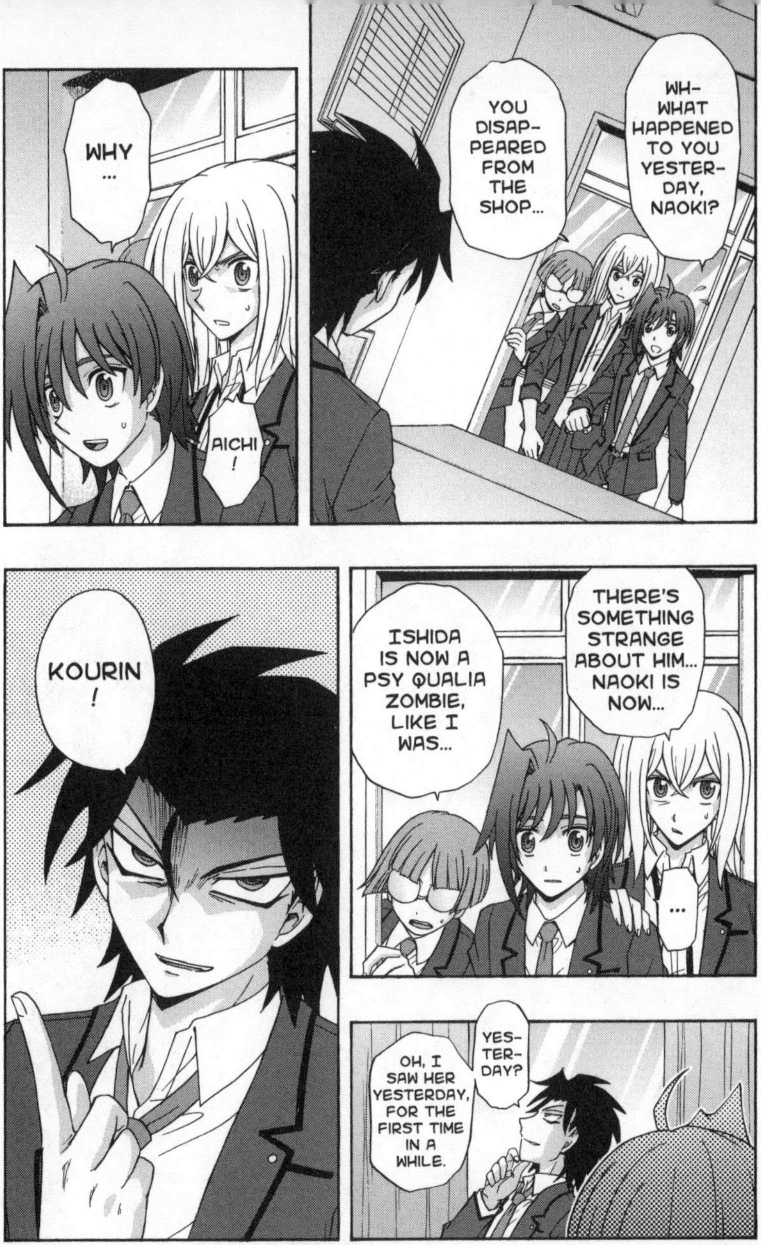
WH- WHAT HAPPENED TO YOU YESTER- DAY, NAOKI?
YOU DISAP- PEARED FROM THE SHOP...
WHY ...
AICHI !
THERE'S SOMETHING STRANGE ABOUT HIM... NAOKI IS NOW...
ISHIDA IS NOW A PSY QUALIA ZOMBIE, LIKE I WAS...
...
YES- TER- DAY?
OH, I SAW HER YESTERDAY, FOR THE FIRST TIME IN A WHILE.
KOURIN !

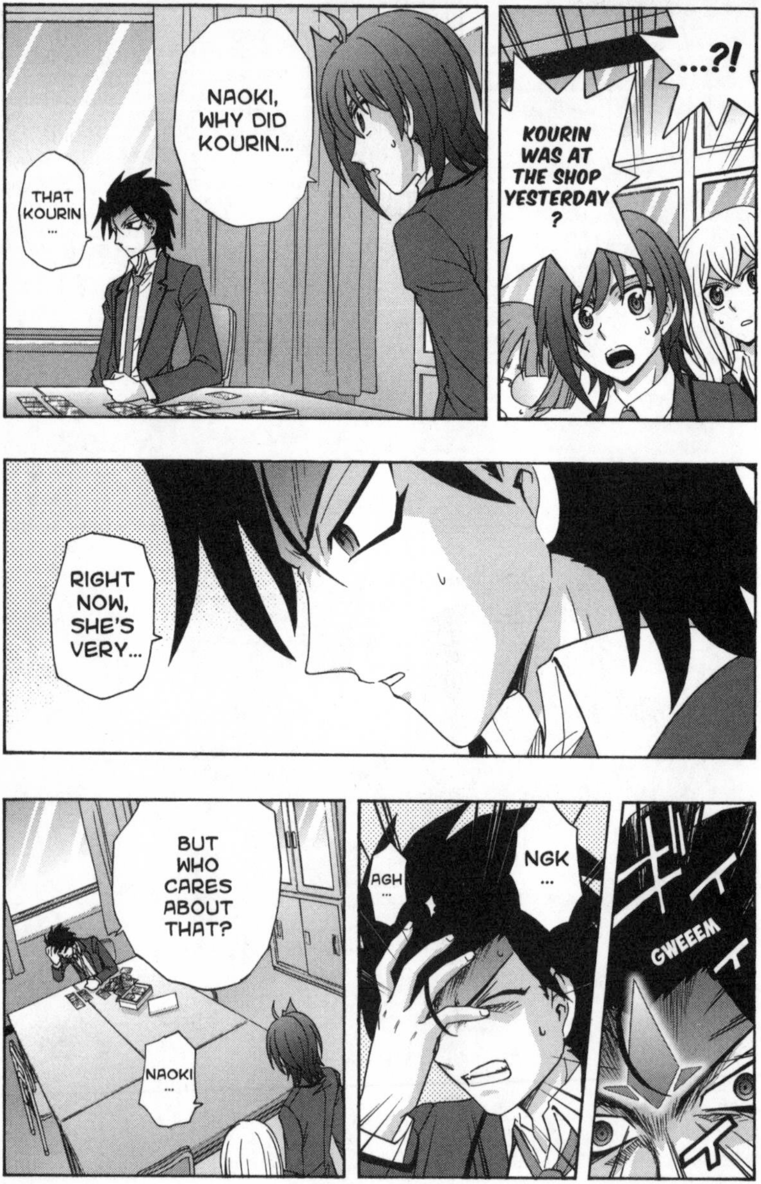
...?!
KOURIN WAS AT THE SHOP YESTERDAY?
NAOKI, WHY DID KOURIN...
THAT KOURIN...
RIGHT NOW, SHE'S VERY...
GWEEEM
NGK...
AGH...
BUT WHO CARES ABOUT THAT?
NAOKI...

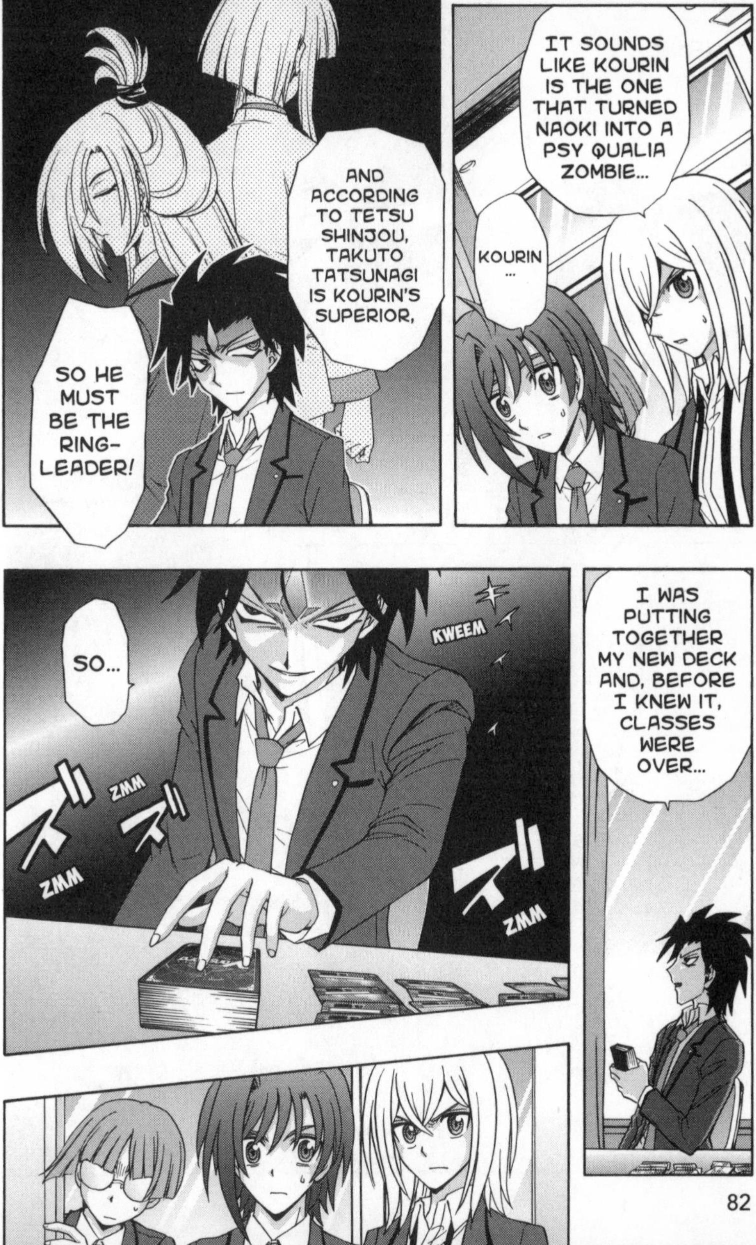
IT SOUNDS LIKE KOURIN IS THE ONE THAT TURNED NAOKI INTO A PSY QUALIA ZOMBIE...
KOURIN ...
AND ACCORDING TO TETSU SHINJOU, TAKUTO TATSUNAGI IS KOURIN'S SUPERIOR,
SO HE MUST BE THE RING-LEADER!
I WAS PUTTING TOGETHER MY NEW DECK AND, BEFORE I KNEW IT, CLASSES WERE OVER...
SO...
KWEEM
ZMM
ZMM
ZMM

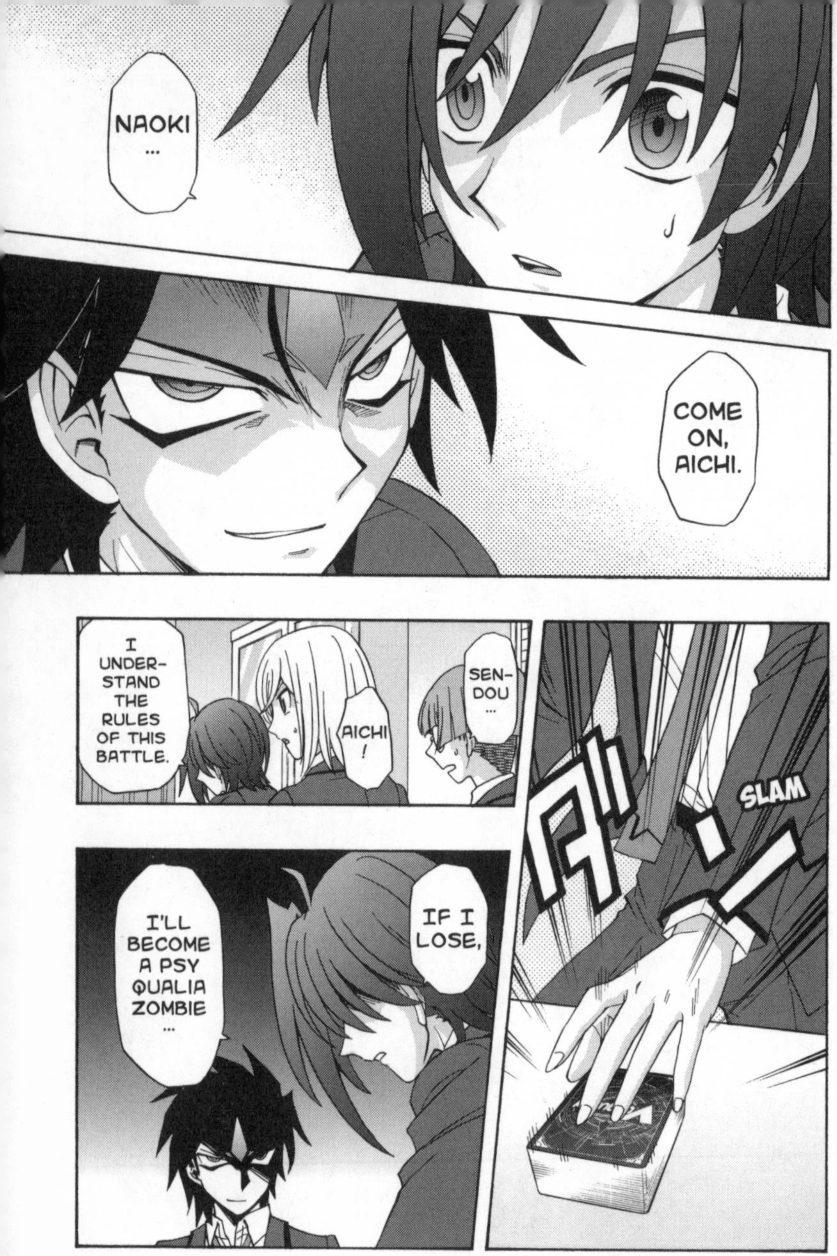
NAOKI ...
COME ON, AICHI.
SLAM
SEN-DOU ...
AICHI!
I UNDER-STAND THE RULES OF THIS BATTLE.
IF I LOSE,
I'LL BECOME A PSY QUALIA ZOMBIE ...

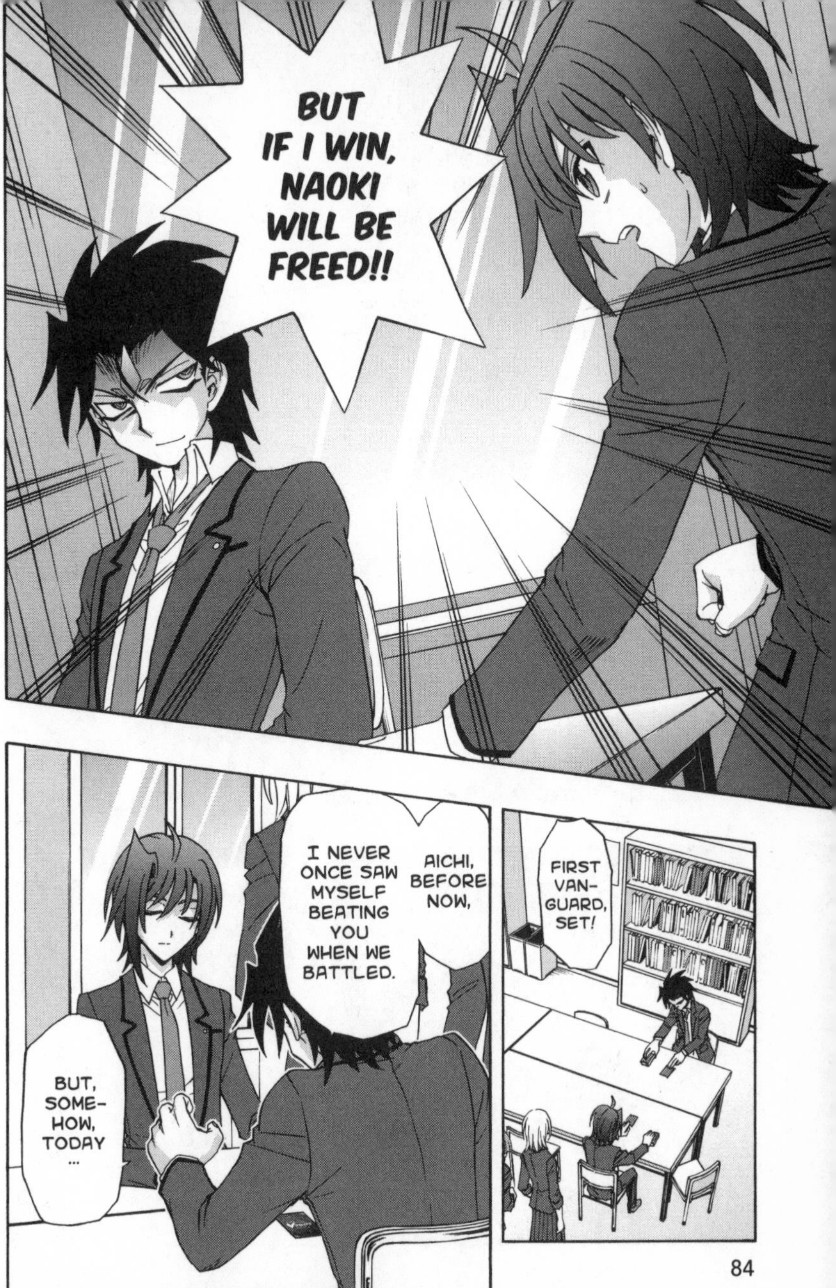
BUT IF I WIN, NAOKI WILL BE FREED!!
FIRST VAN-GUARD, SET!
AICHI, BEFORE NOW,
I NEVER ONCE SAW MYSELF BEATING YOU WHEN WE BATTLED.
BUT, SOME-HOW, TODAY ...

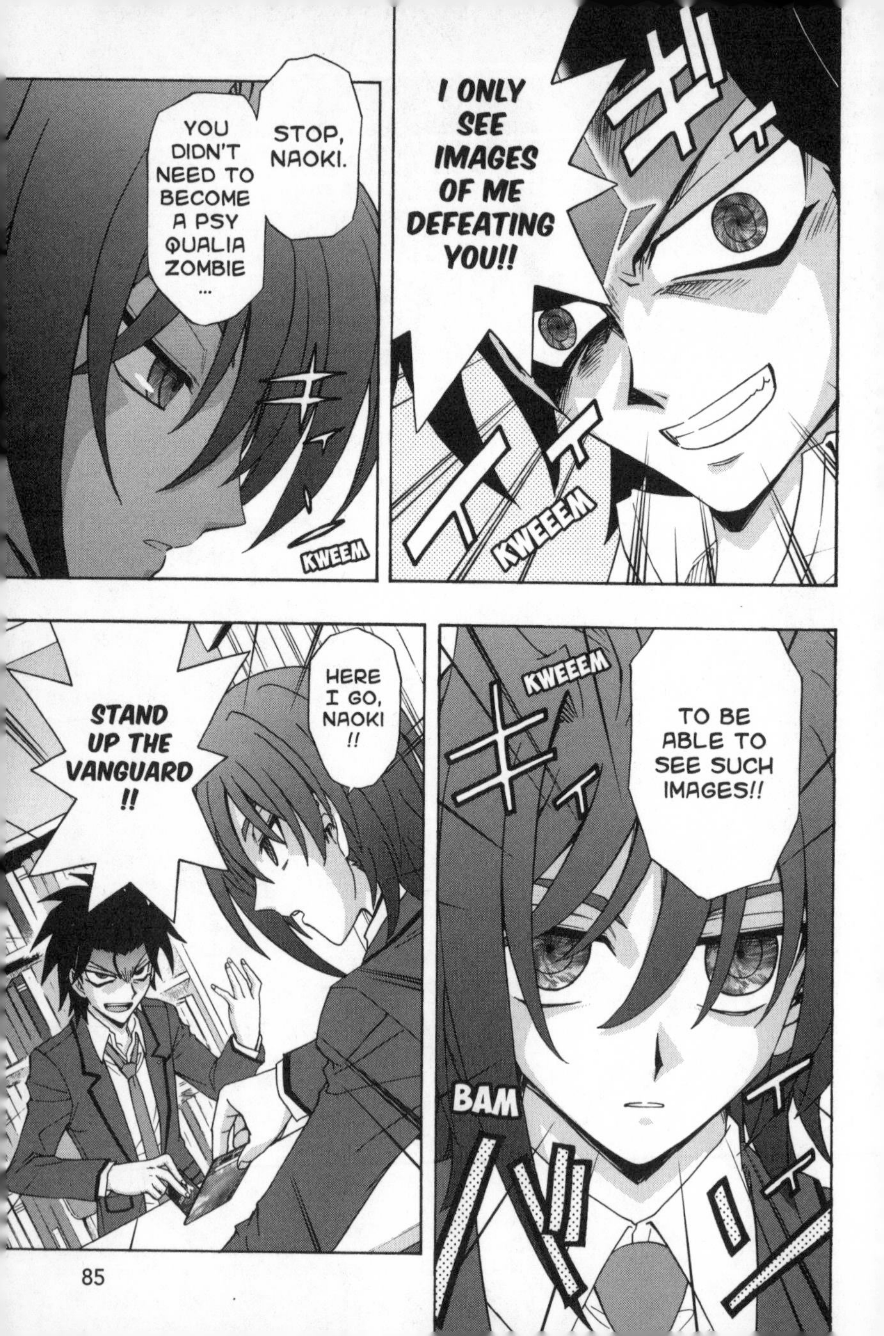
I ONLY SEE IMAGES OF ME DEFEATING YOU!!
KWEEEM
STOP, NAOKI.
YOU DIDN'T NEED TO BECOME A PSY QUALIA ZOMBIE ...
KWEEM
KWEEEM
TO BE ABLE TO SEE SUCH IMAGES!!
BAM
HERE I GO, NAOKI !!
STAND UP THE VANGUARD !!

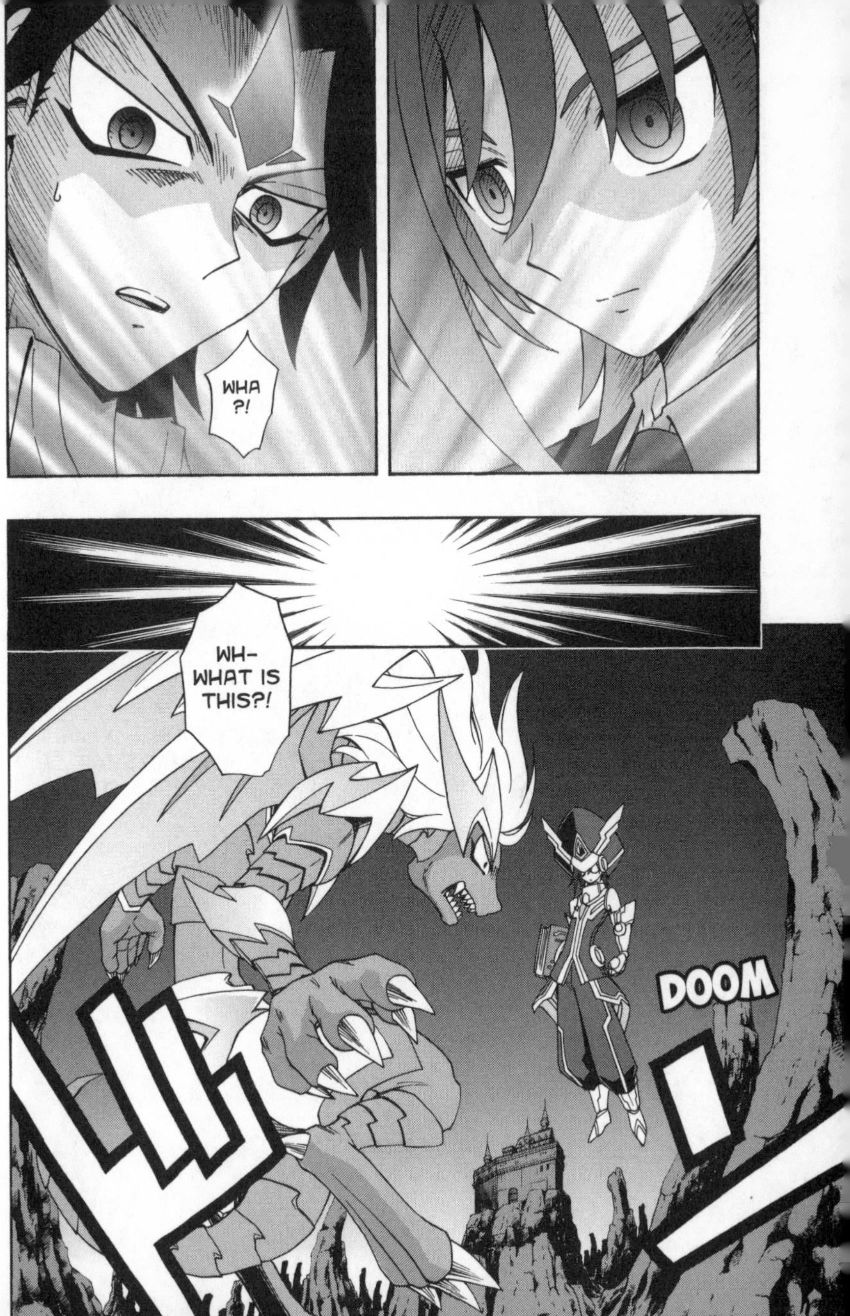
WHA ?!
WH- WHAT IS THIS?!
DOOM

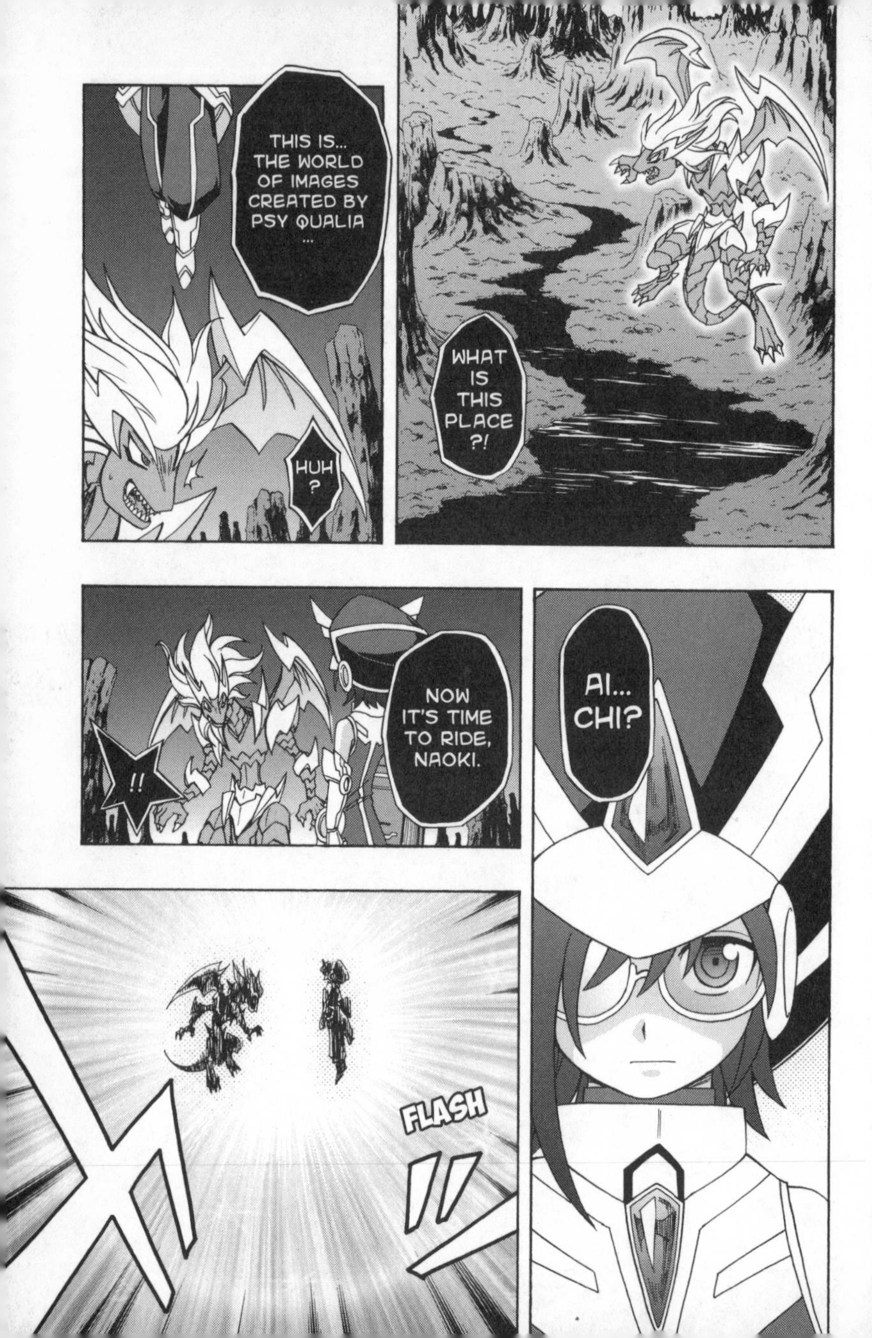
WHAT IS THIS PLACE?!
THIS IS... THE WORLD OF IMAGES CREATED BY PSY QUALIA...
HUH?
AI... CHI?
NOW IT'S TIME TO RIDE, NAOKI.
!!
FLASH

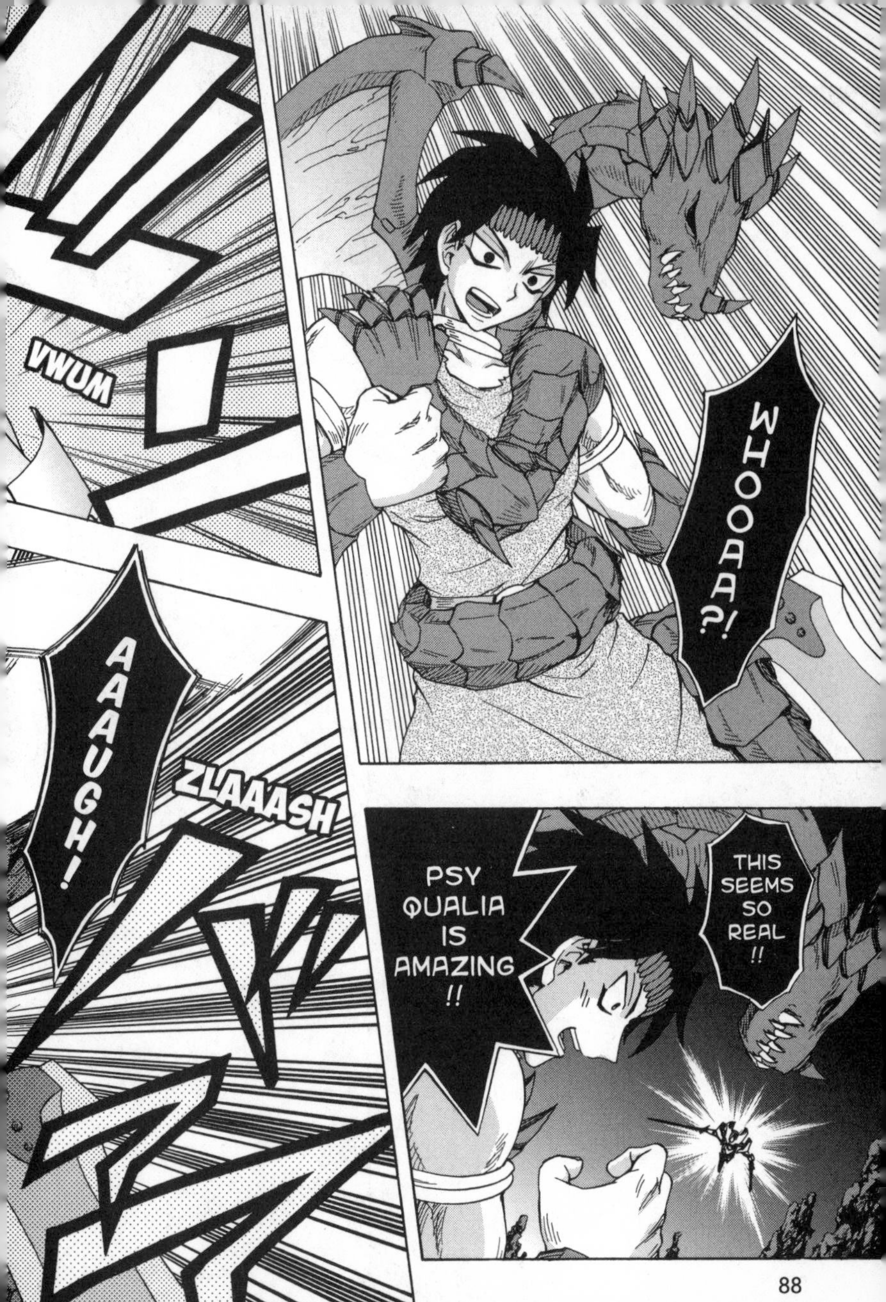
WHOOAAA?!
THIS SEEMS SO REAL!!
PSY QUALIA IS AMAZING!!
VWUM
AAAAUGH!
ZLAAASH

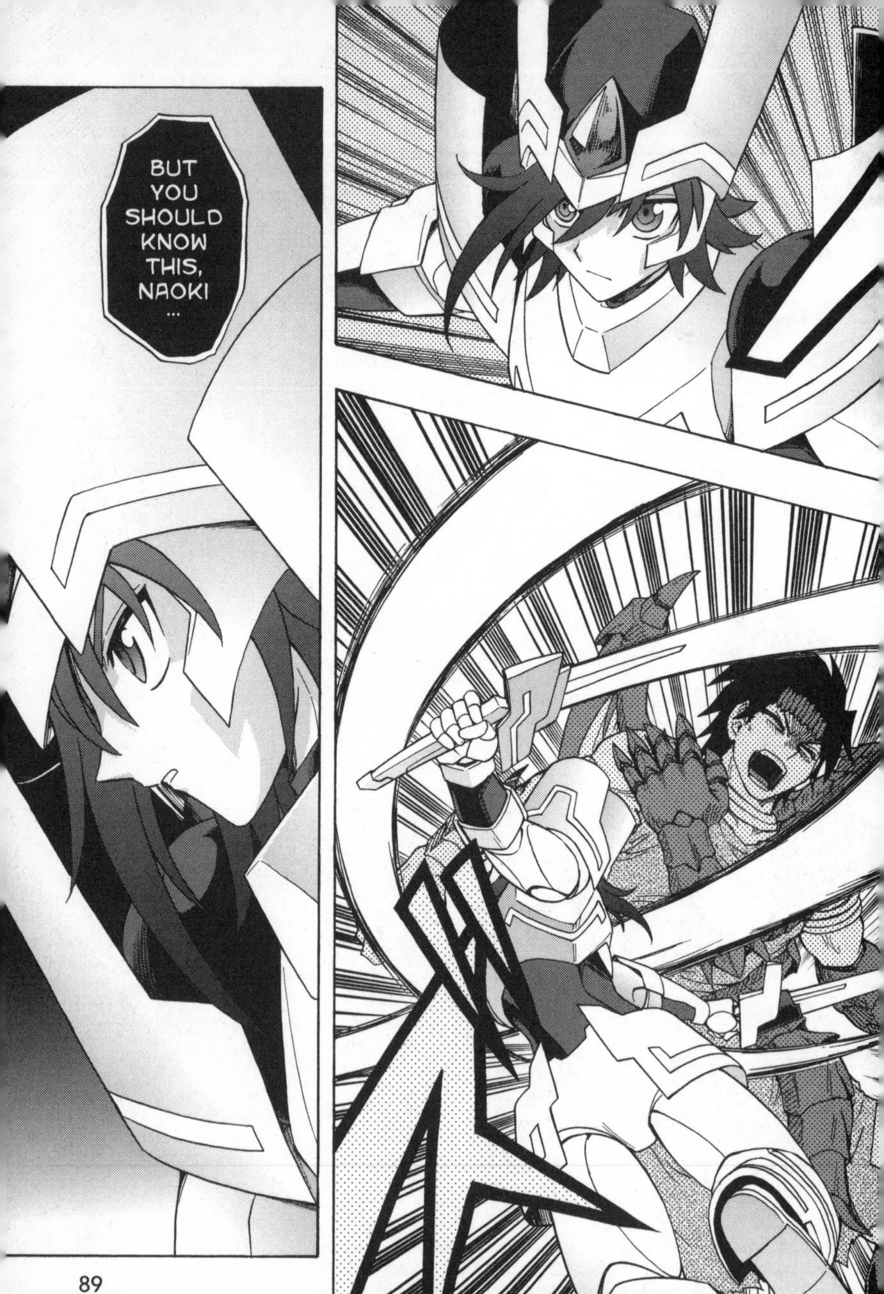
BUT YOU SHOULD KNOW THIS, NAOKI ...

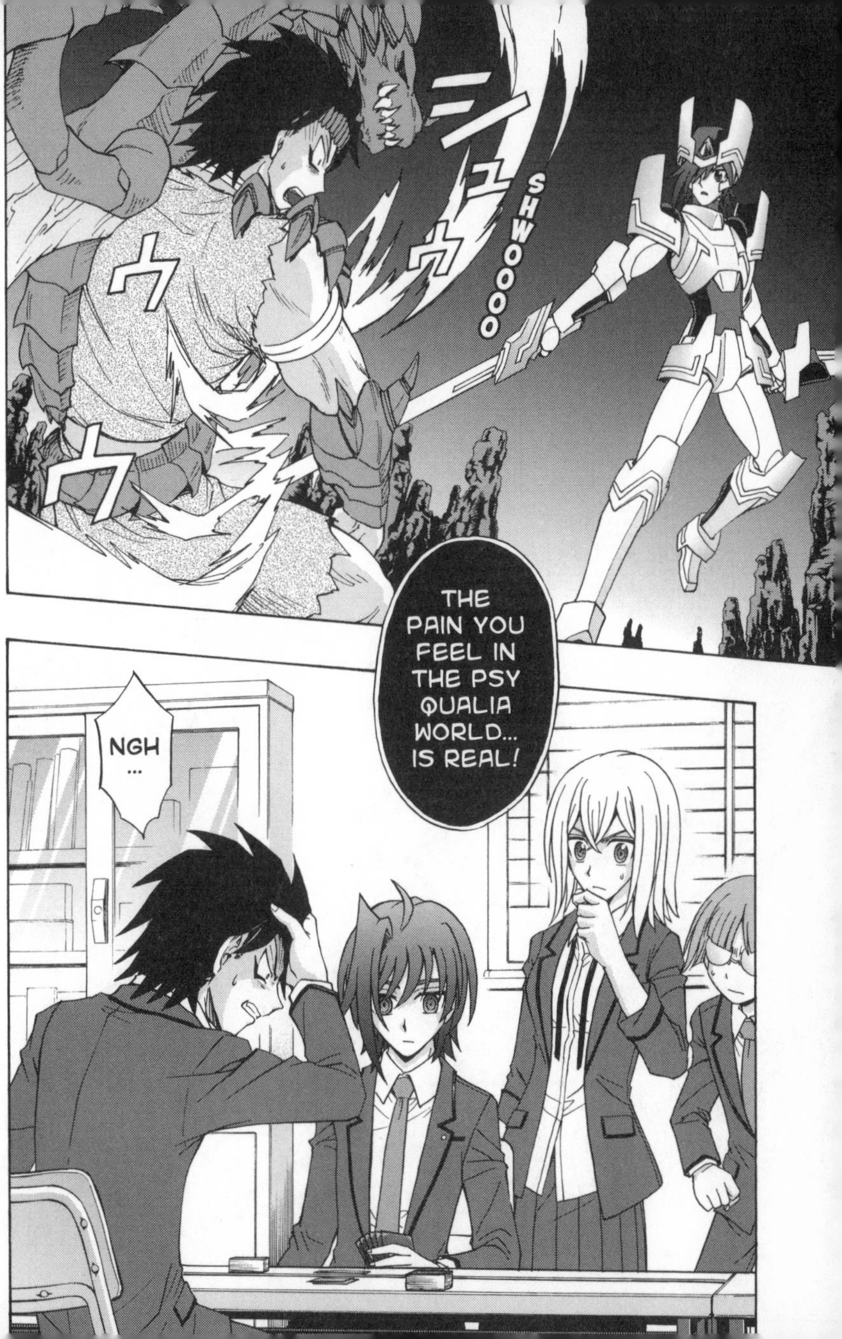
SHWOOOOO
THE PAIN YOU FEEL IN THE PSY QUALIA WORLD... IS REAL!
NGH ...

CARDFIGHT!!
Vanguard

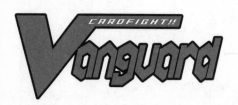

BONUS! CARDFIGHT!! Vanguard

NEVER-BEFORE-SEEN IMAGE BOARDS

I drew these sketches of the Q4 because I thought they might appear early on in Vanguard G. (Itou)

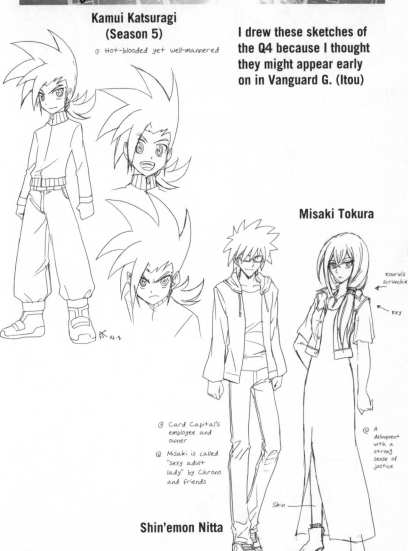

Kamui Katsuragi (Season 5)

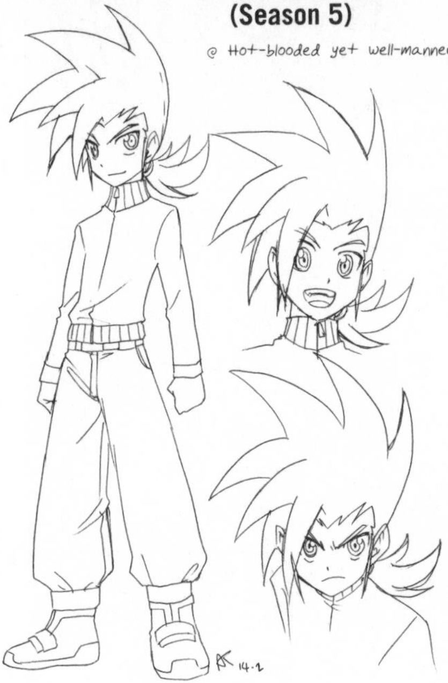

@ Hot-blooded yet well-mannered
AK 14.2

Misaki Tokura

Shin'emon Nitta

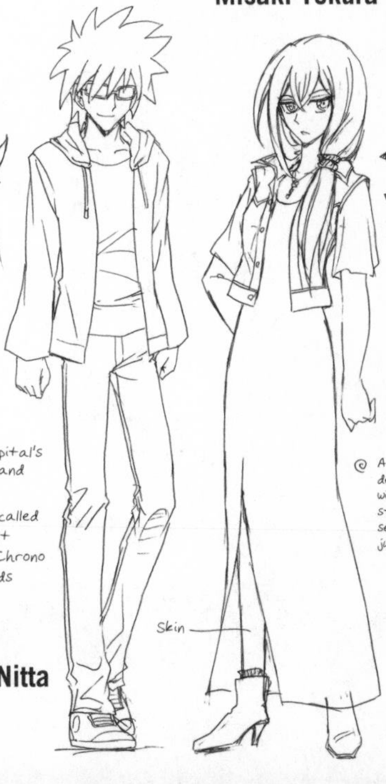

Kourin's scrunchie
Key
@ A delinquent with a strong sense of justice
@ Card Capital's employee and owner
@ Misaki is called "sexy adult lady" by Chrono and friends
Skin

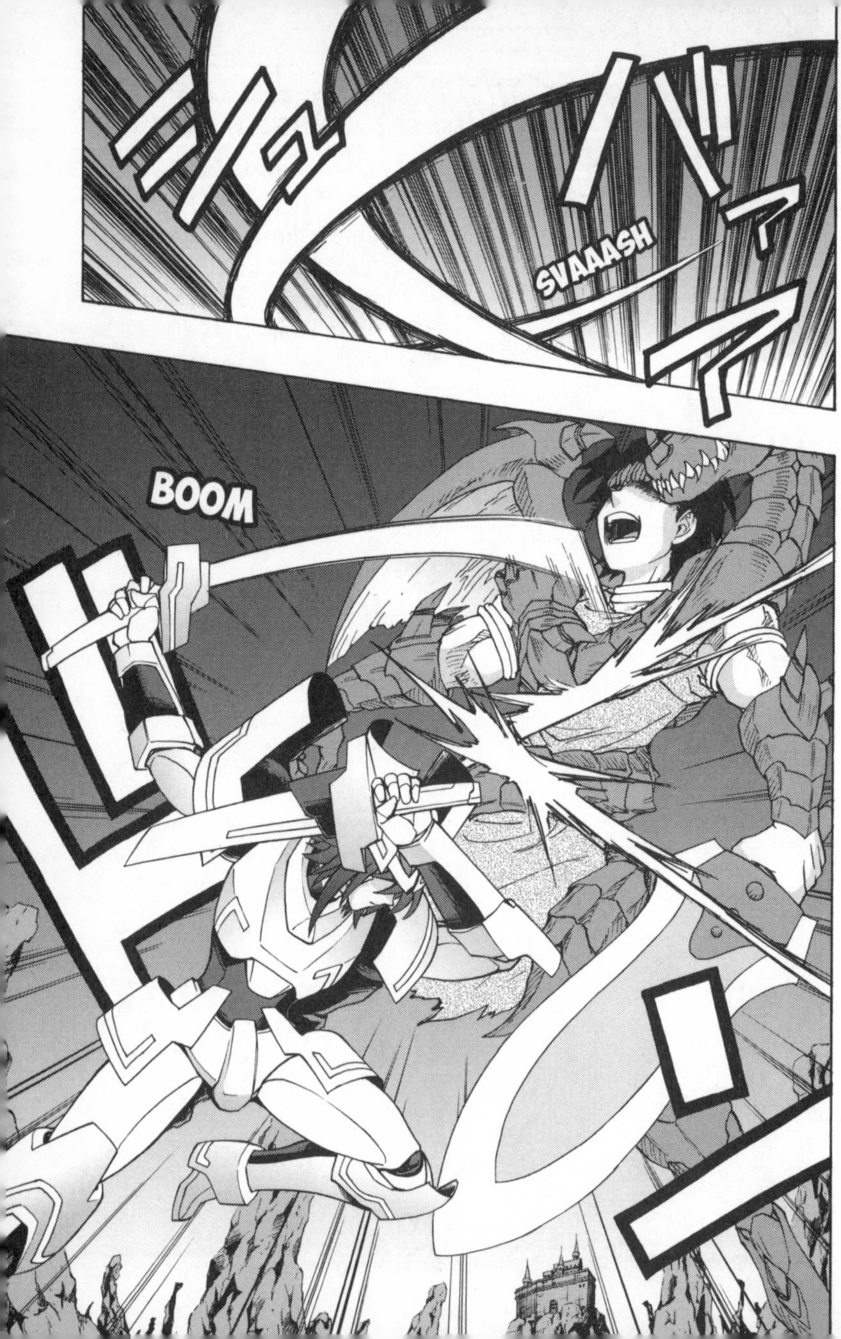
SVAAASH
BOOM

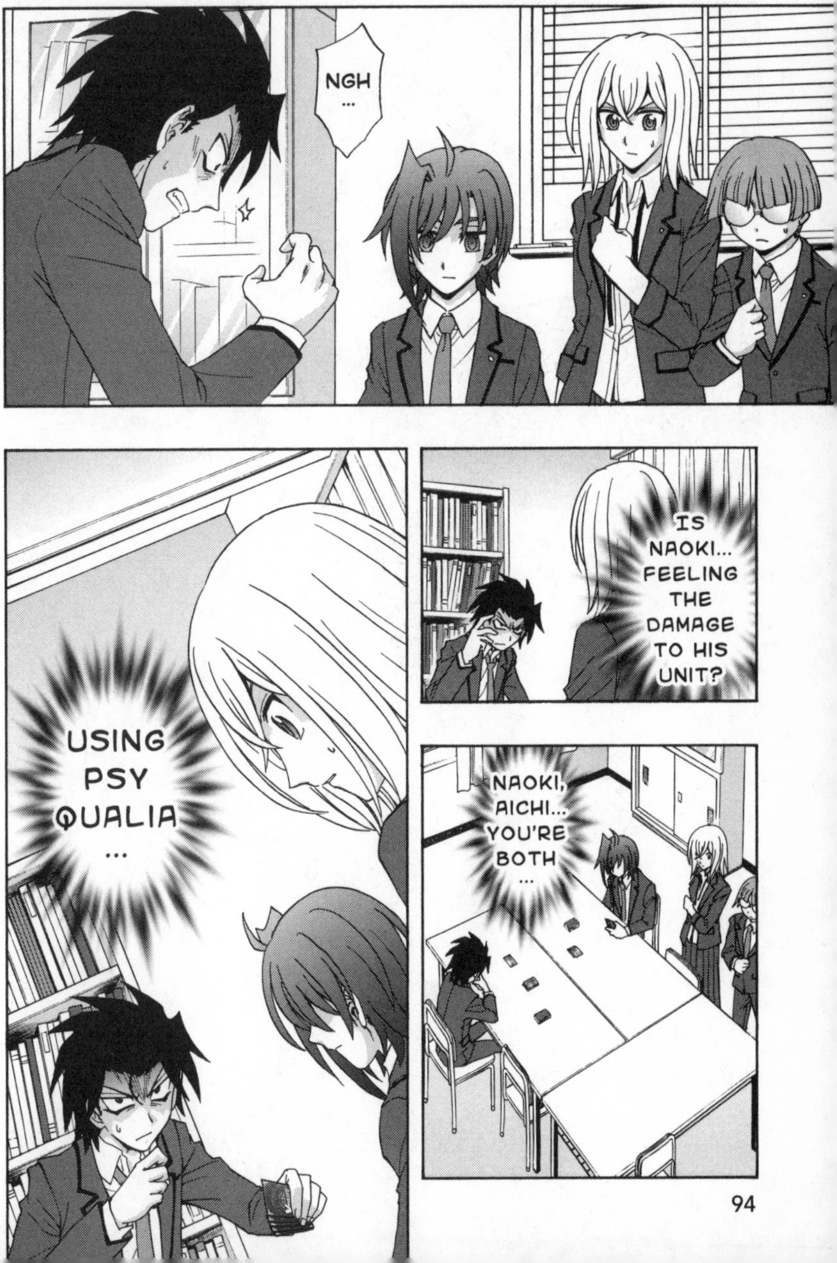
NGH ...
IS NAOKI... FEELING THE DAMAGE TO HIS UNIT?
NAOKI, AICHI... YOU'RE BOTH ...
USING PSY QUALIA ...

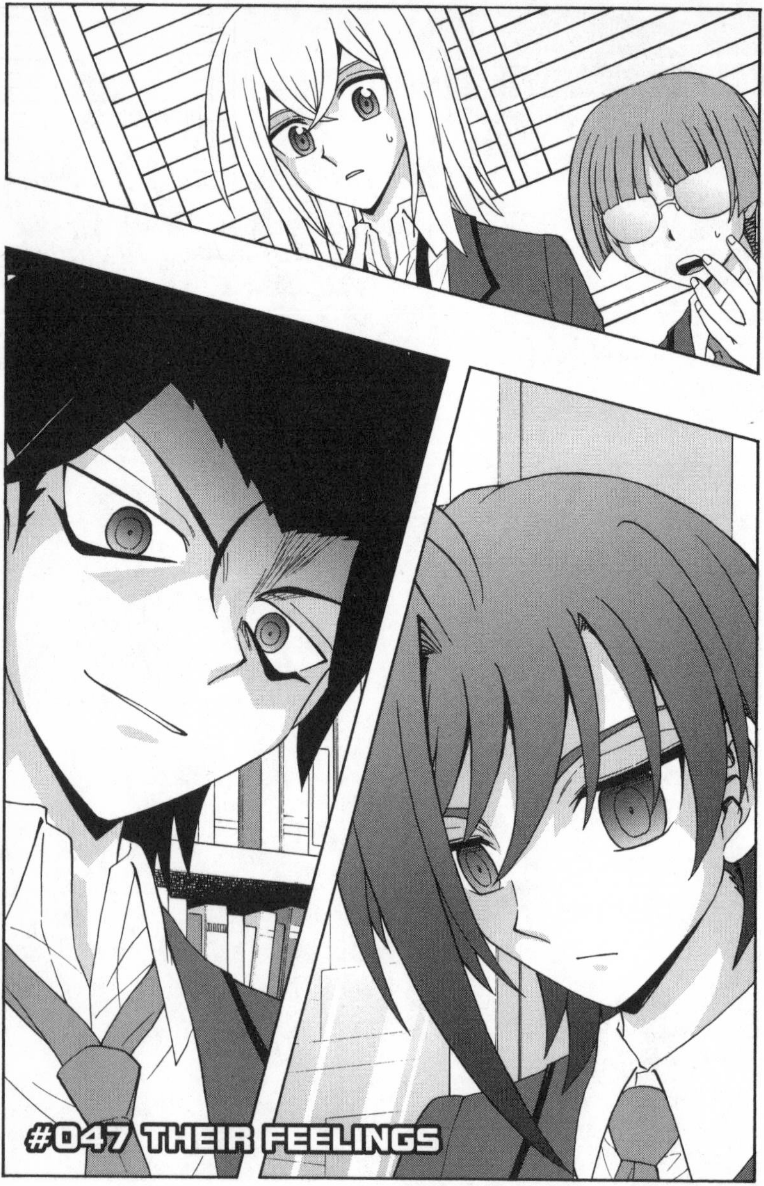
#047 THEIR FEELINGS

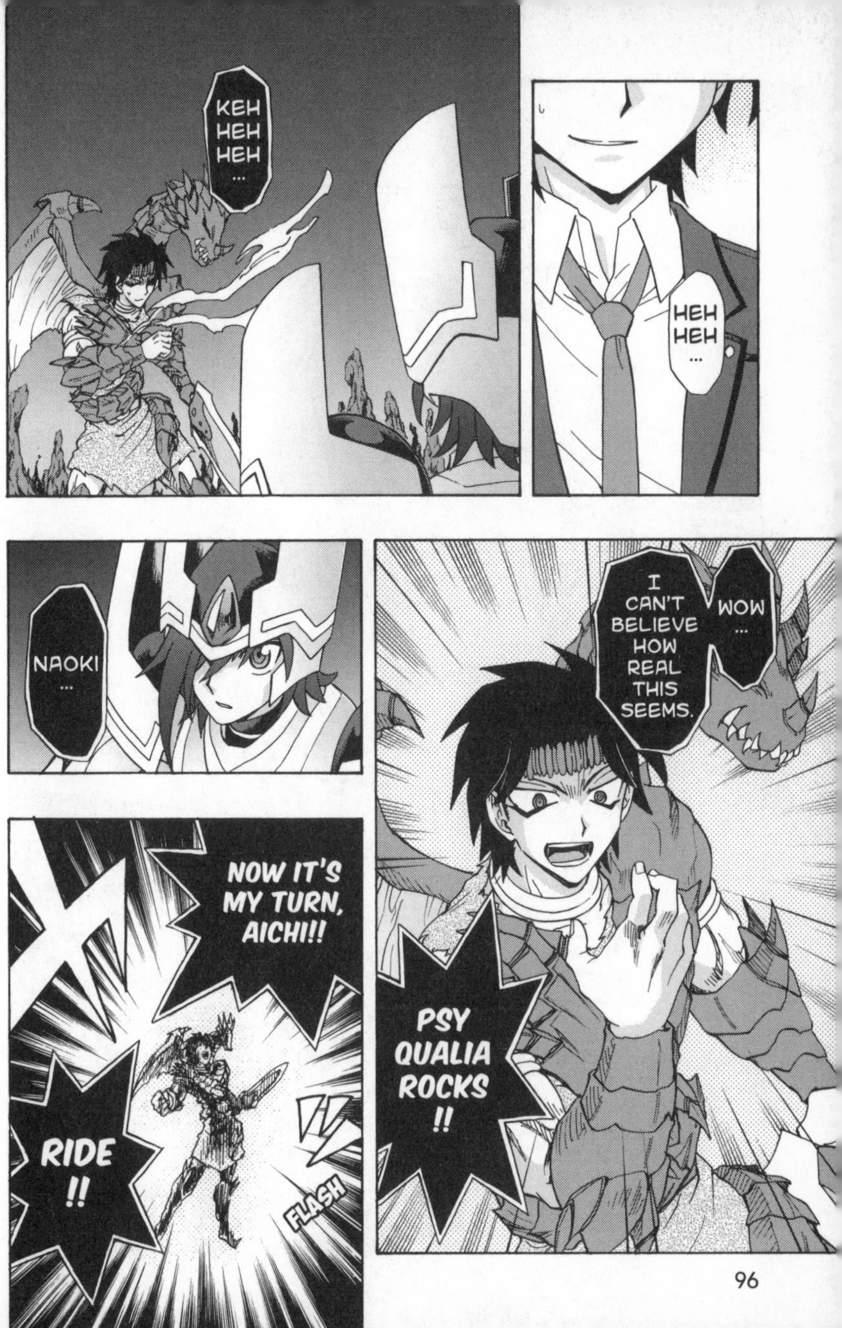
HEH HEH ...
KEH HEH HEH ...
WOW ...
I CAN'T BELIEVE HOW REAL THIS SEEMS.
PSY QUALIA ROCKS !!
NAOKI ...
NOW IT'S MY TURN, AICHI!!
RIDE !!
FLASH

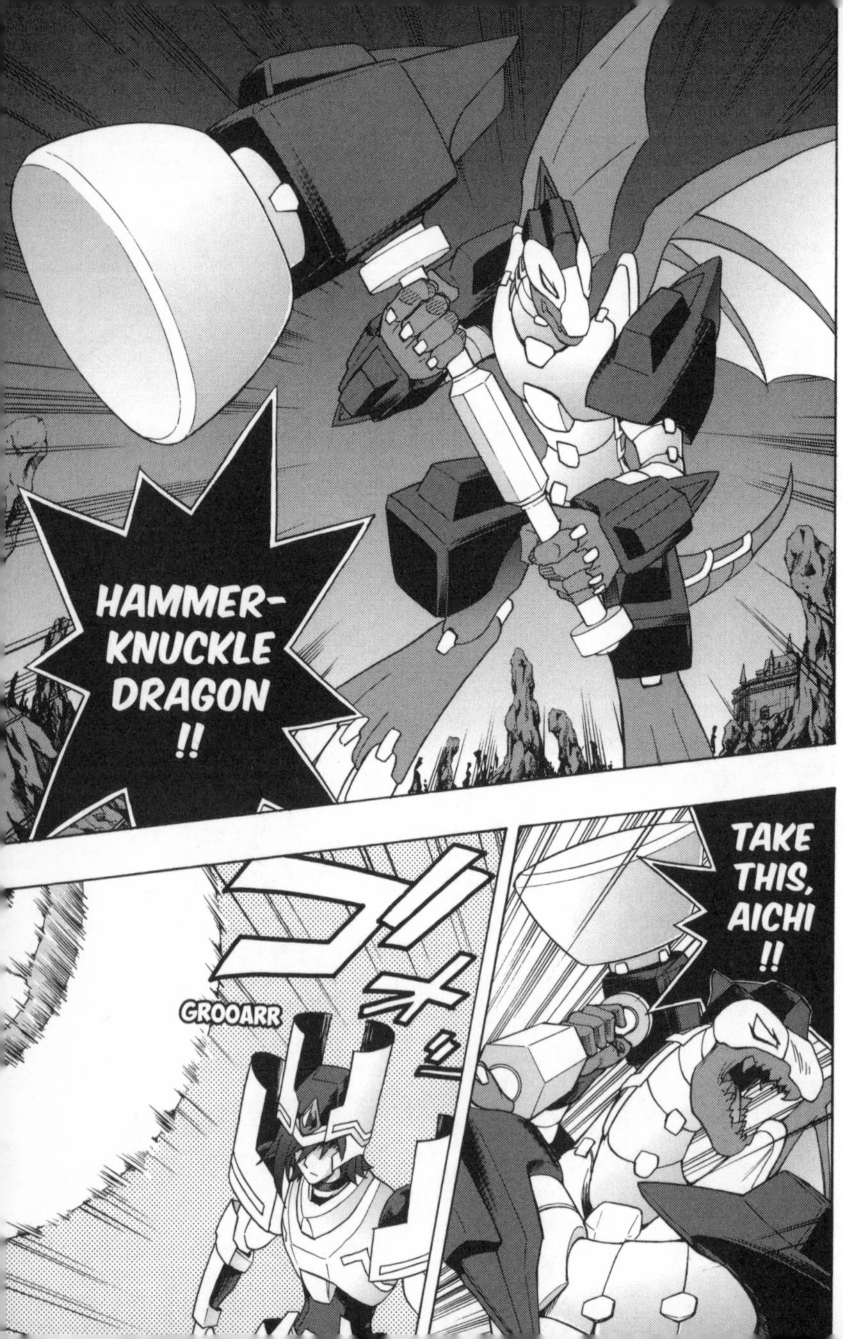
HAMMER-KNUCKLE DRAGON !!
TAKE THIS, AICHI !!
GROOARR

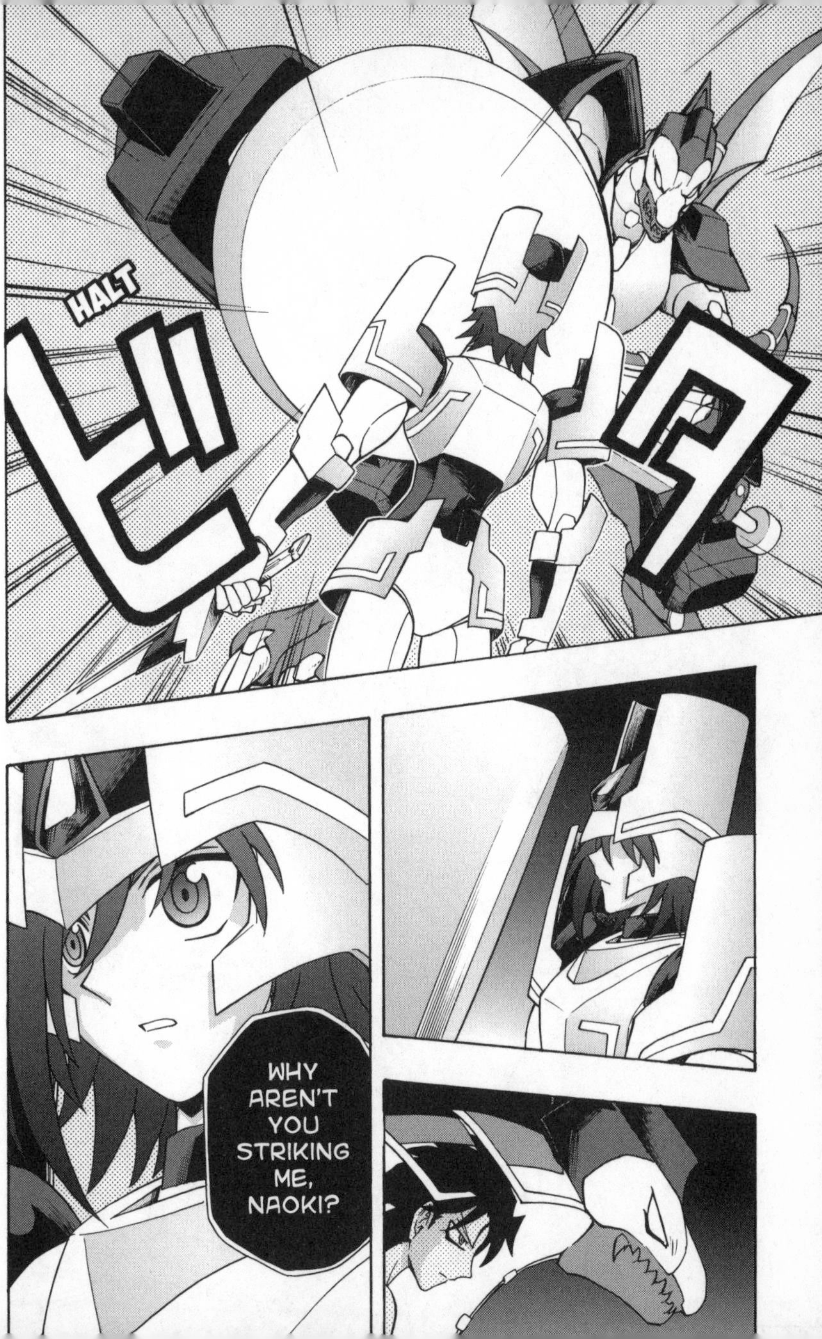
HALT
WHY AREN'T YOU STRIKING ME, NAOKI?

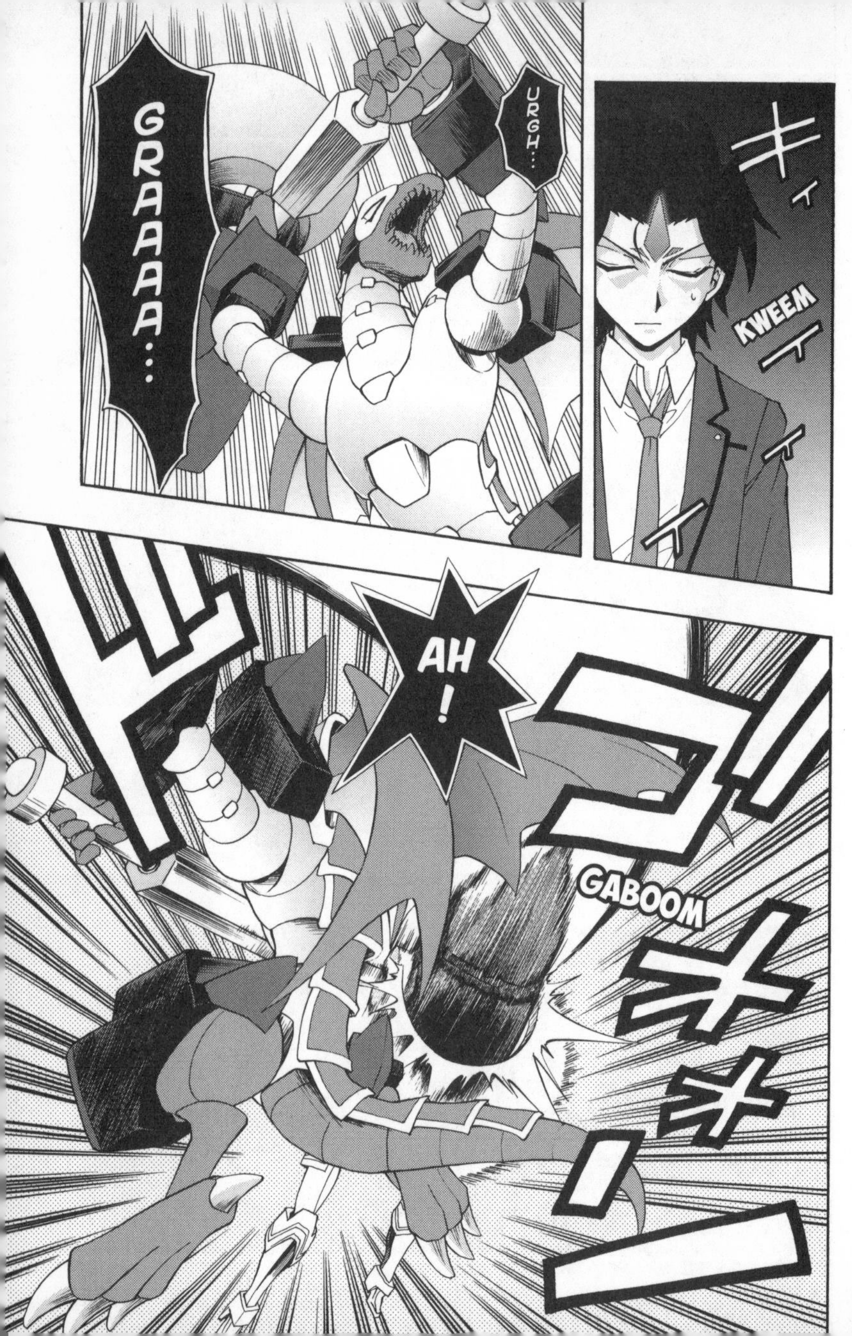
KWEEM
URGH...
GRAAAAAA...
AH!
GABOOM

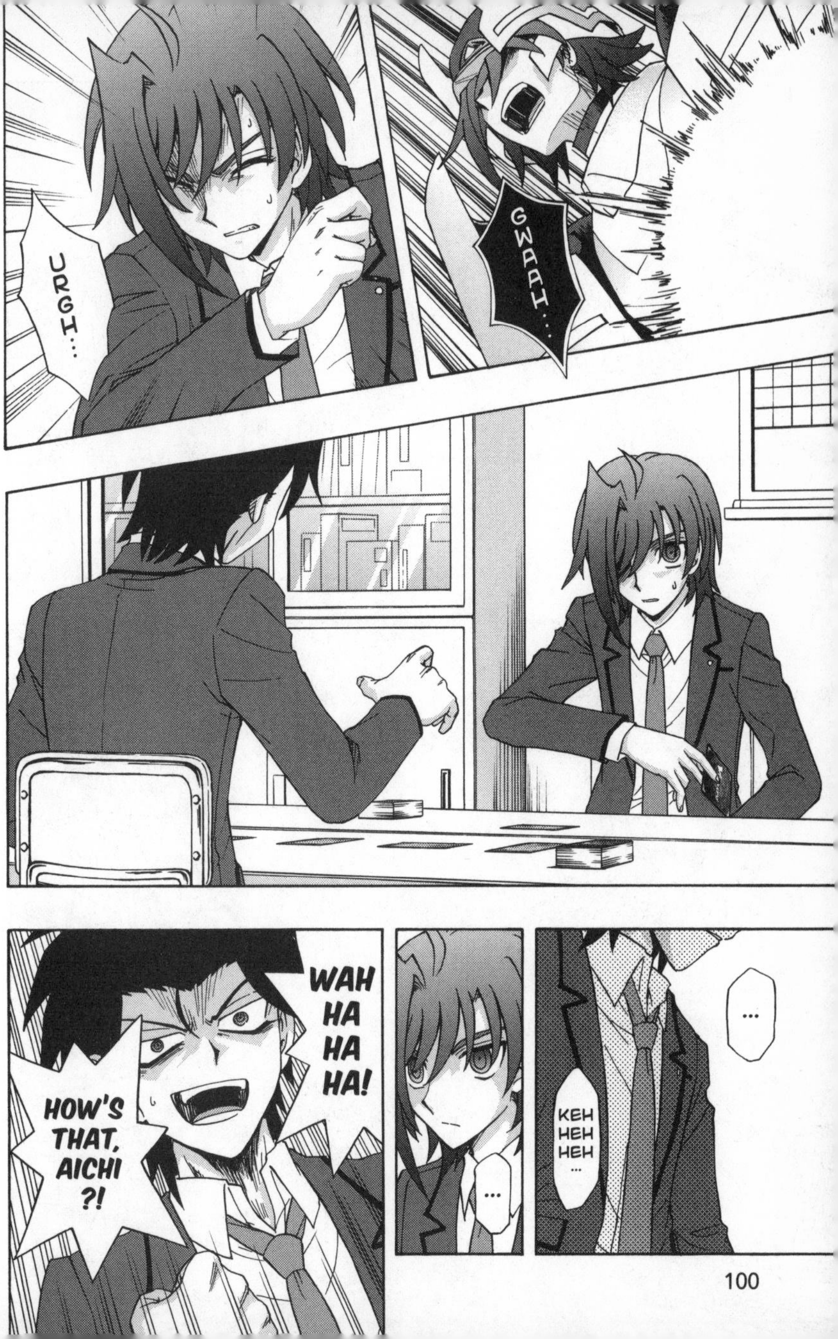
GWAAH...
URGH...
...
KEH HEH HEH...
...
WAH HA HA HA!
HOW'S THAT, AICHI?!

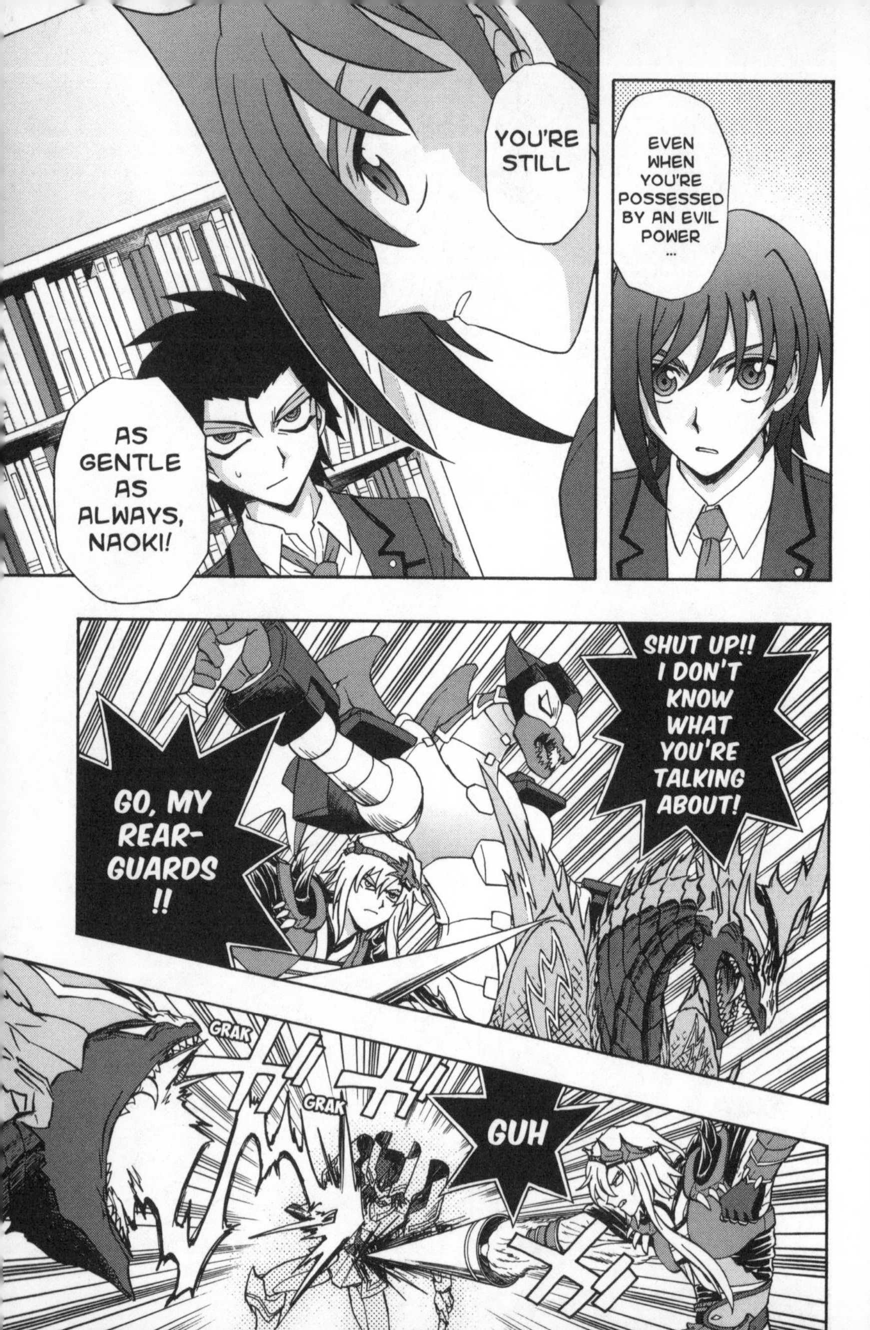
EVEN WHEN YOU'RE POSSESSED BY AN EVIL POWER ...
YOU'RE STILL
AS GENTLE AS ALWAYS, NAOKI!
SHUT UP!! I DON'T KNOW WHAT YOU'RE TALKING ABOUT!
GO, MY REAR-GUARDS !!
GRAK
GRAK
GUH

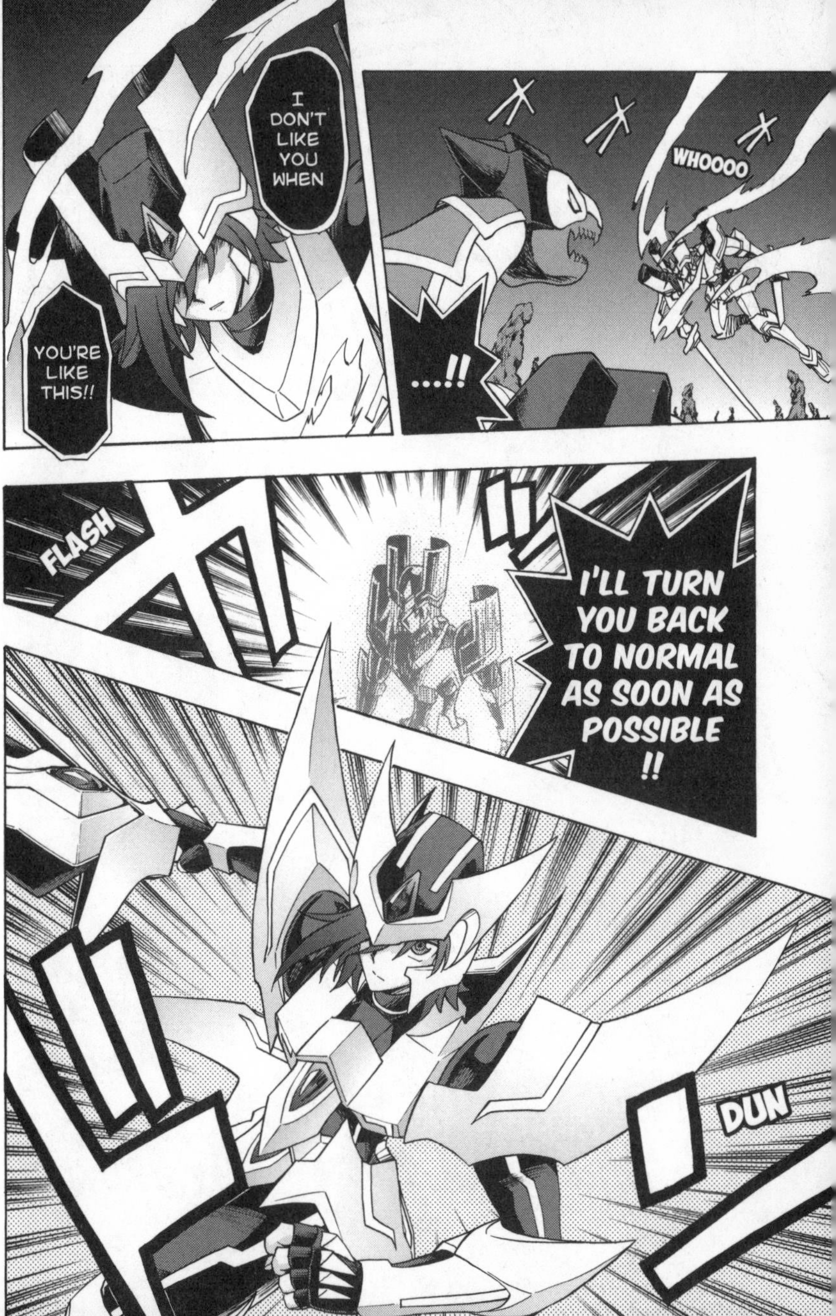
WHOOOO
....!!
I DON'T LIKE YOU WHEN
YOU'RE LIKE THIS!!
FLASH
I'LL TURN YOU BACK TO NORMAL AS SOON AS POSSIBLE !!
DUN

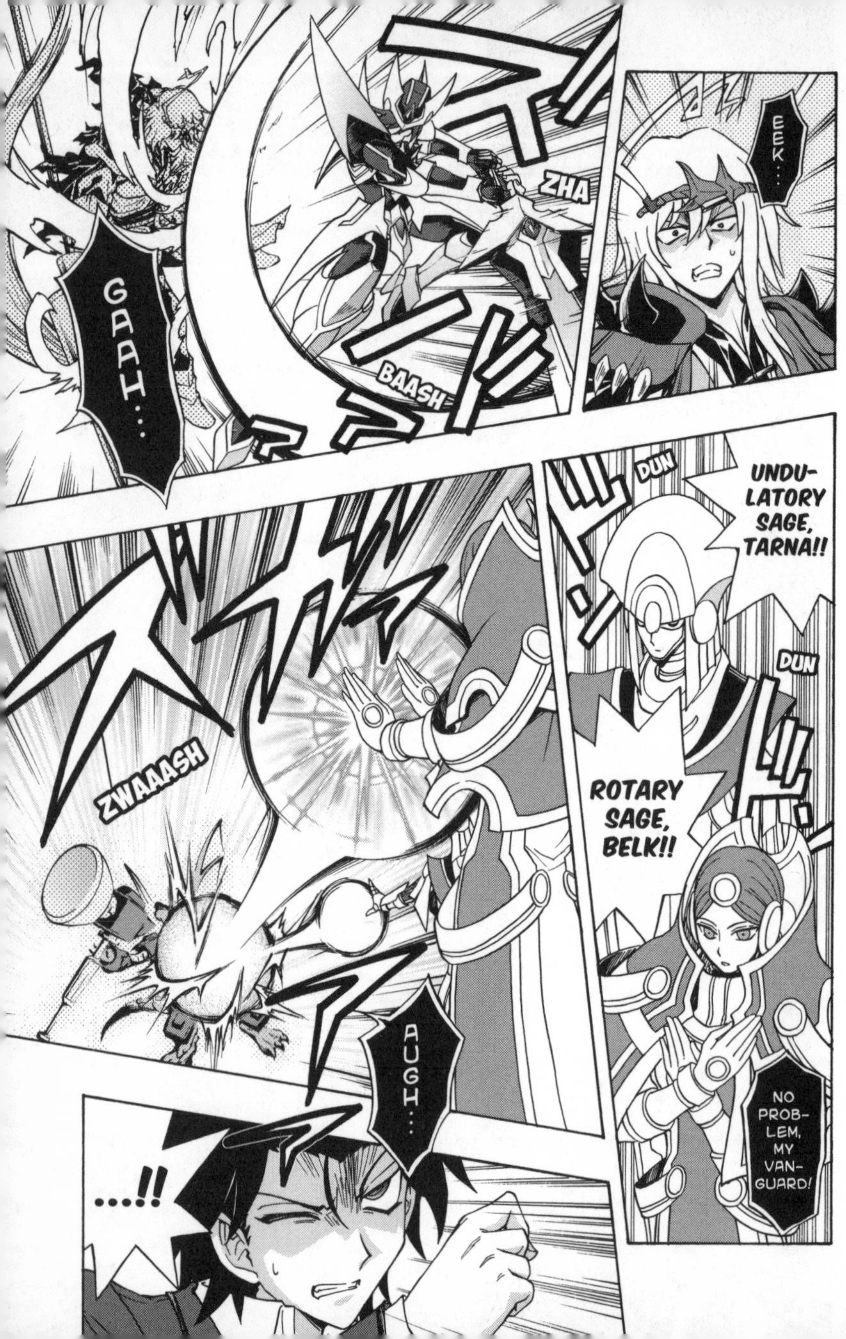
EEK...
ZHA
BAASH
GAAH...
DUN
UNDULATORY SAGE, TARNA!!
DUN
ROTARY SAGE, BELK!!
NO PROBLEM, MY VANGUARD!
ZWAAASH
AUGH...
...!!

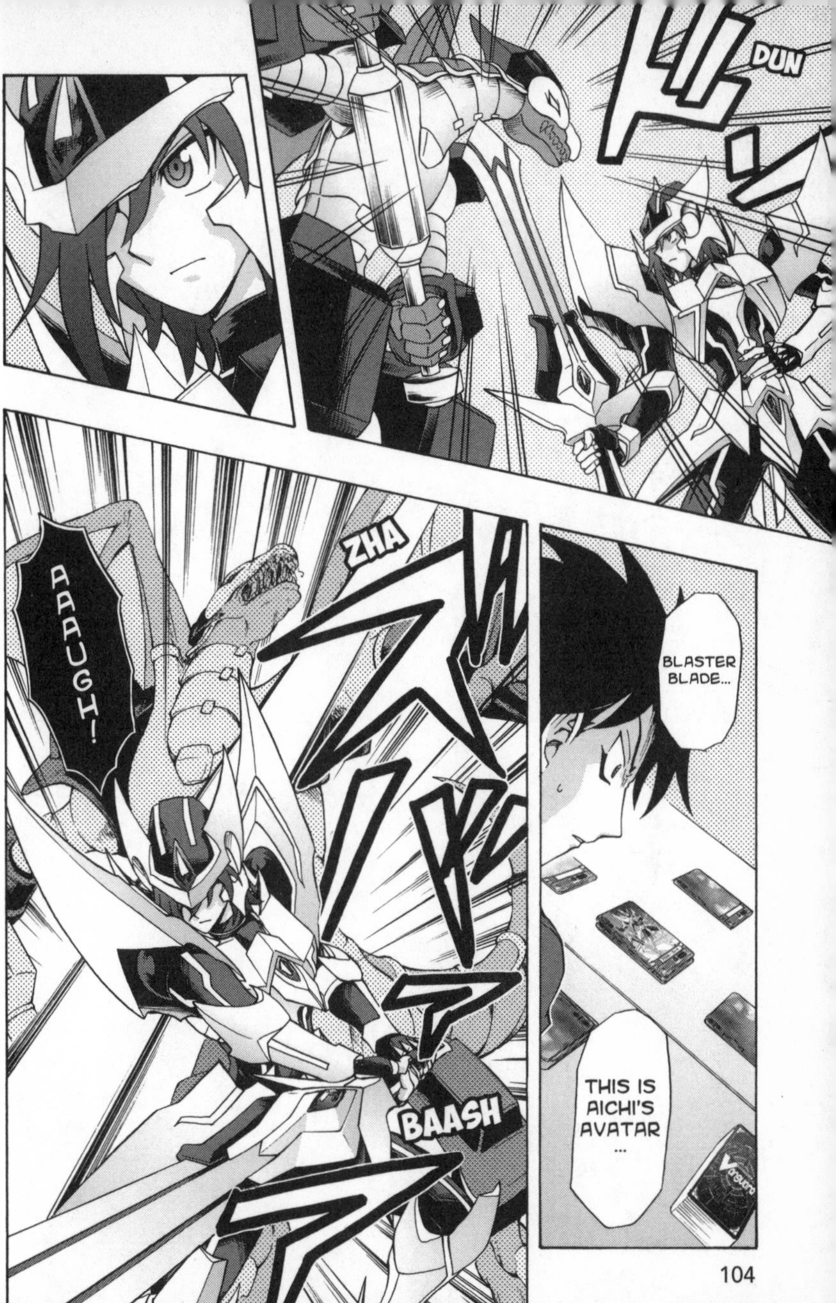
DUN
BLASTER BLADE...
THIS IS AICHI'S AVATAR ...
ZHA
AAAUGH!
BAASH

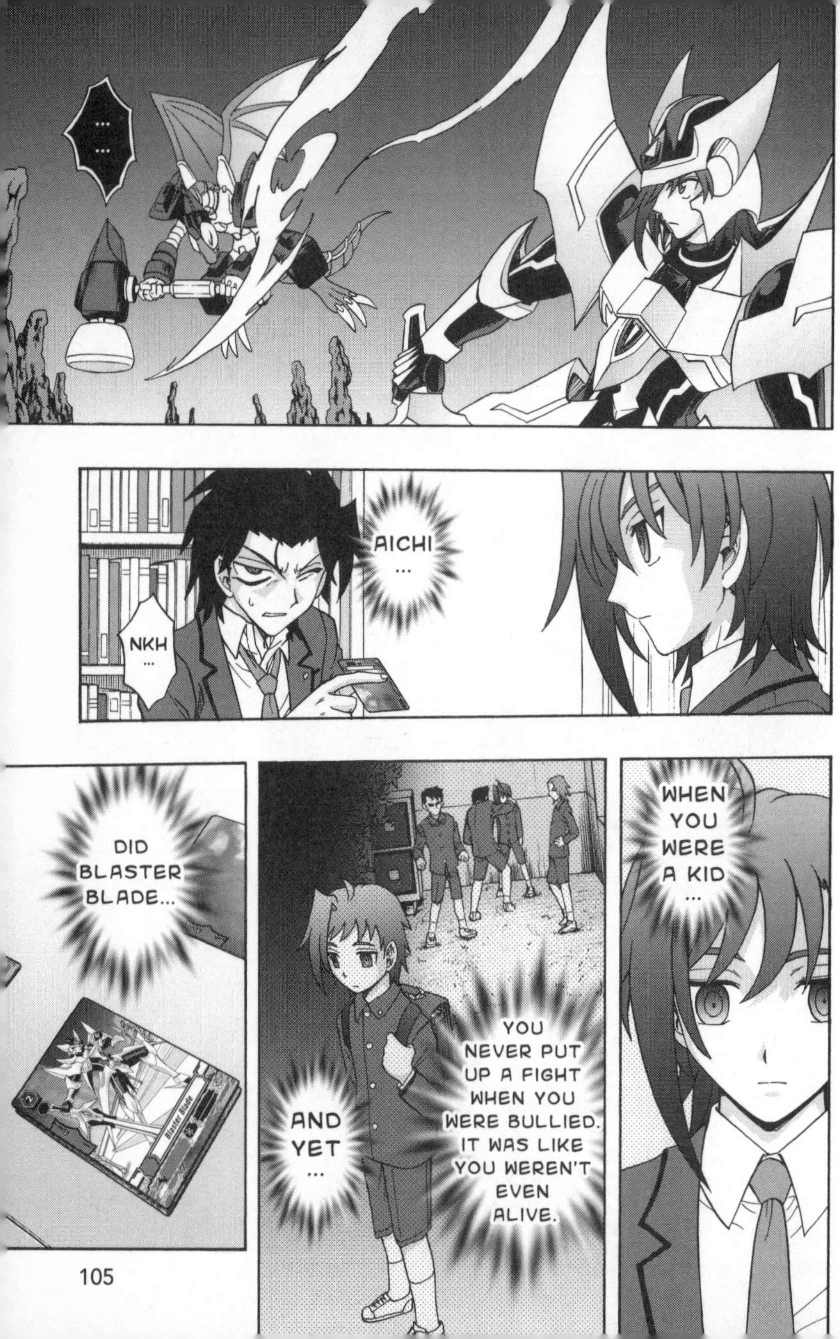
...
...
AICHI ...
NKH ...
WHEN YOU WERE A KID ...
YOU NEVER PUT UP A FIGHT WHEN YOU WERE BULLIED. IT WAS LIKE YOU WEREN'T EVEN ALIVE.
AND YET ...
DID BLASTER BLADE...
Blaster Blade

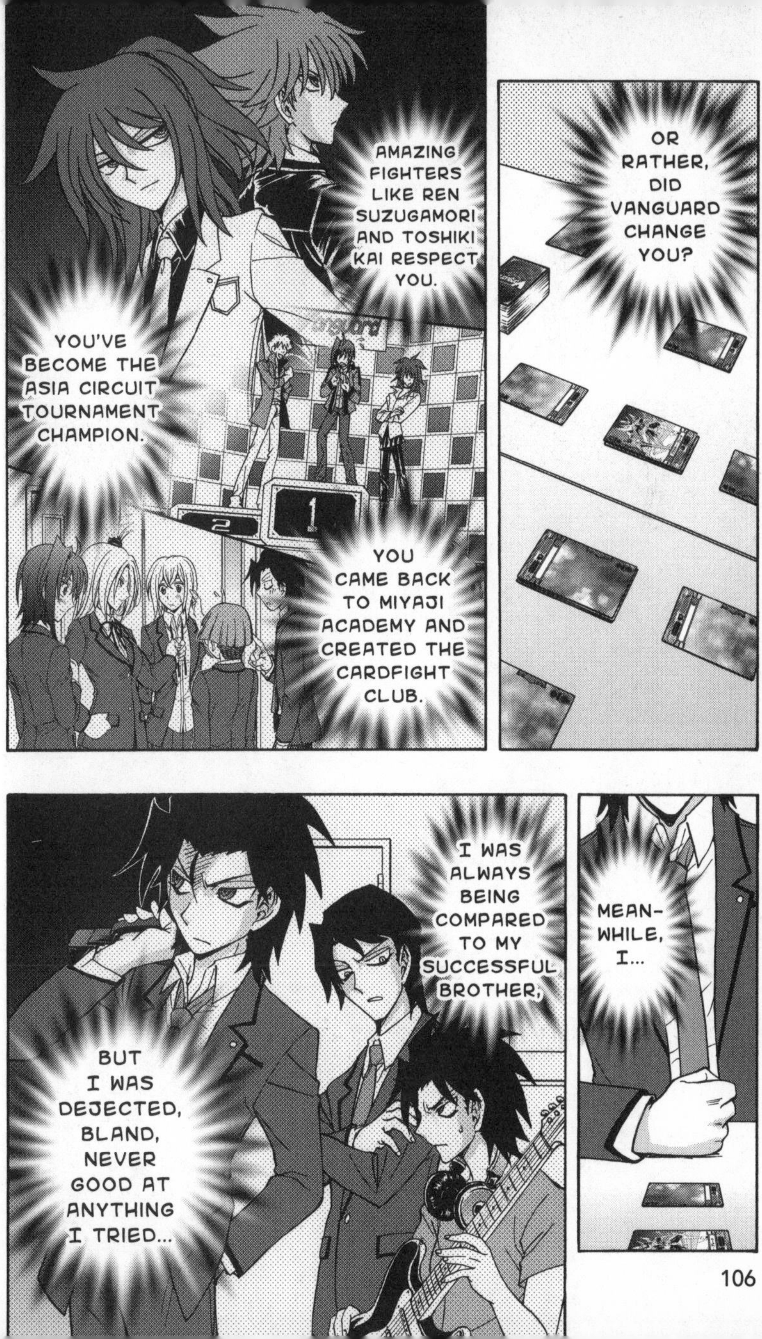
OR RATHER, DID VANGUARD CHANGE YOU?
AMAZING FIGHTERS LIKE REN SUZUGAMORI AND TOSHIKI KAI RESPECT YOU.
YOU'VE BECOME THE ASIA CIRCUIT TOURNAMENT CHAMPION.
YOU CAME BACK TO MIYAJI ACADEMY AND CREATED THE CARDFIGHT CLUB.
MEAN-WHILE, I...
I WAS ALWAYS BEING COMPARED TO MY SUCCESSFUL BROTHER,
BUT I WAS DEJECTED, BLAND, NEVER GOOD AT ANYTHING I TRIED...

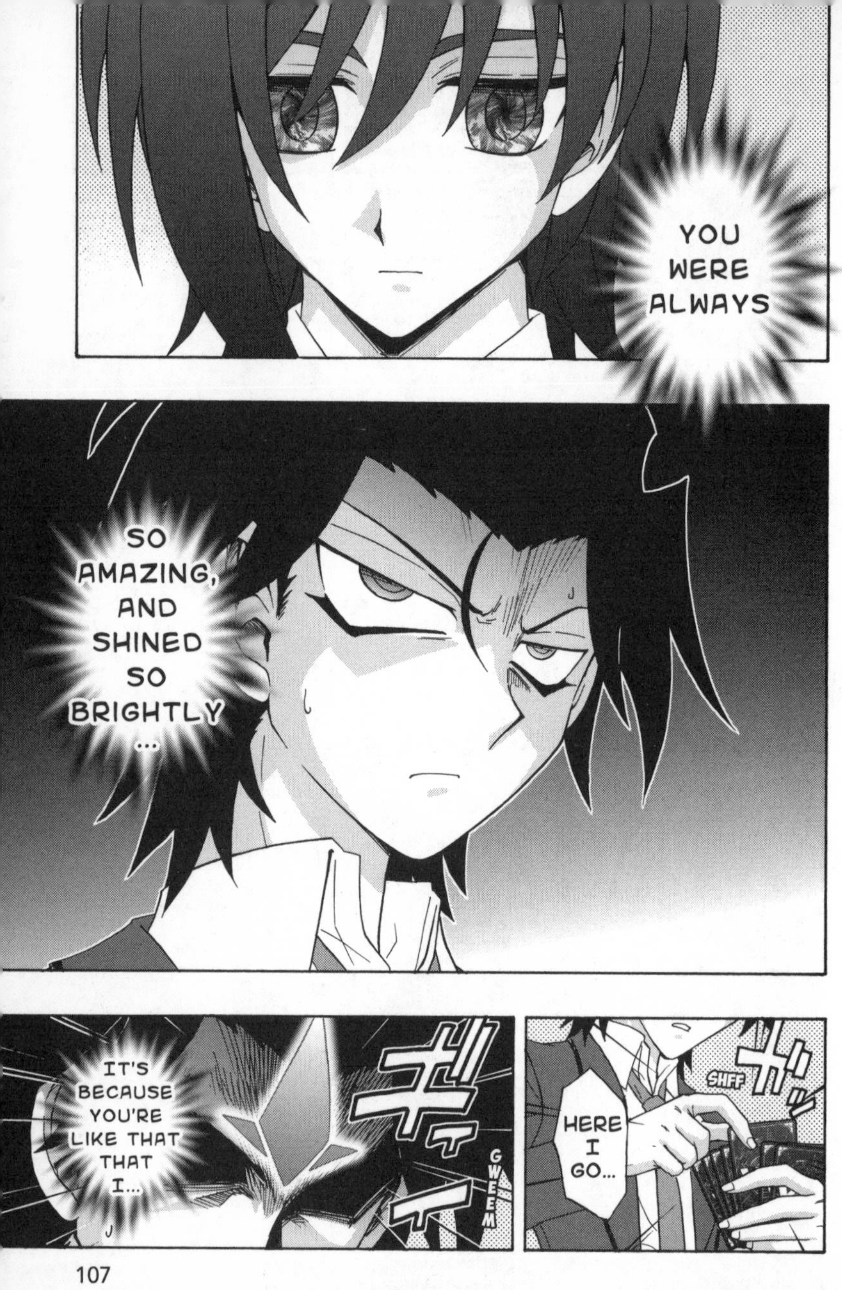
YOU WERE ALWAYS
SO AMAZING, AND SHINED SO BRIGHTLY ...
SHFF
HERE I GO...
IT'S BECAUSE YOU'RE LIKE THAT THAT I...
GWEEM

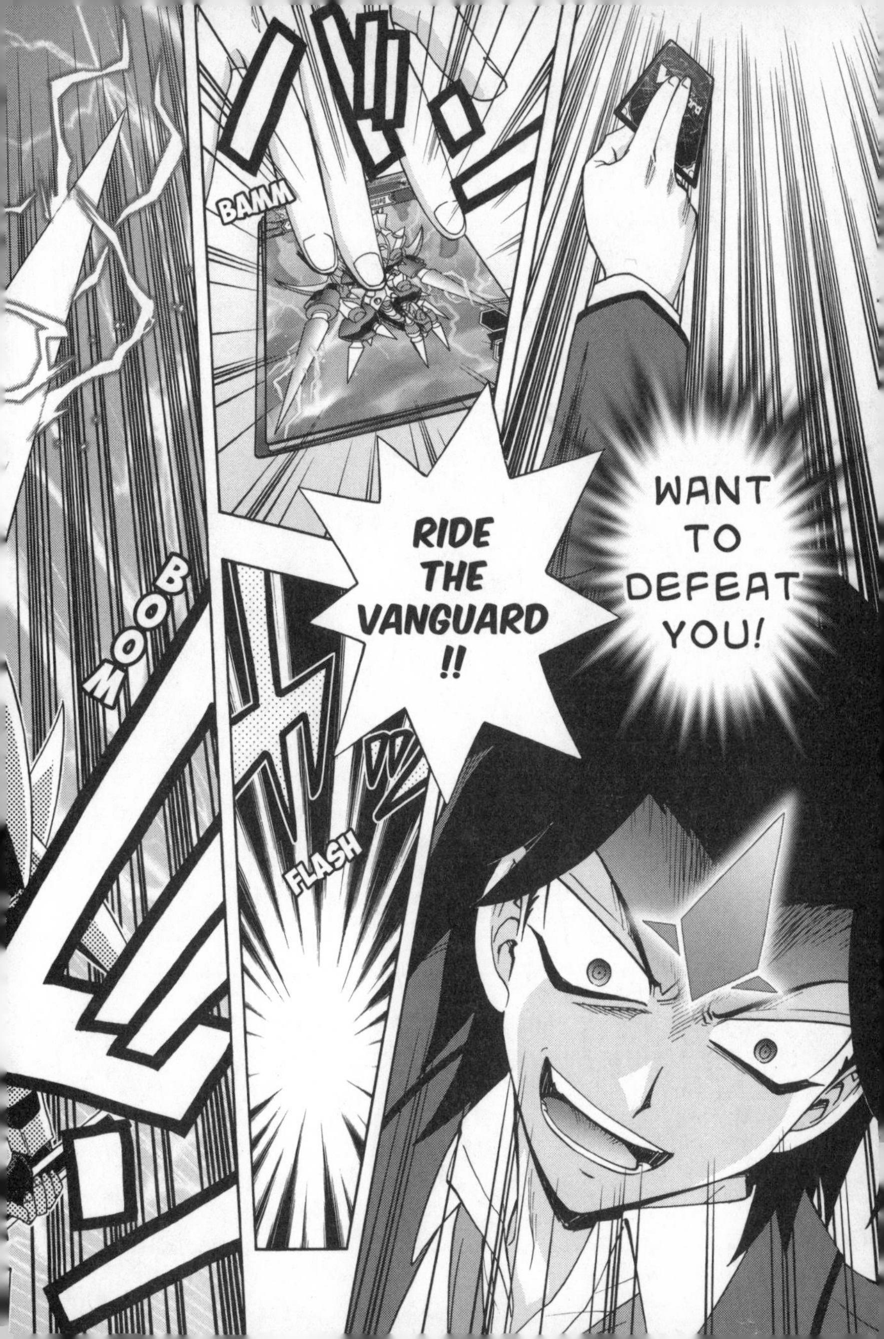
WANT TO DEFEAT YOU!
RIDE THE VANGUARD !!
BAMM
FLASH
BOOM

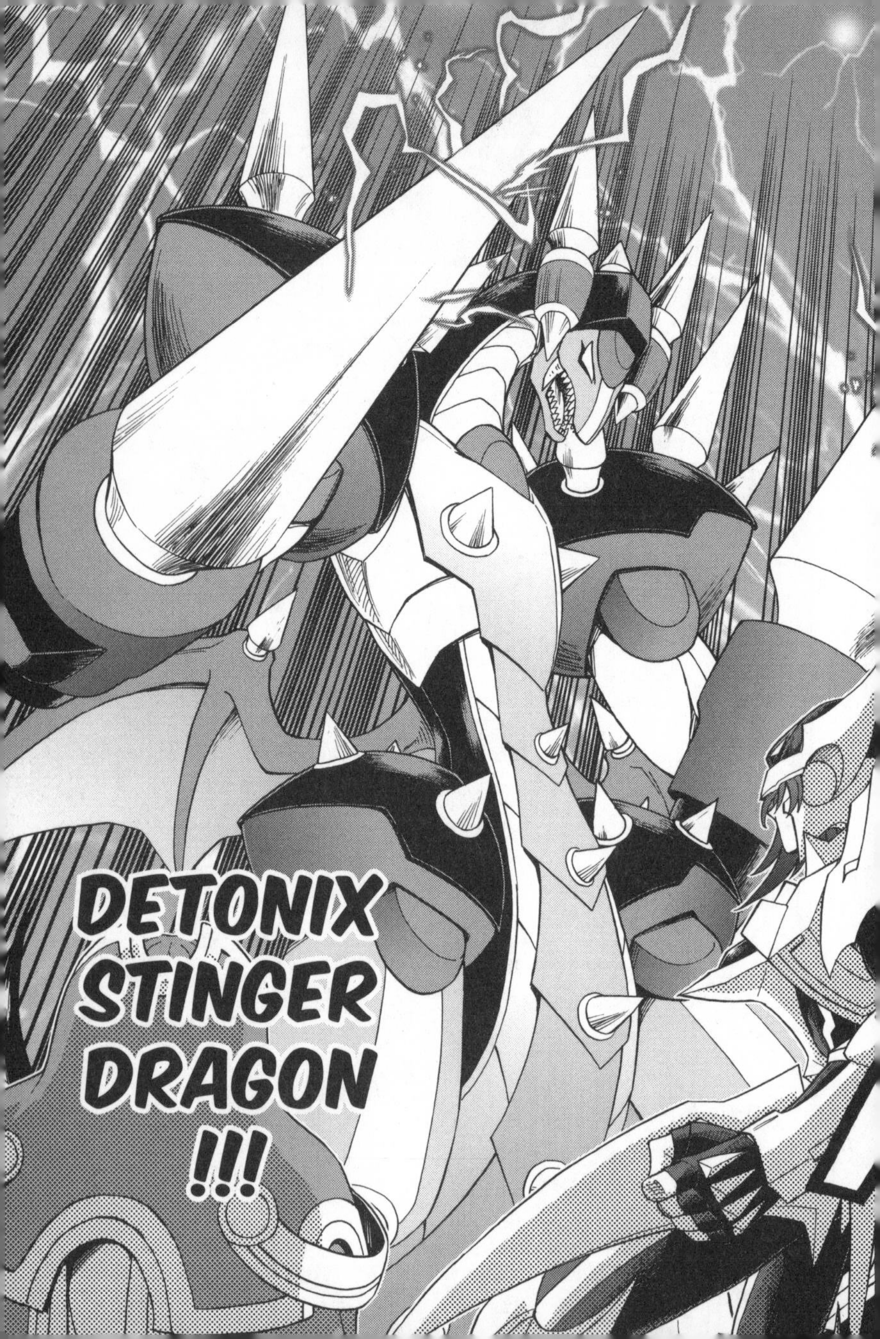
DETONIX
STINGER
DRAGON
!!!

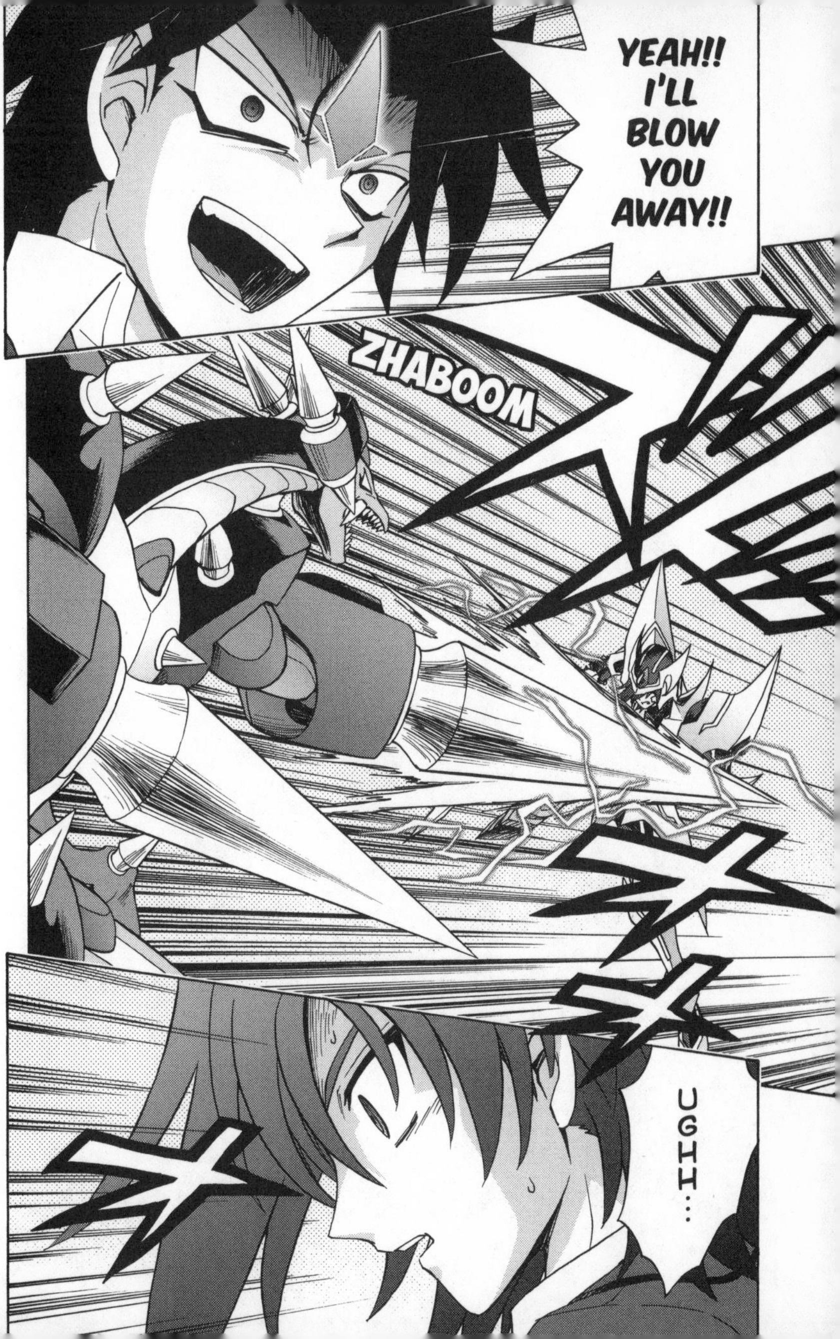

YEAH!! I'LL BLOW YOU AWAY!!
ZHABOOM
UGHH...

CARDFIGHT!!
Vanguard

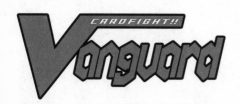

BONUS! CARDFIGHT!! Vanguard

NEVER-BEFORE-SEEN IMAGE BOARDS

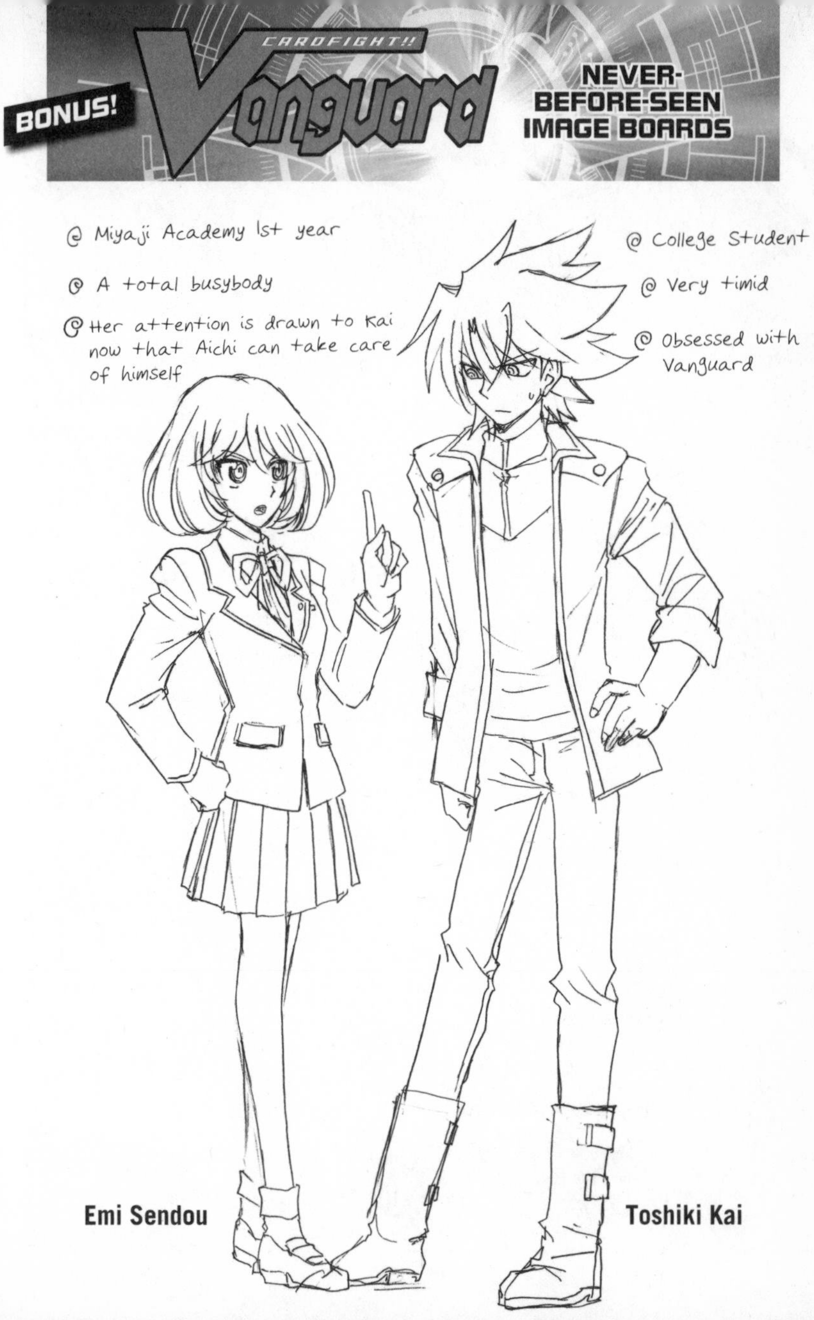
@ Miyaji Academy 1st year
@ A total busybody
@ Her attention is drawn to Kai now that Aichi can take care of himself
@ College Student
@ Very timid
@ Obsessed with Vanguard
Emi Sendou
Toshiki Kai

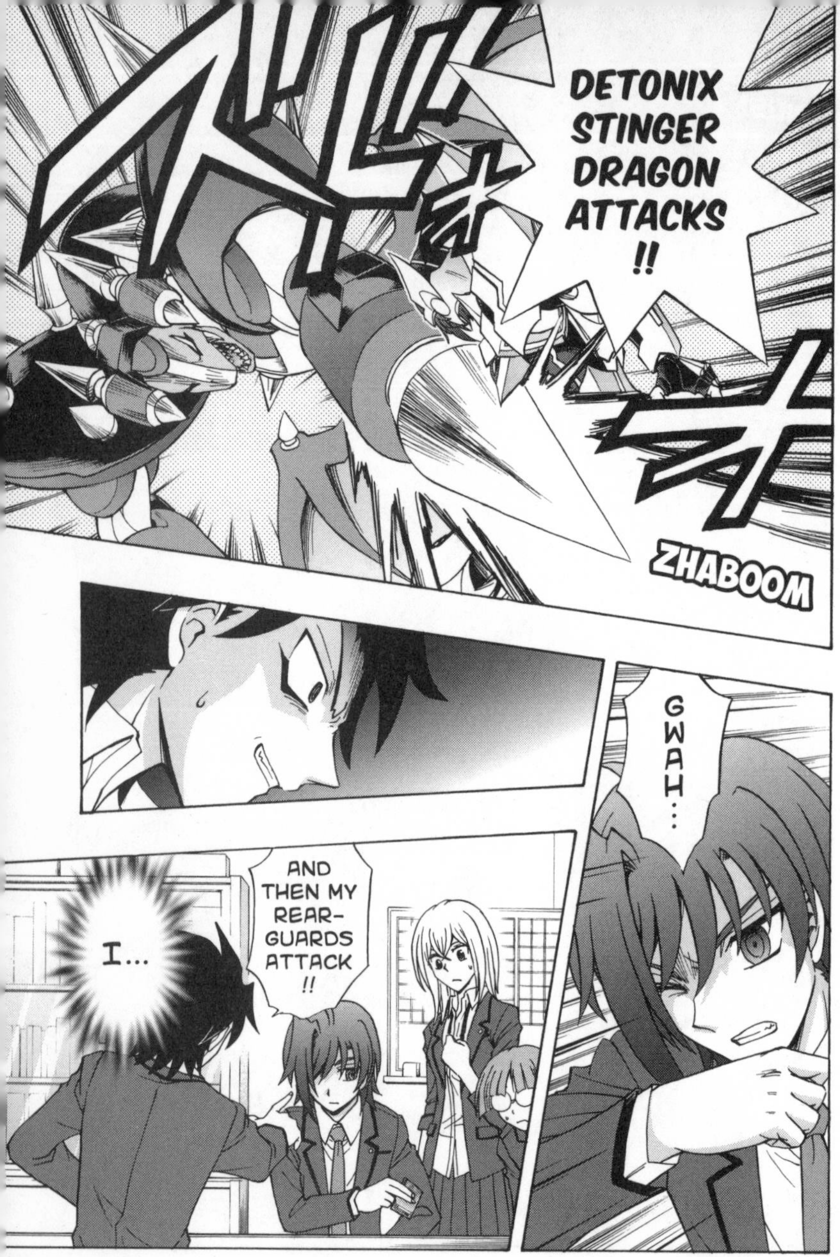
DETONIX STINGER DRAGON ATTACKS !!
ZHABOOM
GWAH...
AND THEN MY REAR-GUARDS ATTACK !!
I...

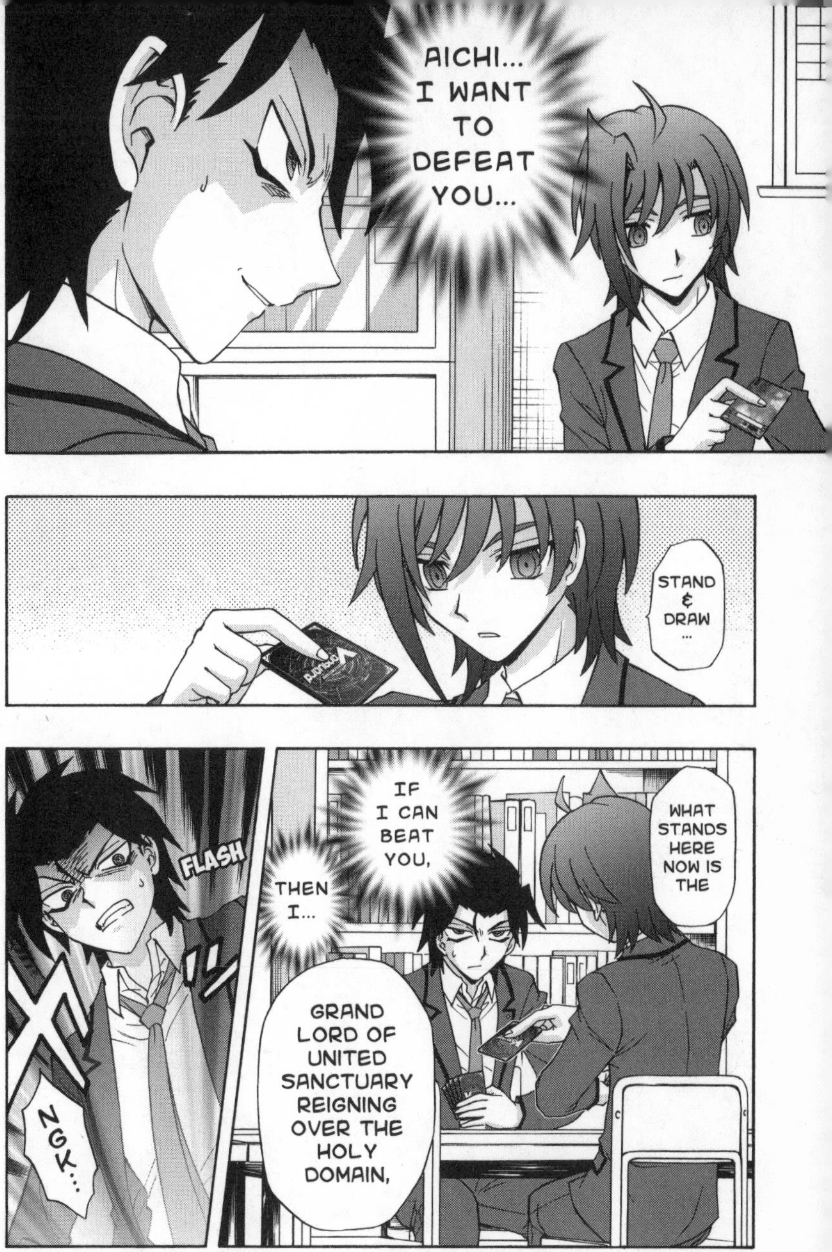
AICHI... I WANT TO DEFEAT YOU...
STAND & DRAW ...
WHAT STANDS HERE NOW IS THE
IF I CAN BEAT YOU,
THEN I...
GRAND LORD OF UNITED SANCTUARY REIGNING OVER THE HOLY DOMAIN,
FLASH
NGK...

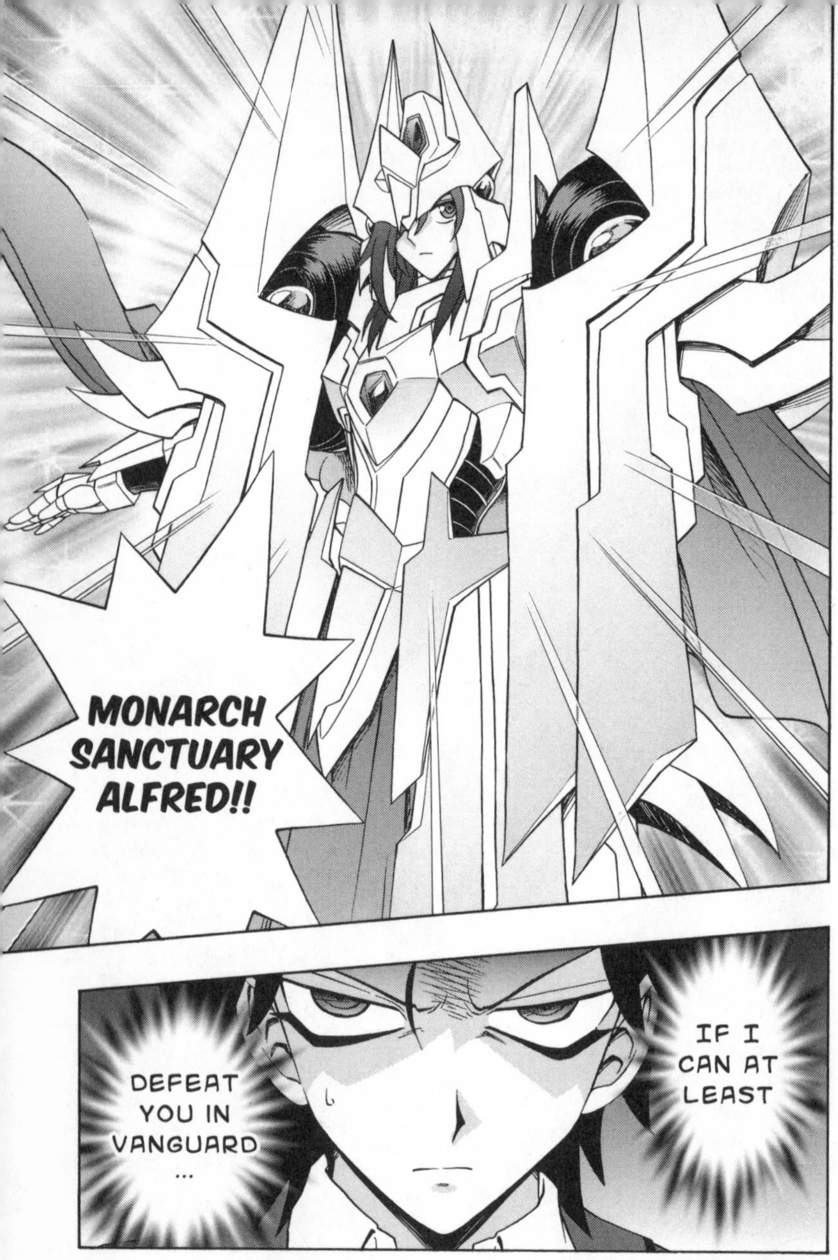
MONARCH SANCTUARY ALFRED!!
IF I CAN AT LEAST
DEFEAT YOU IN VANGUARD ...

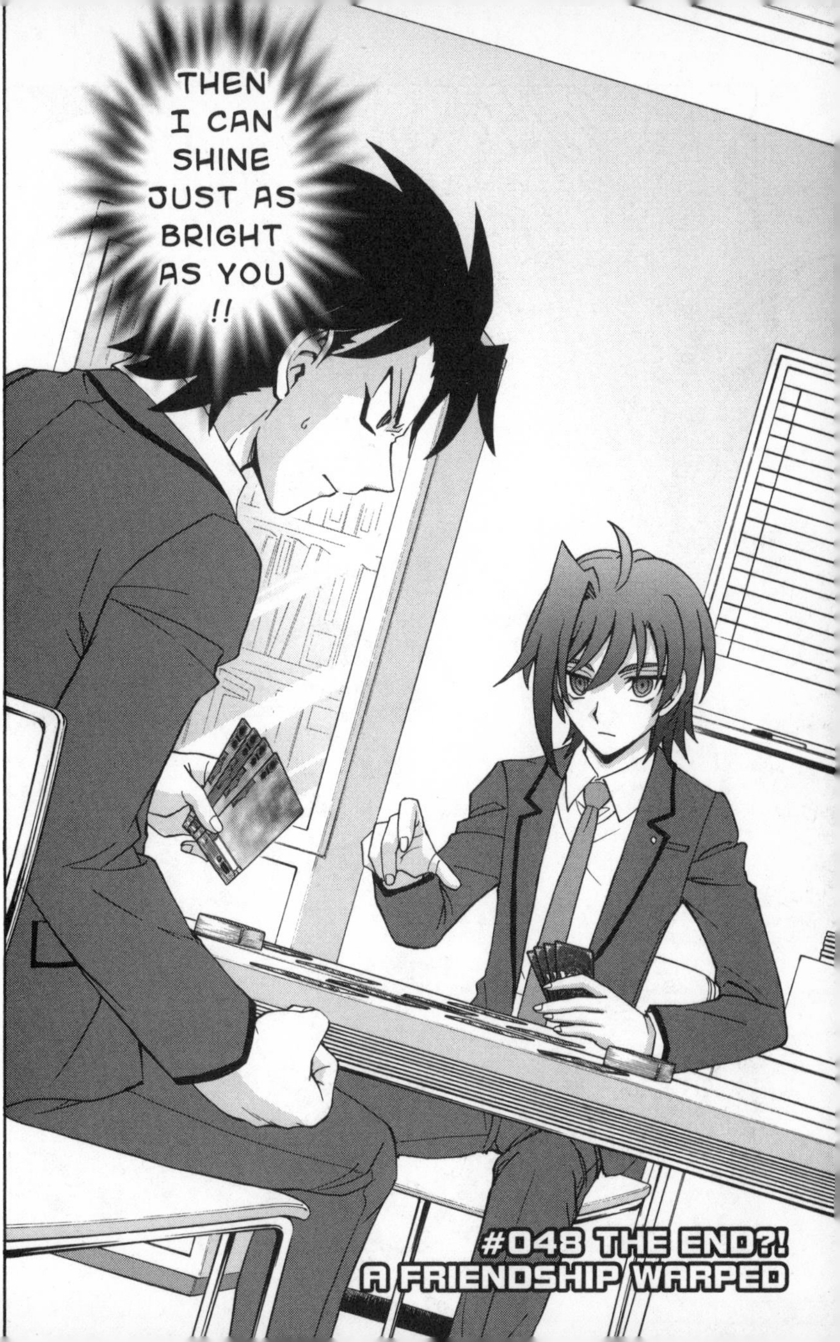
THEN I CAN SHINE JUST AS BRIGHT AS YOU !!
#048 THE END?! A FRIENDSHIP WARPED

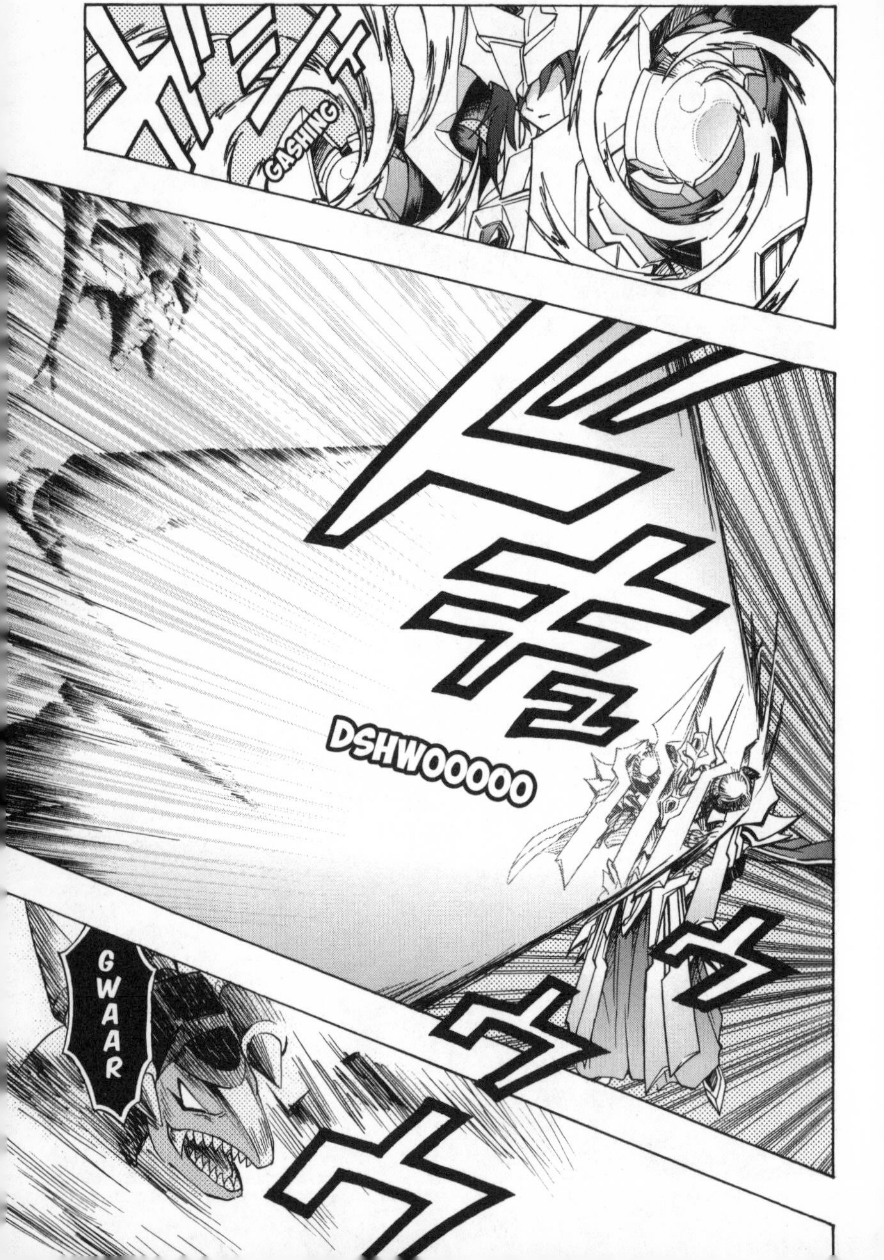
GASHING
DSHWOOOOO
GWAAR

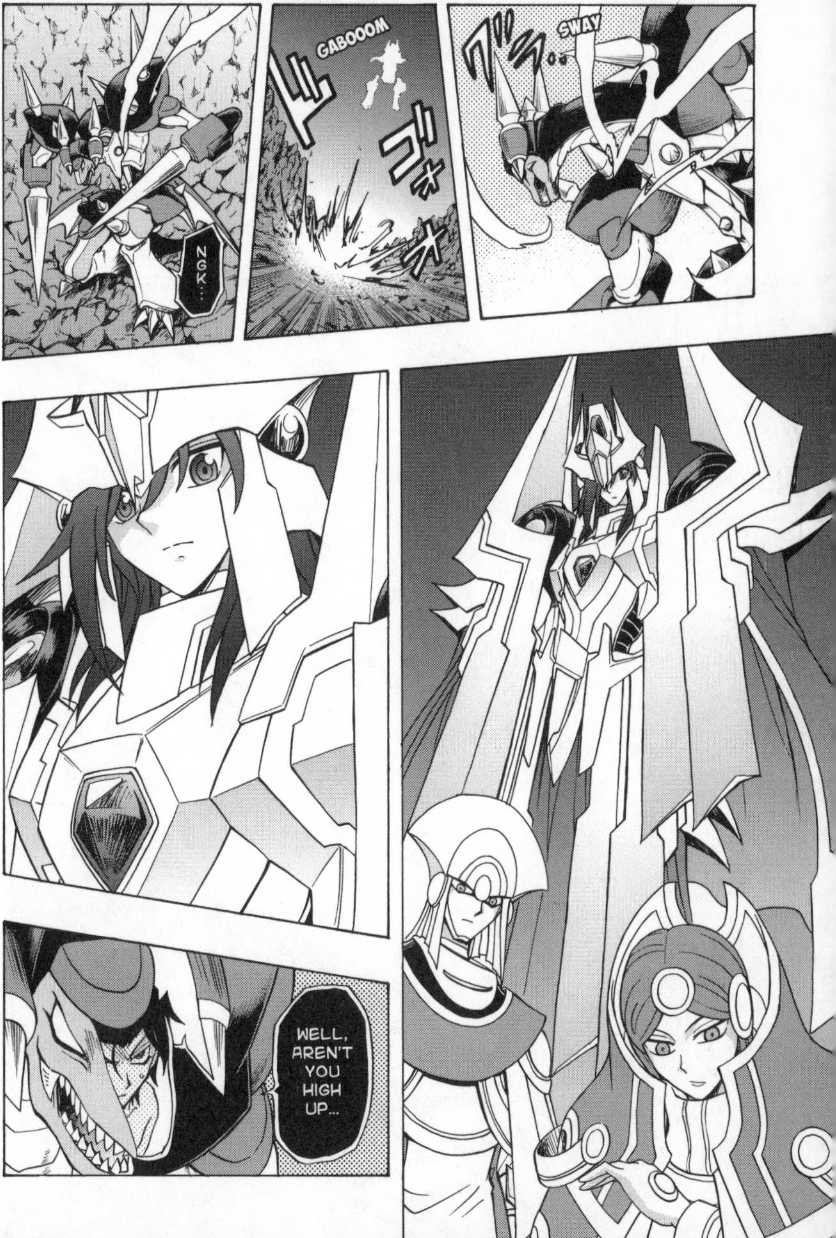
SWAY
GABOOOM
NGK...
WELL, AREN'T YOU HIGH UP...

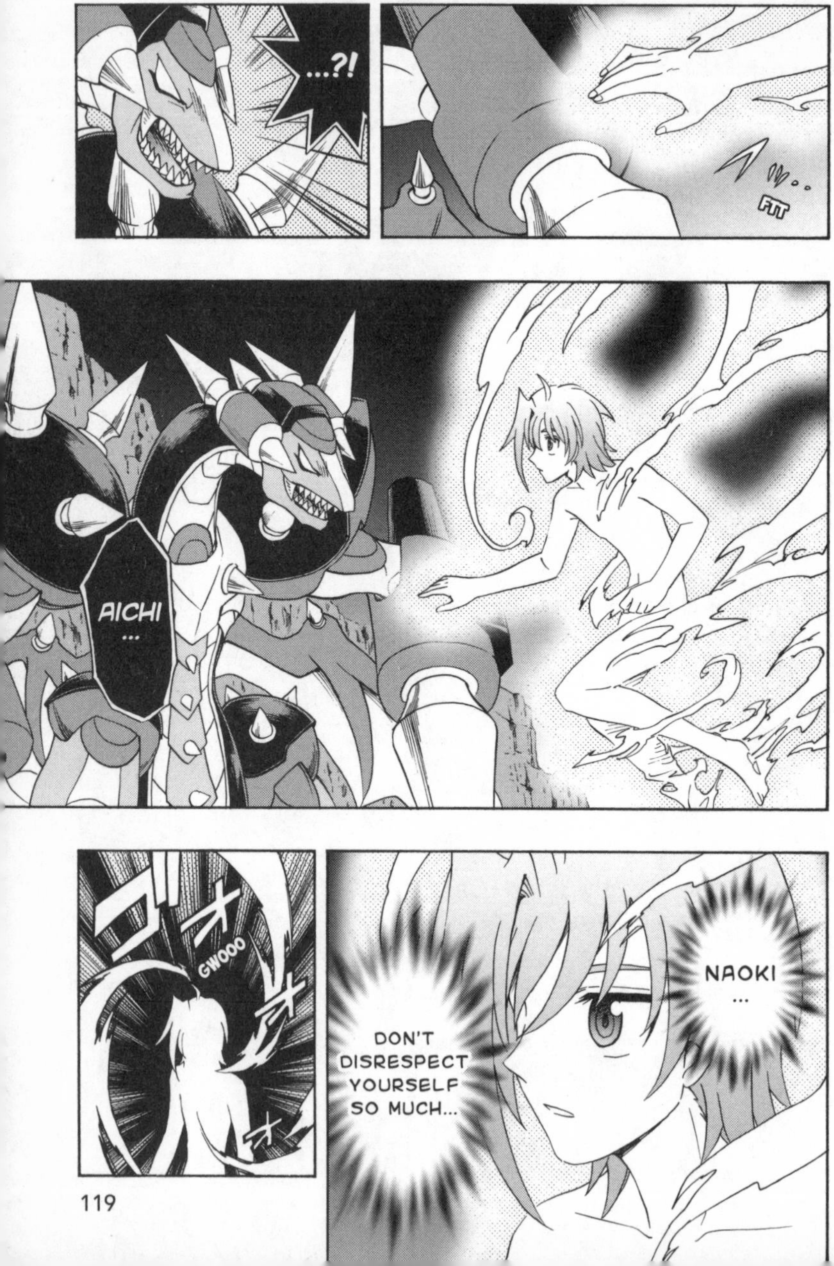
FIT
...?!
AICHI ...
NAOKI ...
DON'T DISRESPECT YOURSELF SO MUCH...
GWOOO

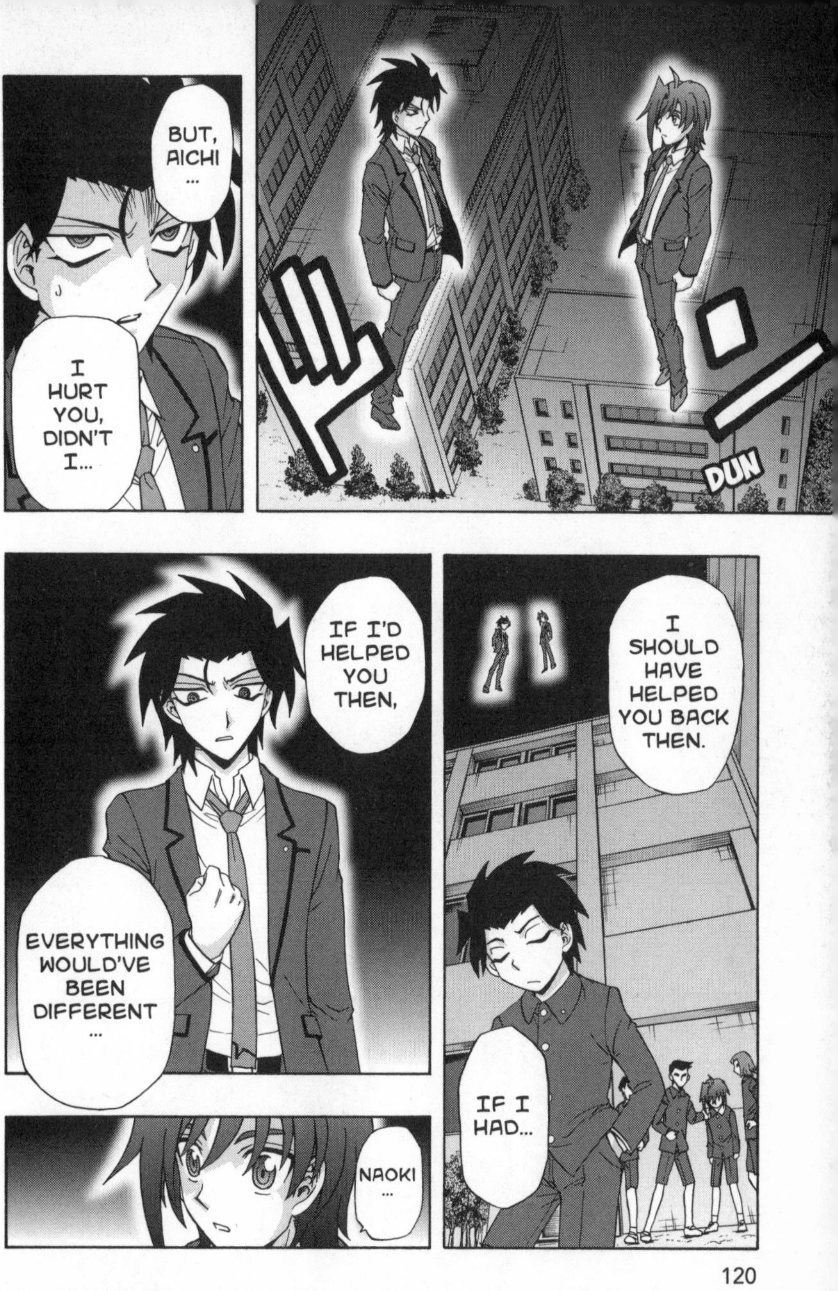
DUN
BUT, AICHI ...
I HURT YOU, DIDN'T I...
I SHOULD HAVE HELPED YOU BACK THEN.
IF I HAD...
IF I'D HELPED YOU THEN,
EVERYTHING WOULD'VE BEEN DIFFERENT ...
NAOKI ...

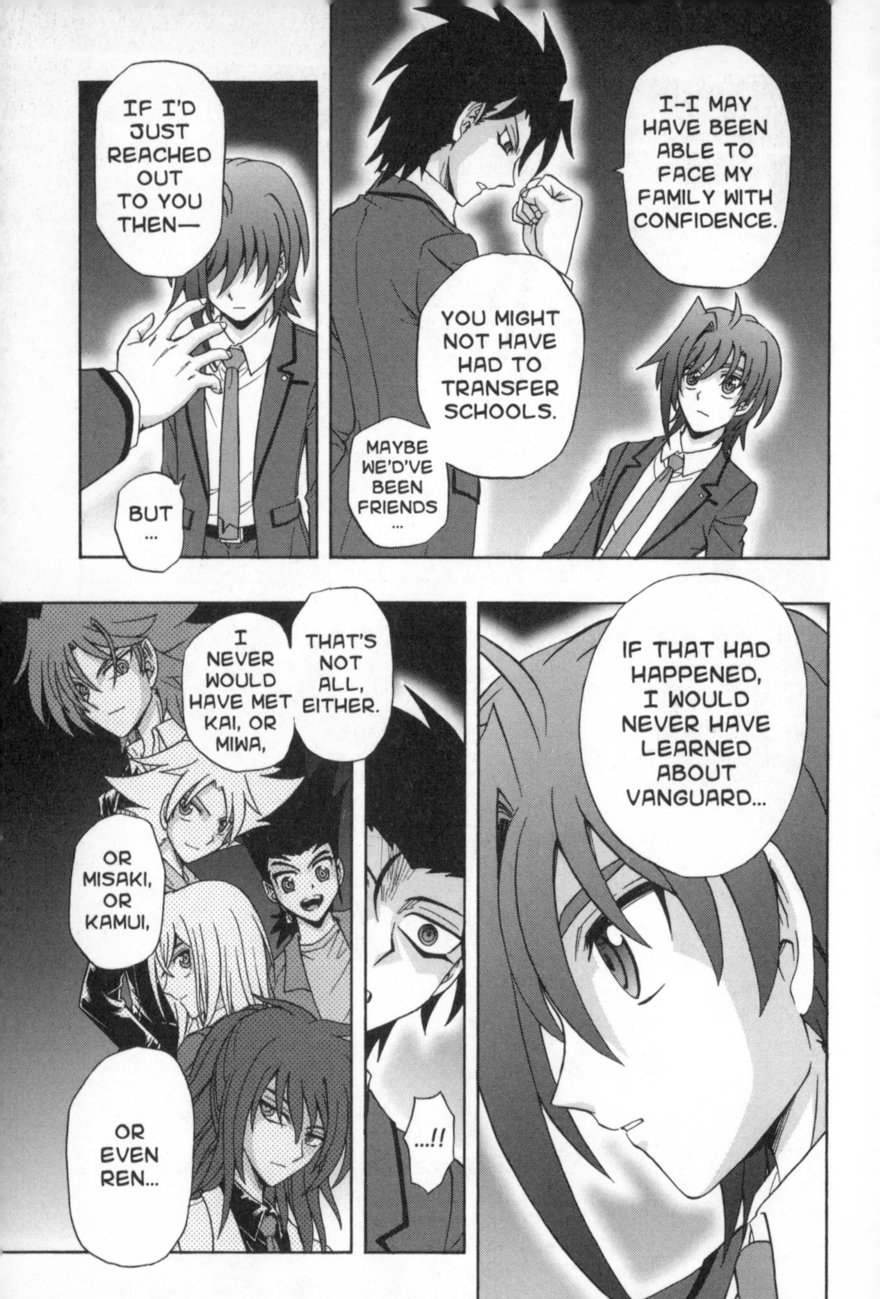
I-I MAY HAVE BEEN ABLE TO FACE MY FAMILY WITH CONFIDENCE.
YOU MIGHT NOT HAVE HAD TO TRANSFER SCHOOLS.
MAYBE WE'D'VE BEEN FRIENDS ...
IF I'D JUST REACHED OUT TO YOU THEN—
BUT ...
IF THAT HAD HAPPENED, I WOULD NEVER HAVE LEARNED ABOUT VANGUARD...
THAT'S NOT ALL, EITHER.
I NEVER WOULD HAVE MET KAI, OR MIWA,
OR MISAKI, OR KAMUI,
...!!
OR EVEN REN...

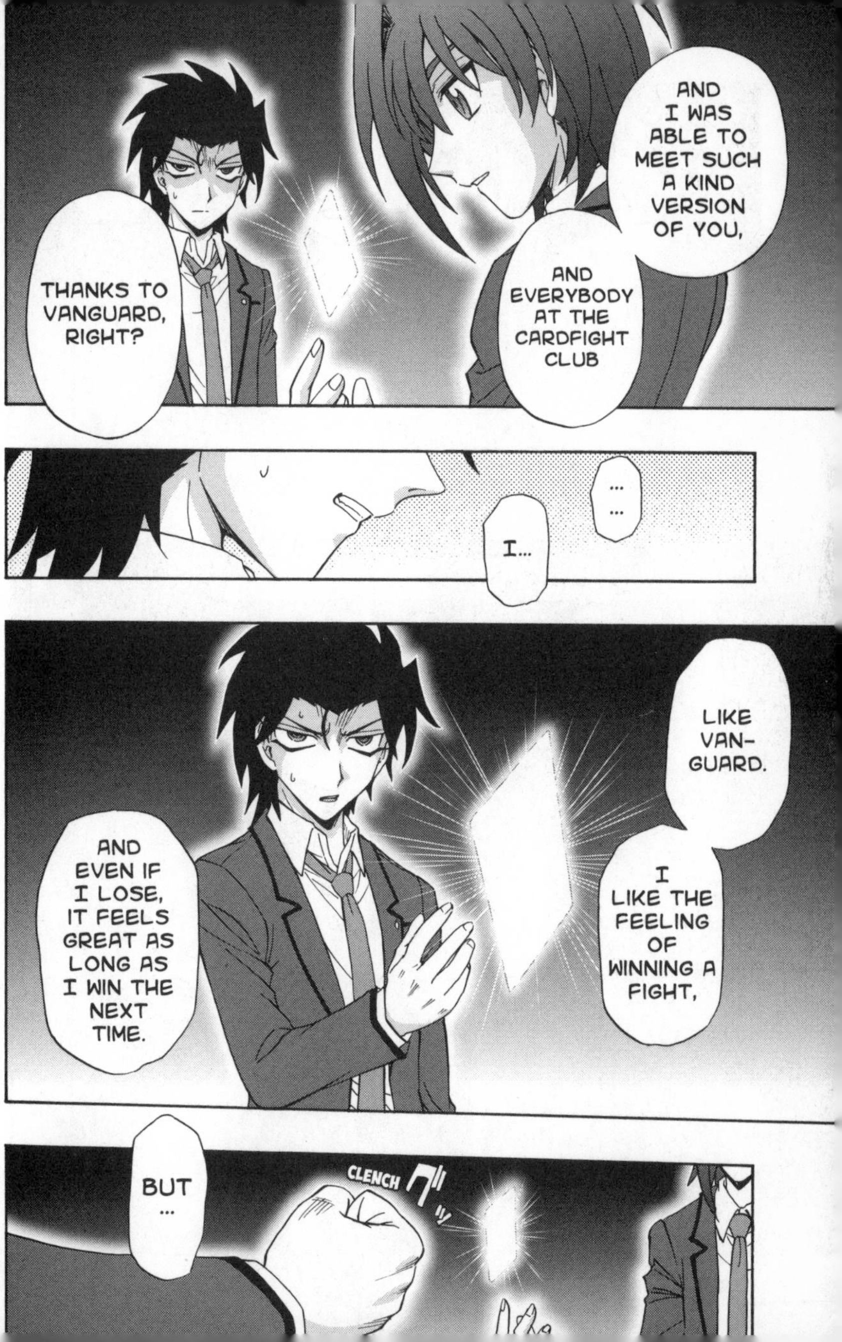
AND I WAS ABLE TO MEET SUCH A KIND VERSION OF YOU,
AND EVERYBODY AT THE CARDFIGHT CLUB
THANKS TO VANGUARD, RIGHT?
……
I...
LIKE VAN-GUARD.
I LIKE THE FEELING OF WINNING A FIGHT,
AND EVEN IF I LOSE, IT FEELS GREAT AS LONG AS I WIN THE NEXT TIME.
BUT ...
CLENCH

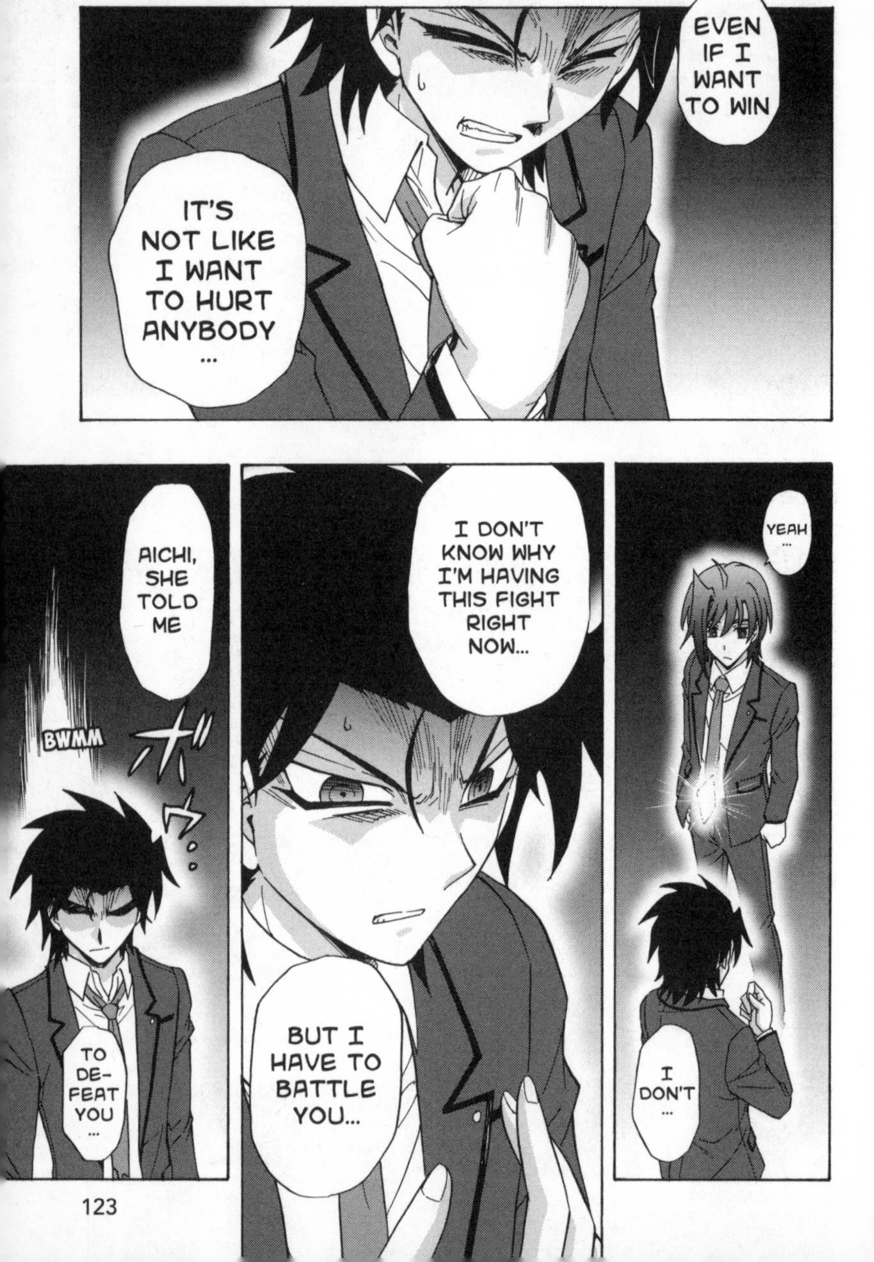
EVEN IF I WANT TO WIN
IT'S NOT LIKE I WANT TO HURT ANYBODY ...
YEAH ...
I DON'T ...
I DON'T KNOW WHY I'M HAVING THIS FIGHT RIGHT NOW...
BUT I HAVE TO BATTLE YOU...
AICHI, SHE TOLD ME
BWMM
TO DE-FEAT YOU ...

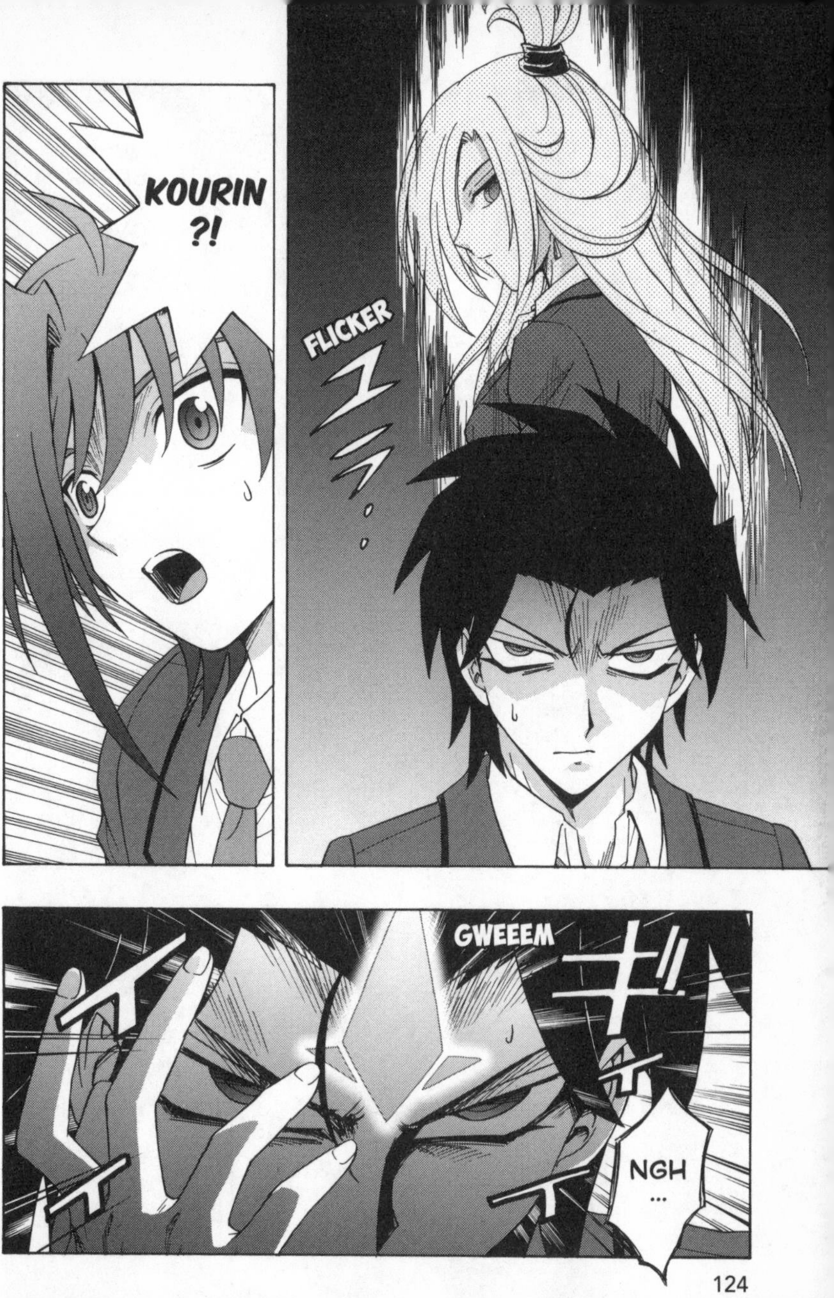
FLICKER
KOURIN ?!
GWEEEM
NGH ...

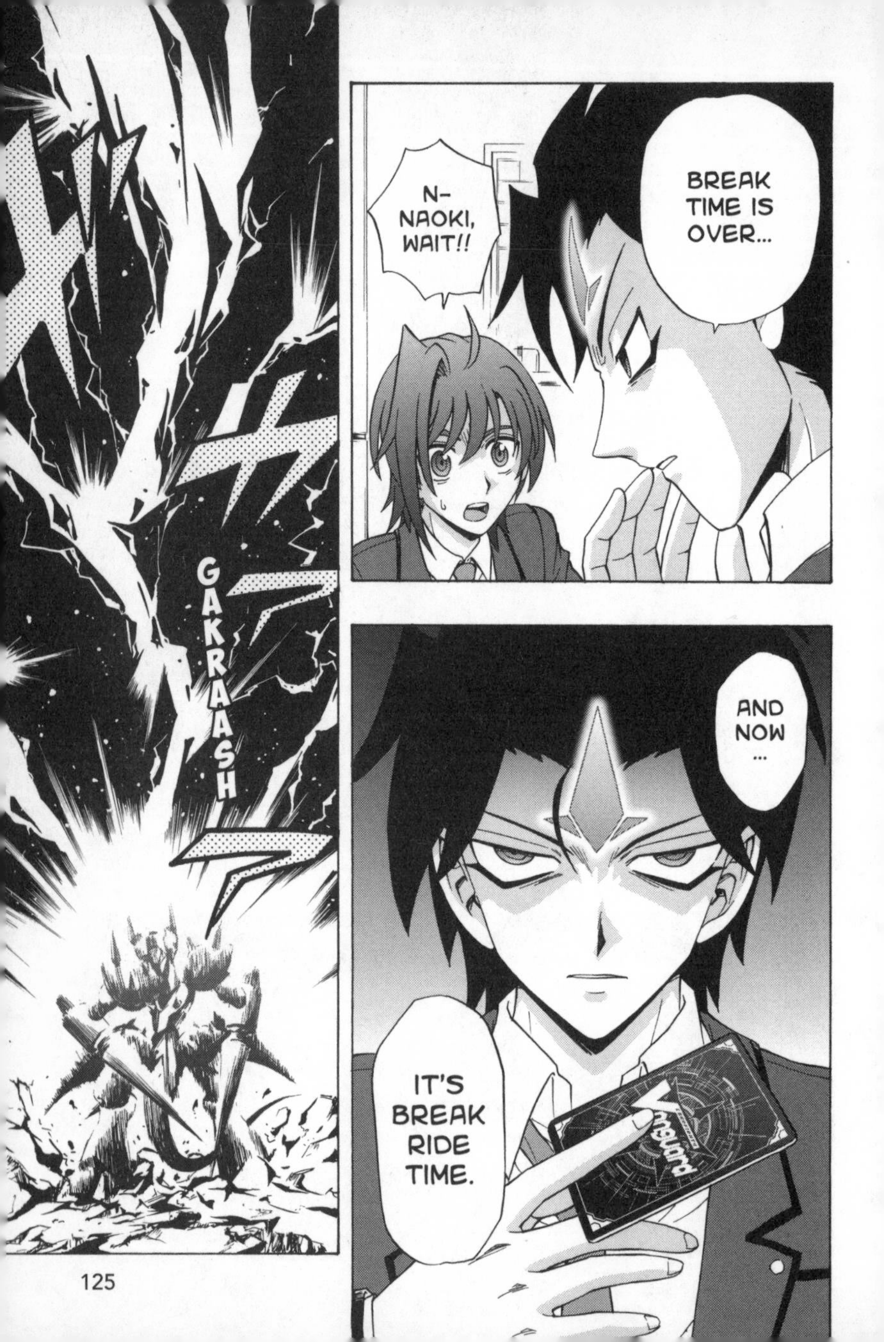
BREAK TIME IS OVER...
N-NAOKI, WAIT!!
AND NOW ...
IT'S BREAK RIDE TIME.
GAKRAASH

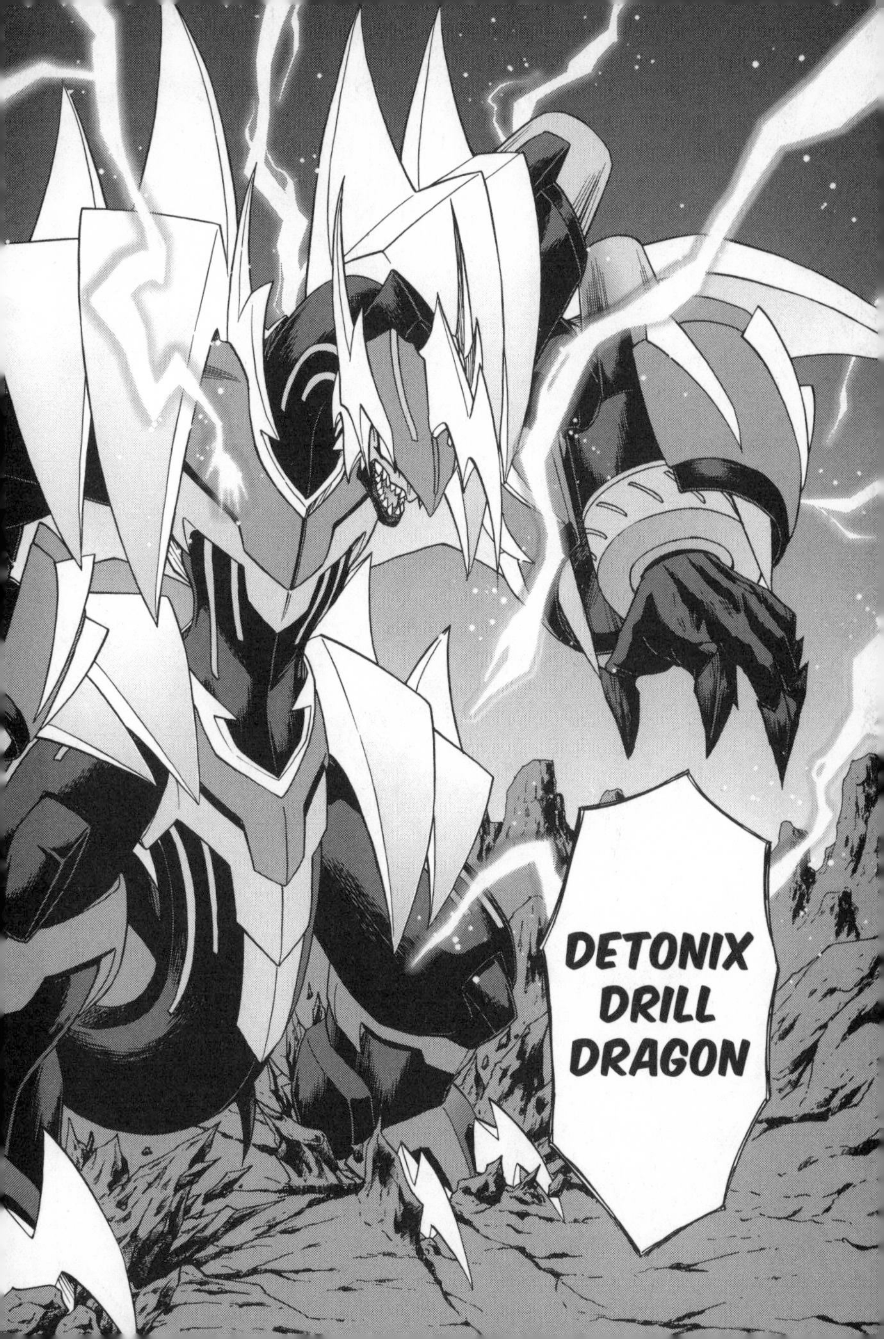
DETONIX DRILL DRAGON

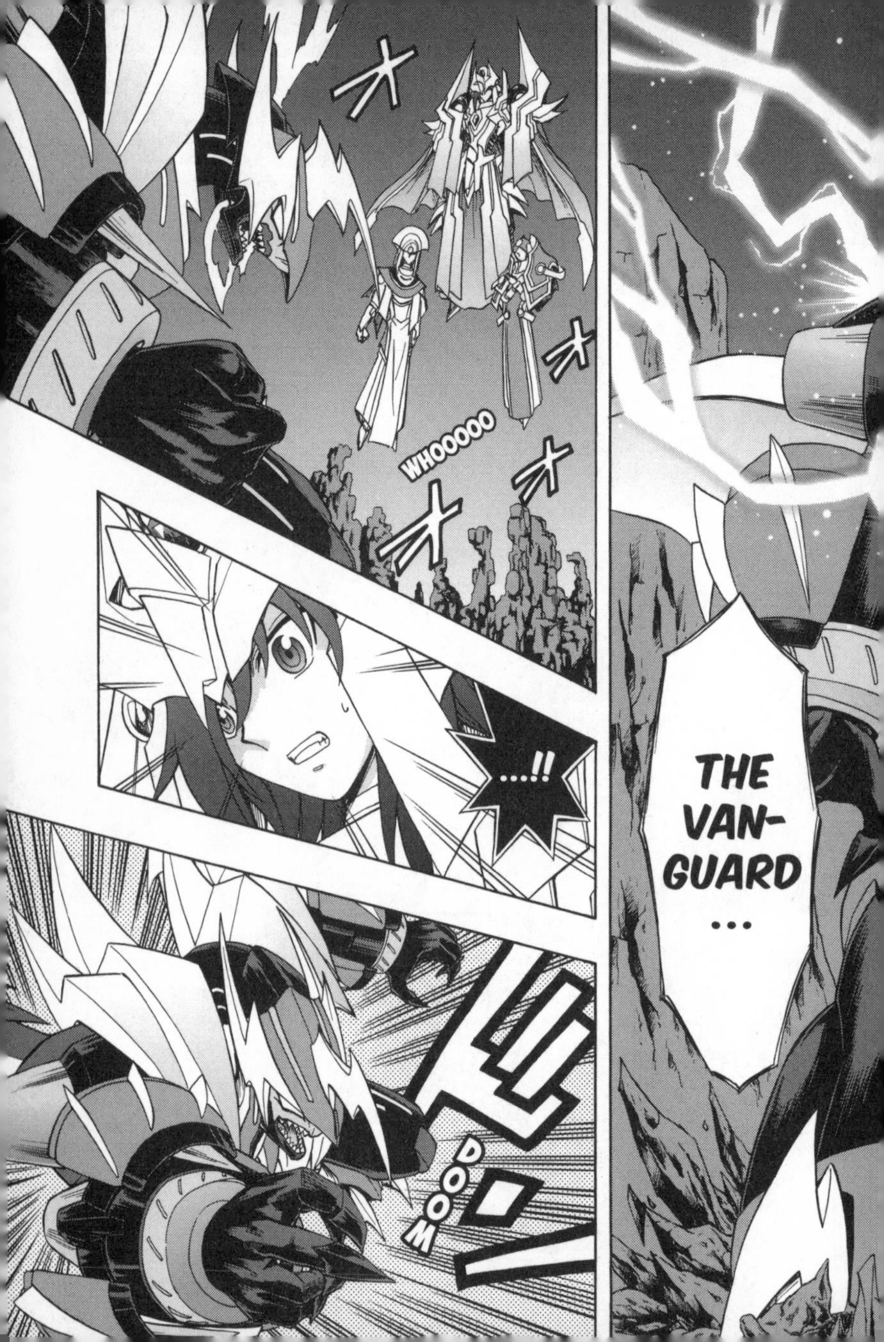
THE VAN-GUARD ...
WHOOOOO
...!!
DOOM

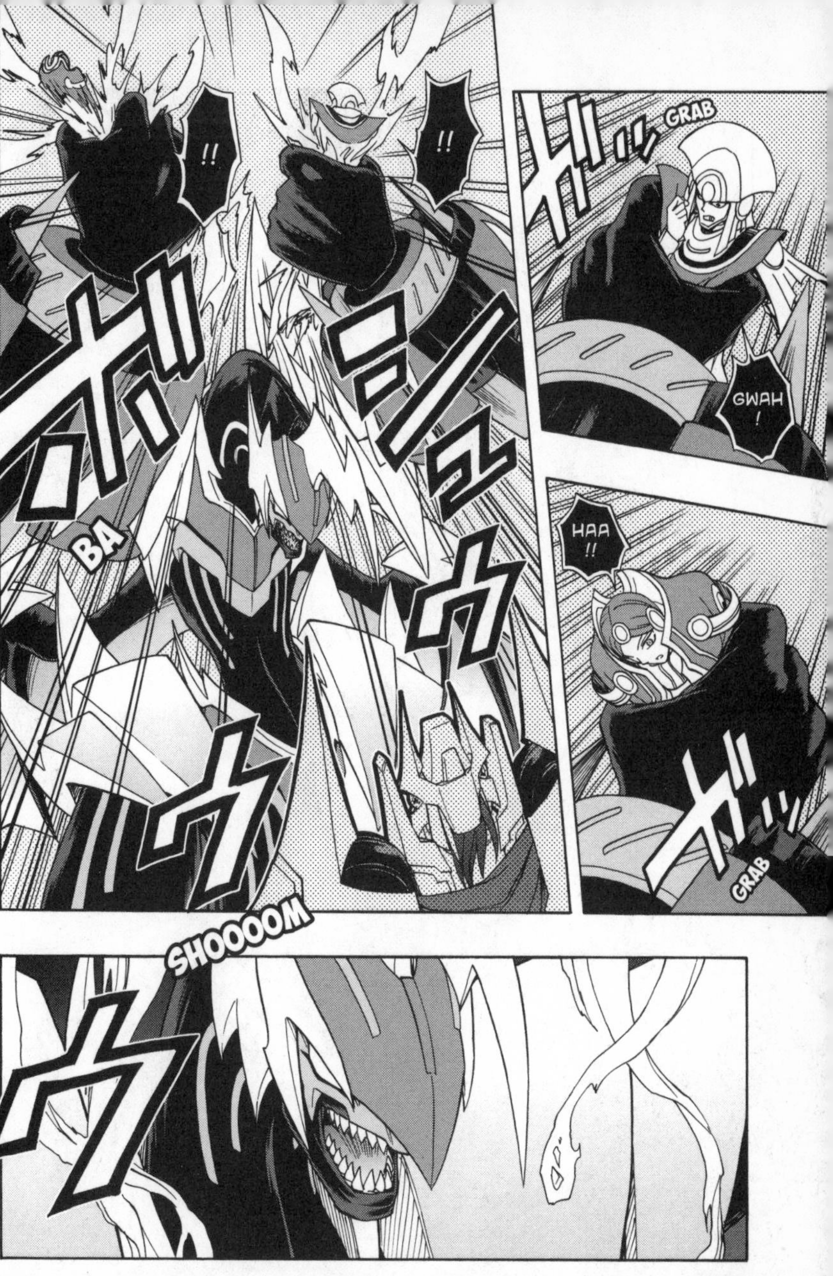
GRAB
GWAH!
HAA!!
GRAB
!!
!!
BA
SHOOOOM

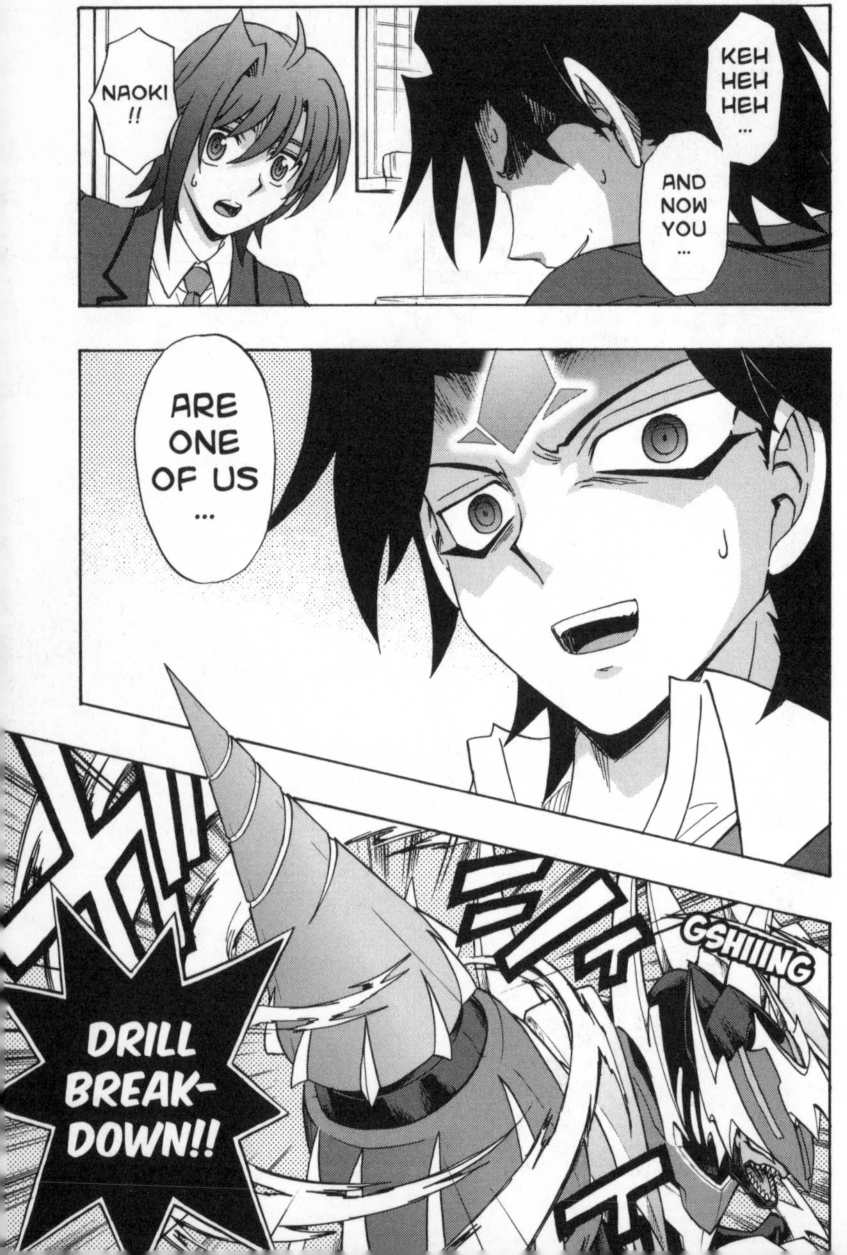
KEH HEH HEH ...
AND NOW YOU ...
NAOKI !!
ARE ONE OF US ...
GSHIIING
DRILL BREAK-DOWN!!

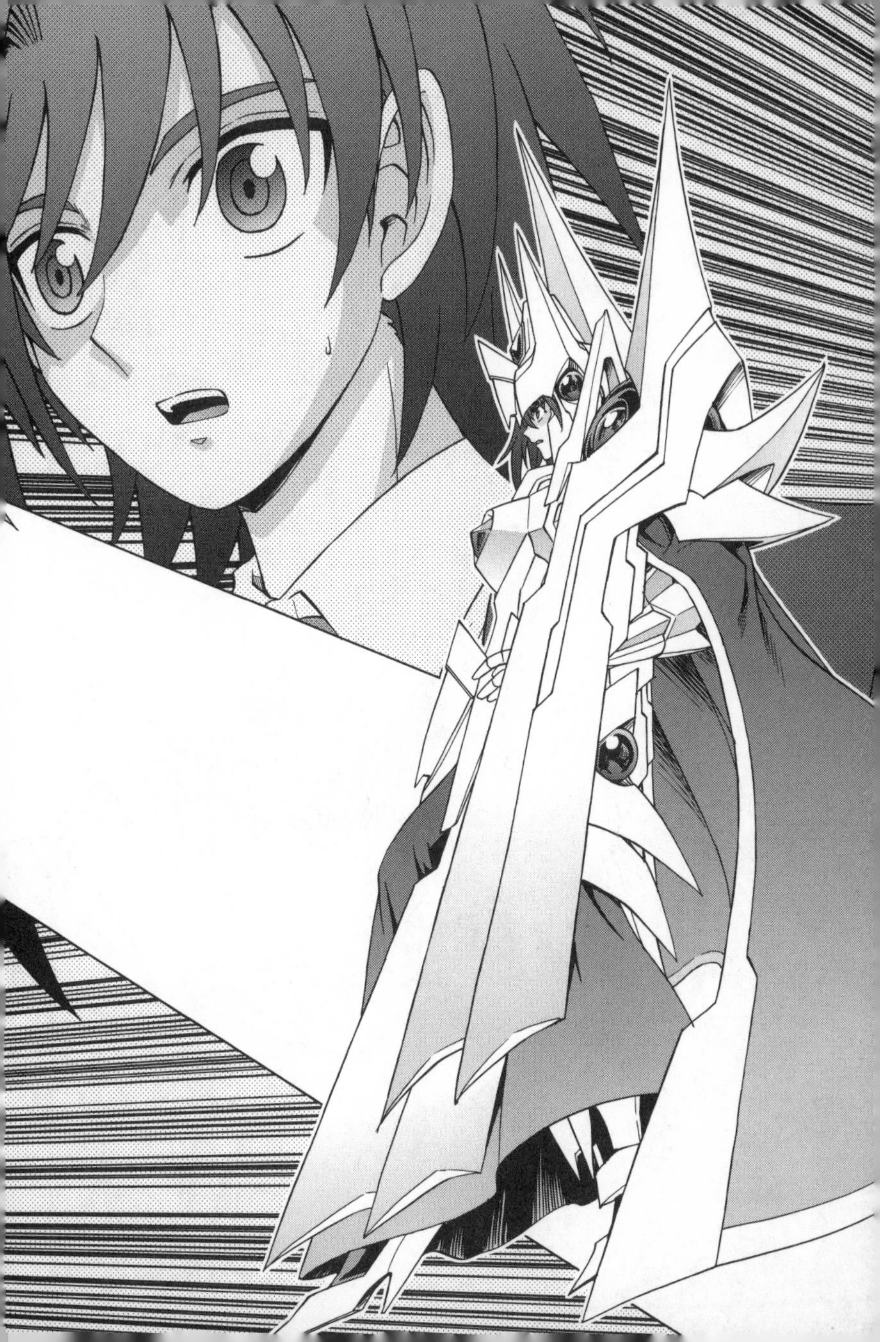

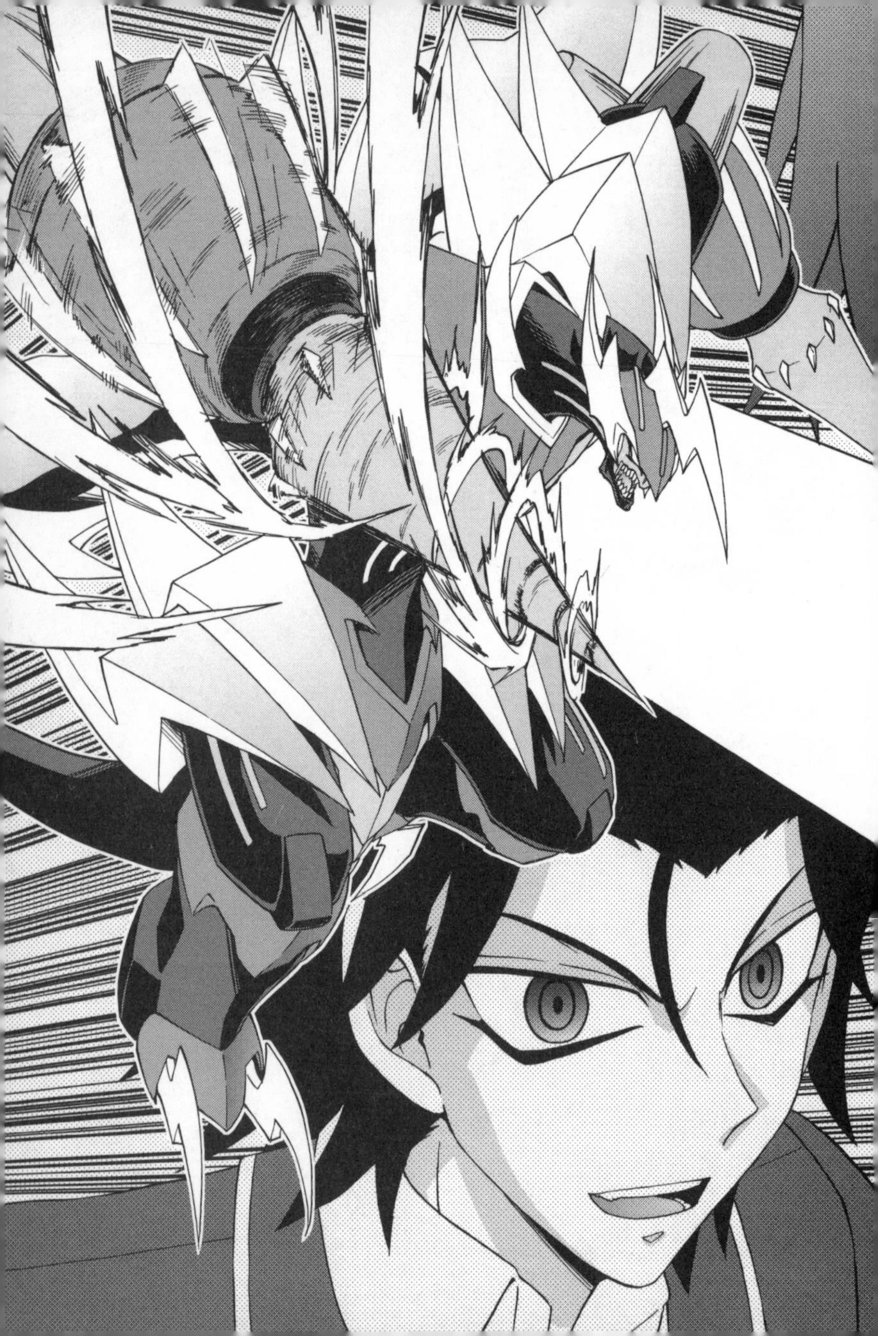

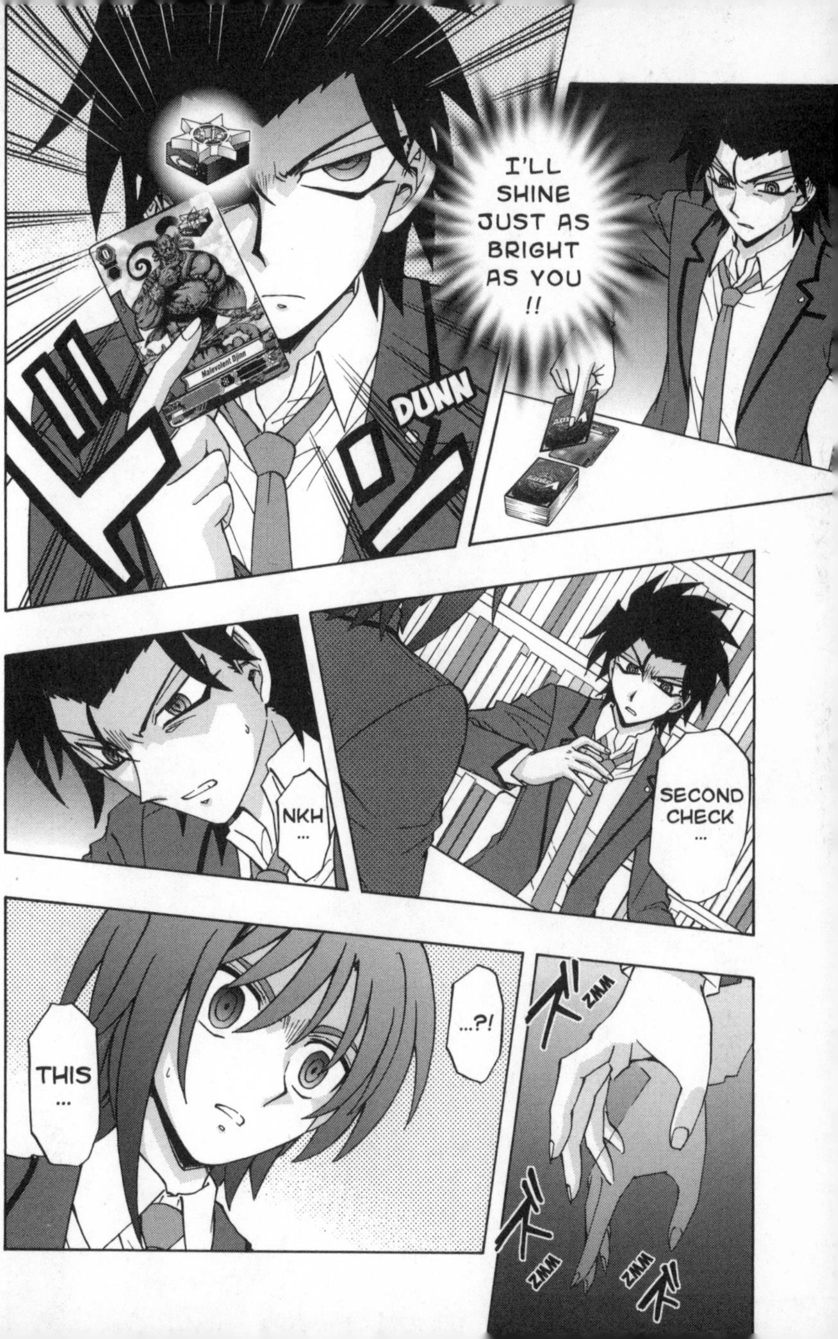
I'LL SHINE JUST AS BRIGHT AS YOU !!
Malevolent Djinn
DUNN
SECOND CHECK ...
NKH ...
ZWW
ZWW
ZWW
ZWW
...?!
THIS ...

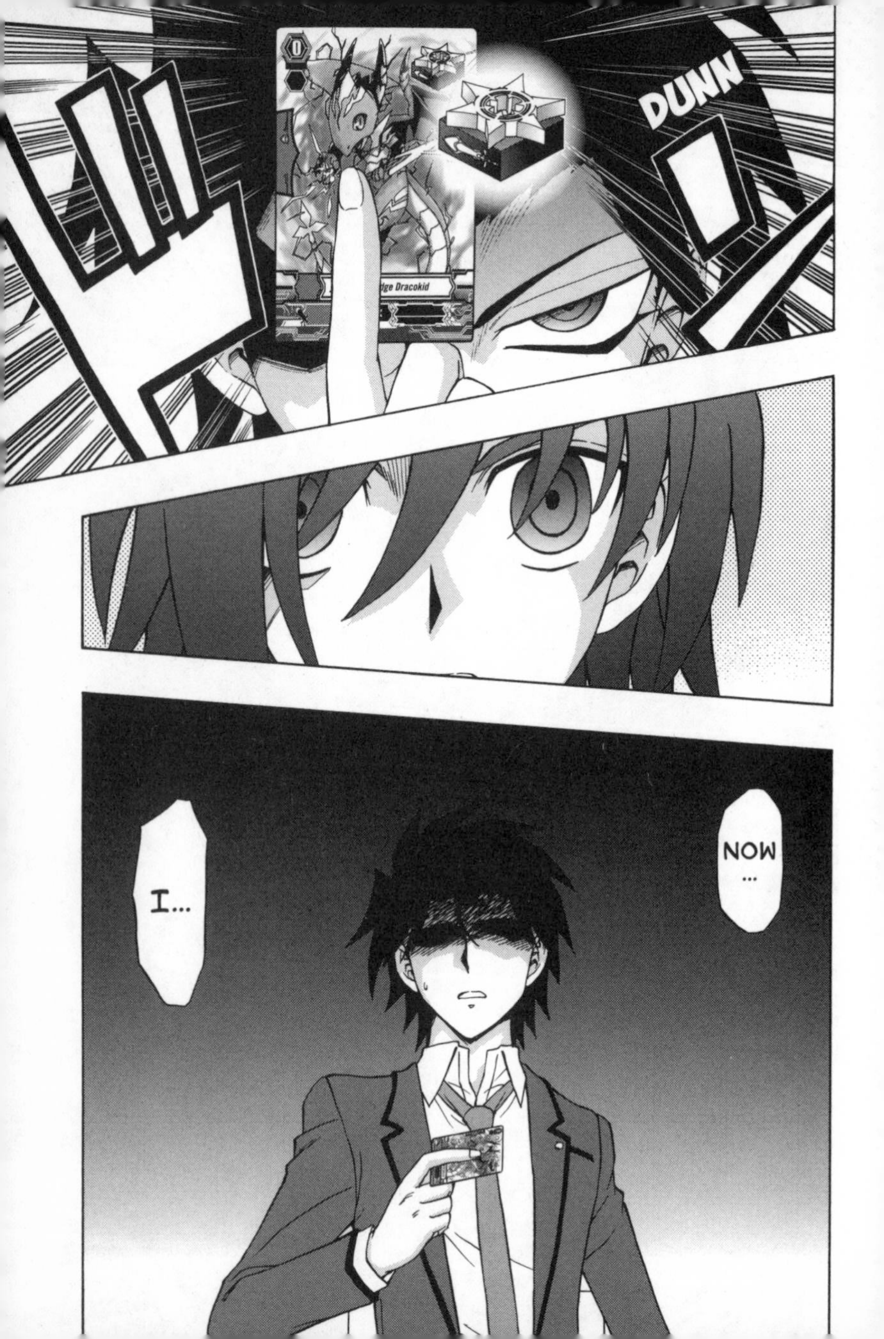
DUNN
NOW...
I...

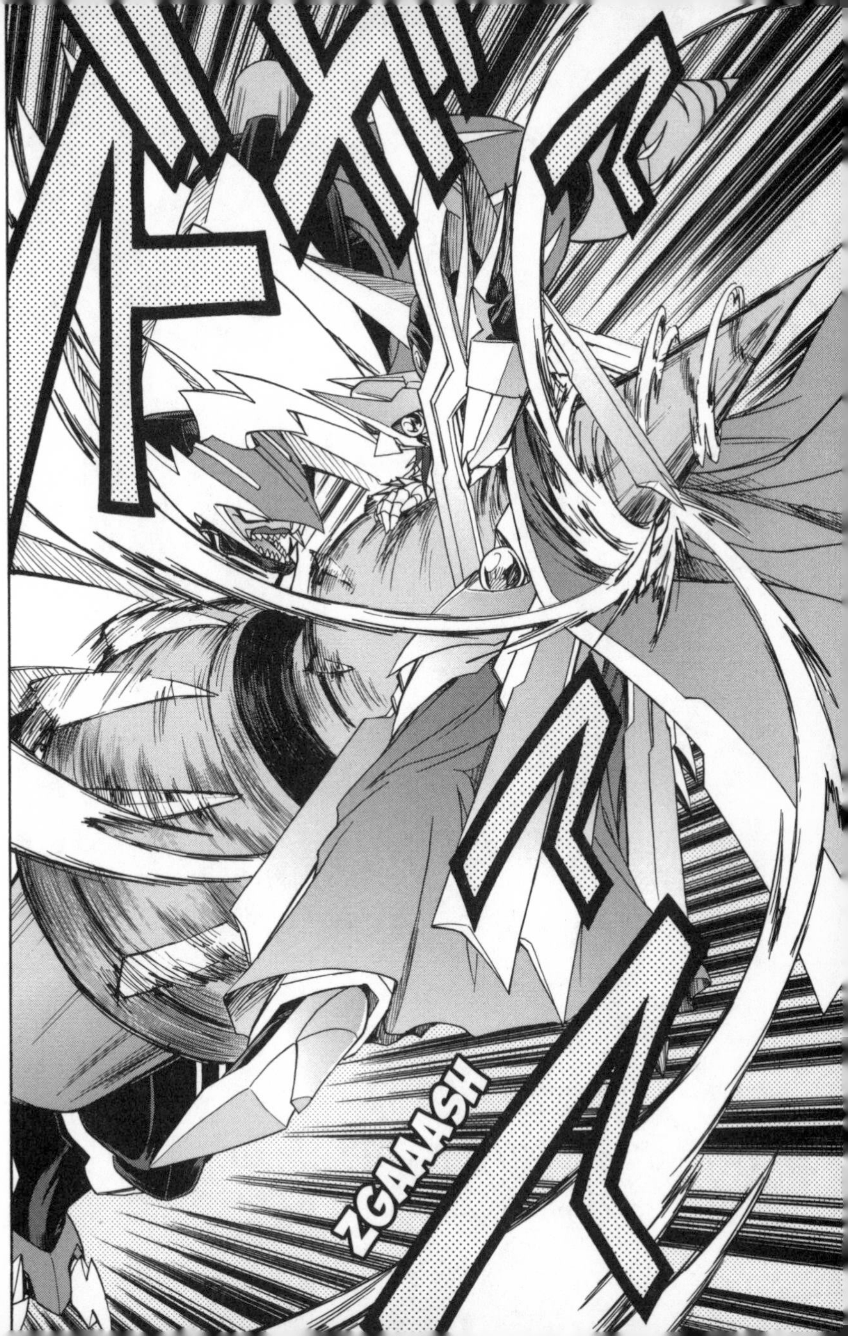
ZGAAASH

CARDFIGHT!! Vanguard

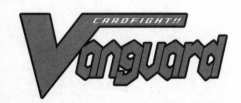

CARDFIGHT!! Vanguard

BONUS!

NEVER-BEFORE-SEEN IMAGE BOARDS

Ren Suzugamori

@ Unemployed

@ Roaming Fighter

Aichi Sendou

@ Studying abroad while living with his father

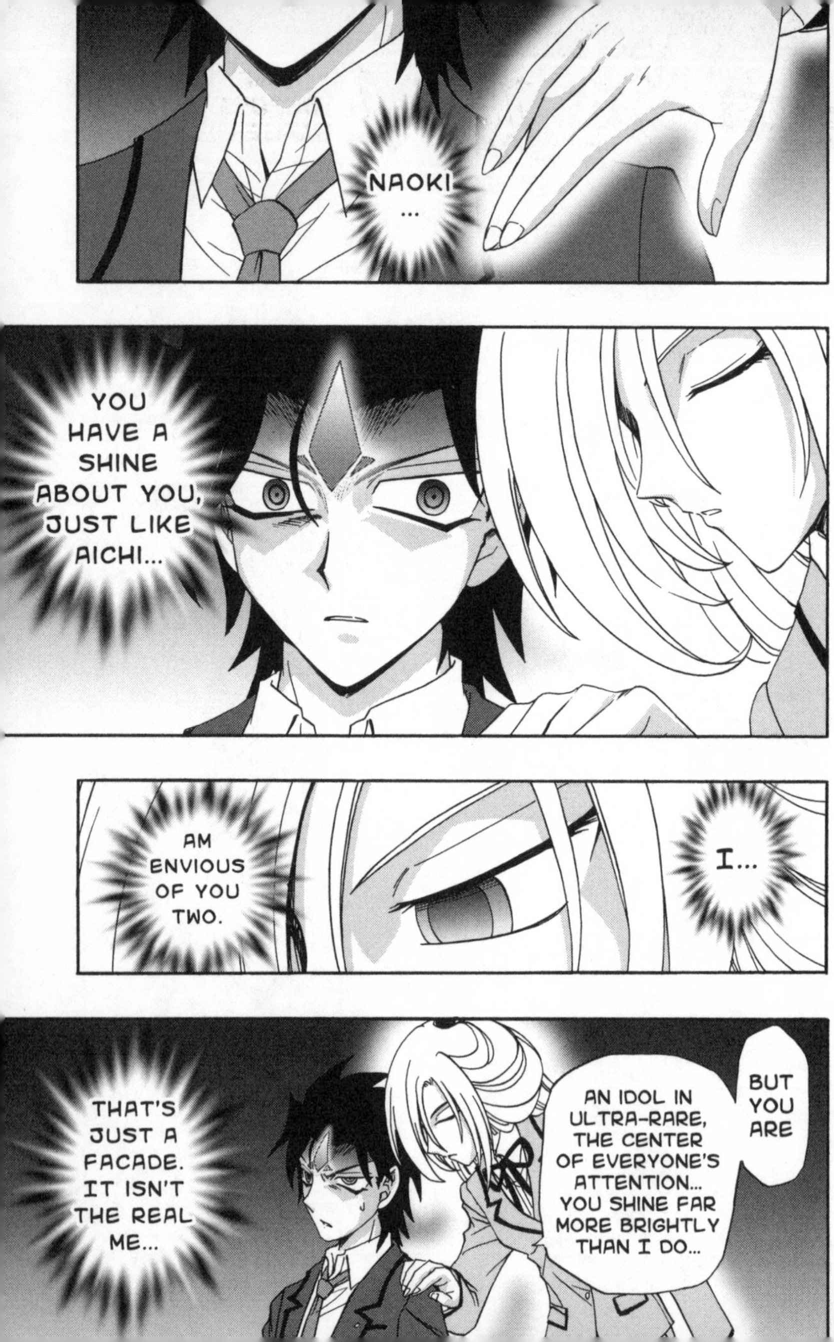
NAOKI...
YOU HAVE A SHINE ABOUT YOU, JUST LIKE AICHI...
I...
AM ENVIOUS OF YOU TWO.
BUT YOU ARE
AN IDOL IN ULTRA-RARE, THE CENTER OF EVERYONE'S ATTENTION... YOU SHINE FAR MORE BRIGHTLY THAN I DO...
THAT'S JUST A FACADE. IT ISN'T THE REAL ME...

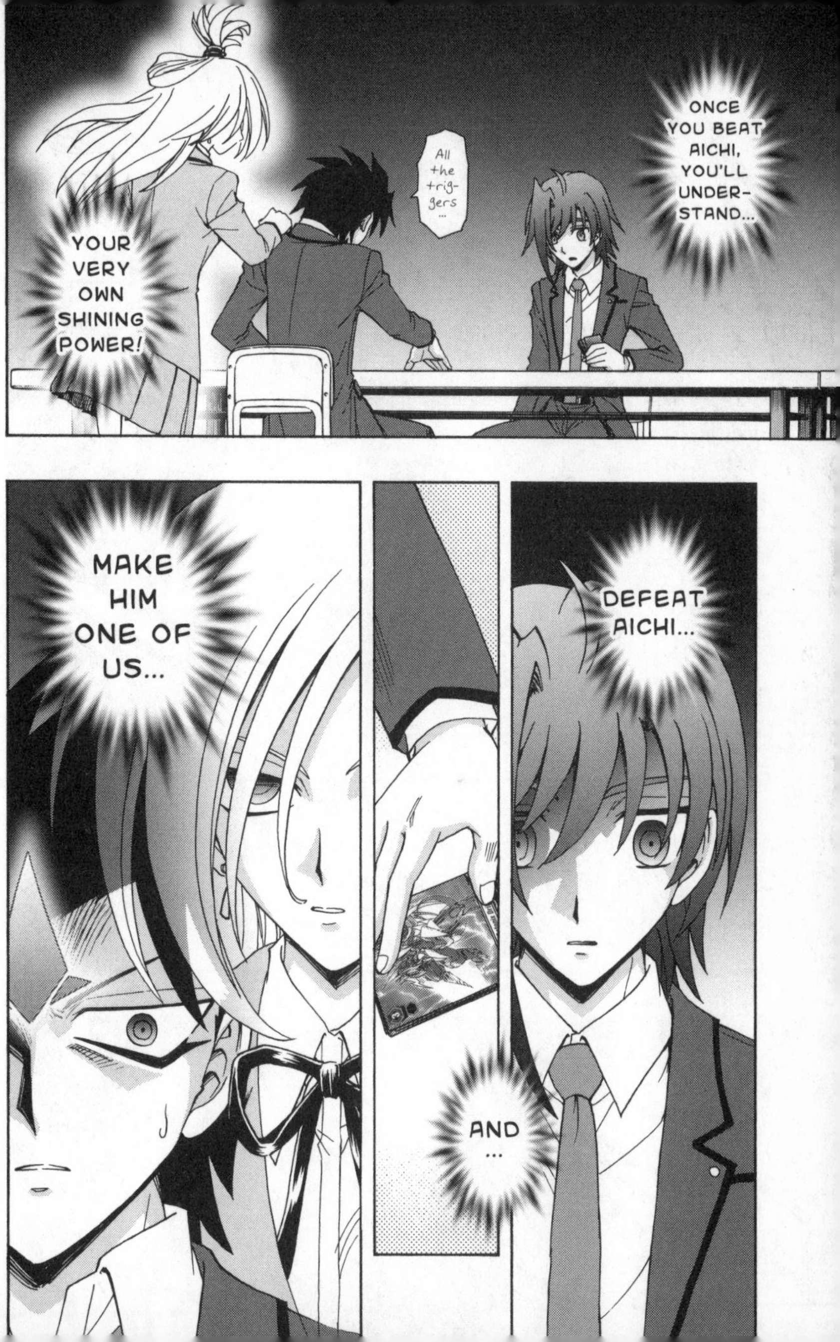
ONCE YOU BEAT AICHI, YOU'LL UNDER-STAND...
All the trig-gers ...
YOUR VERY OWN SHINING POWER!
DEFEAT AICHI...
AND ...
MAKE HIM ONE OF US...

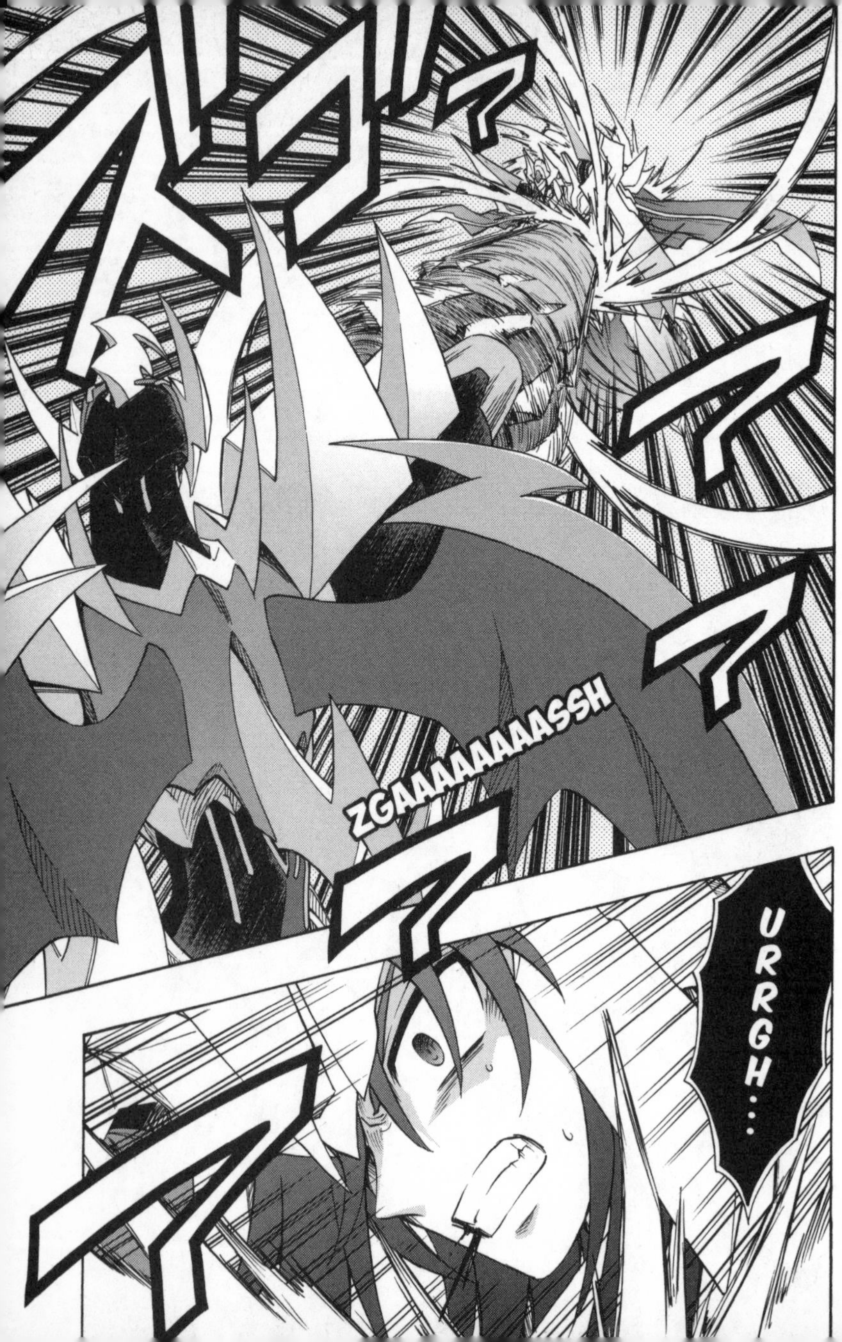
ZGAAAAAAAASSH
URRGH...

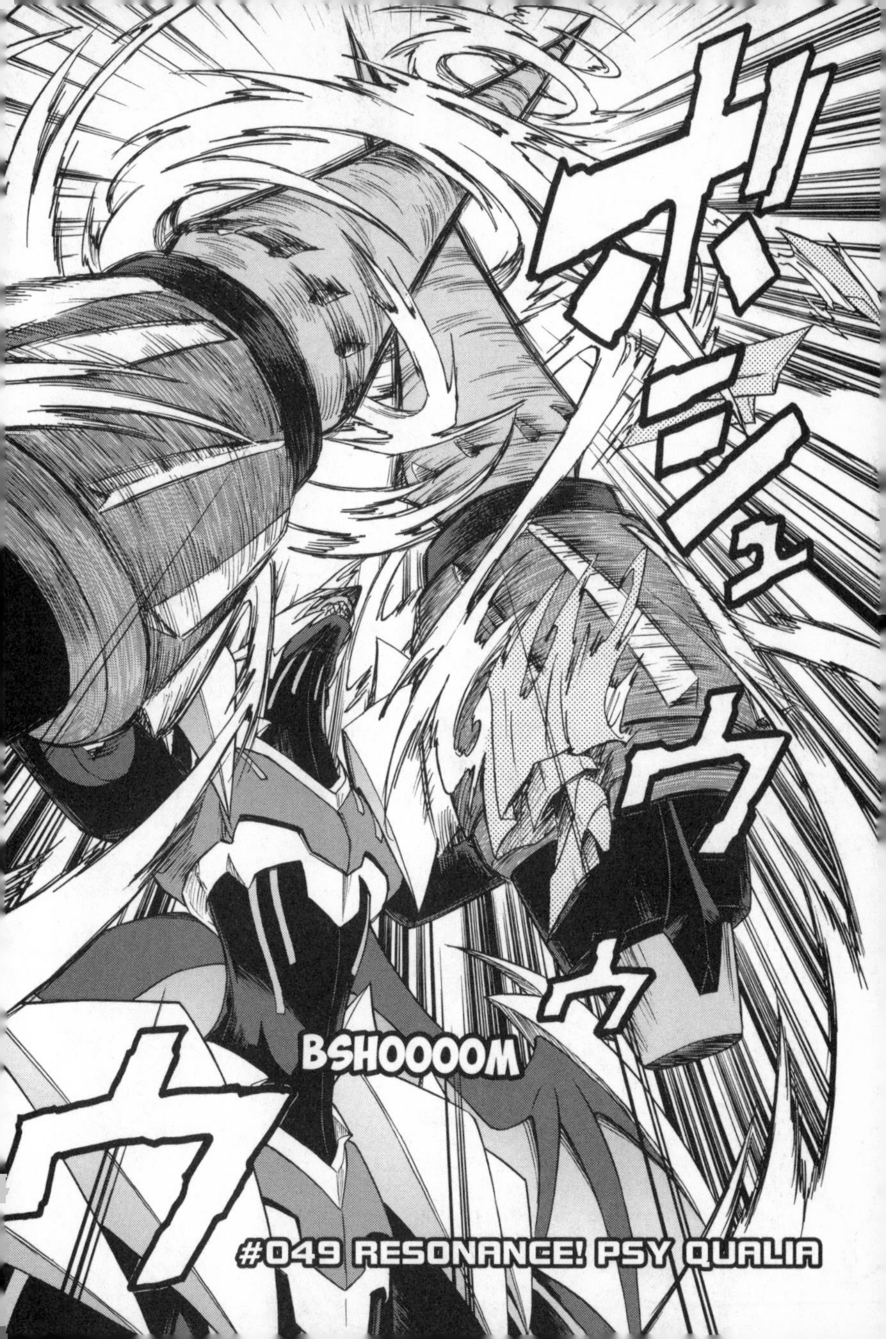
BSHOOOOM

#049 RESONANCE! PSY QUALIA

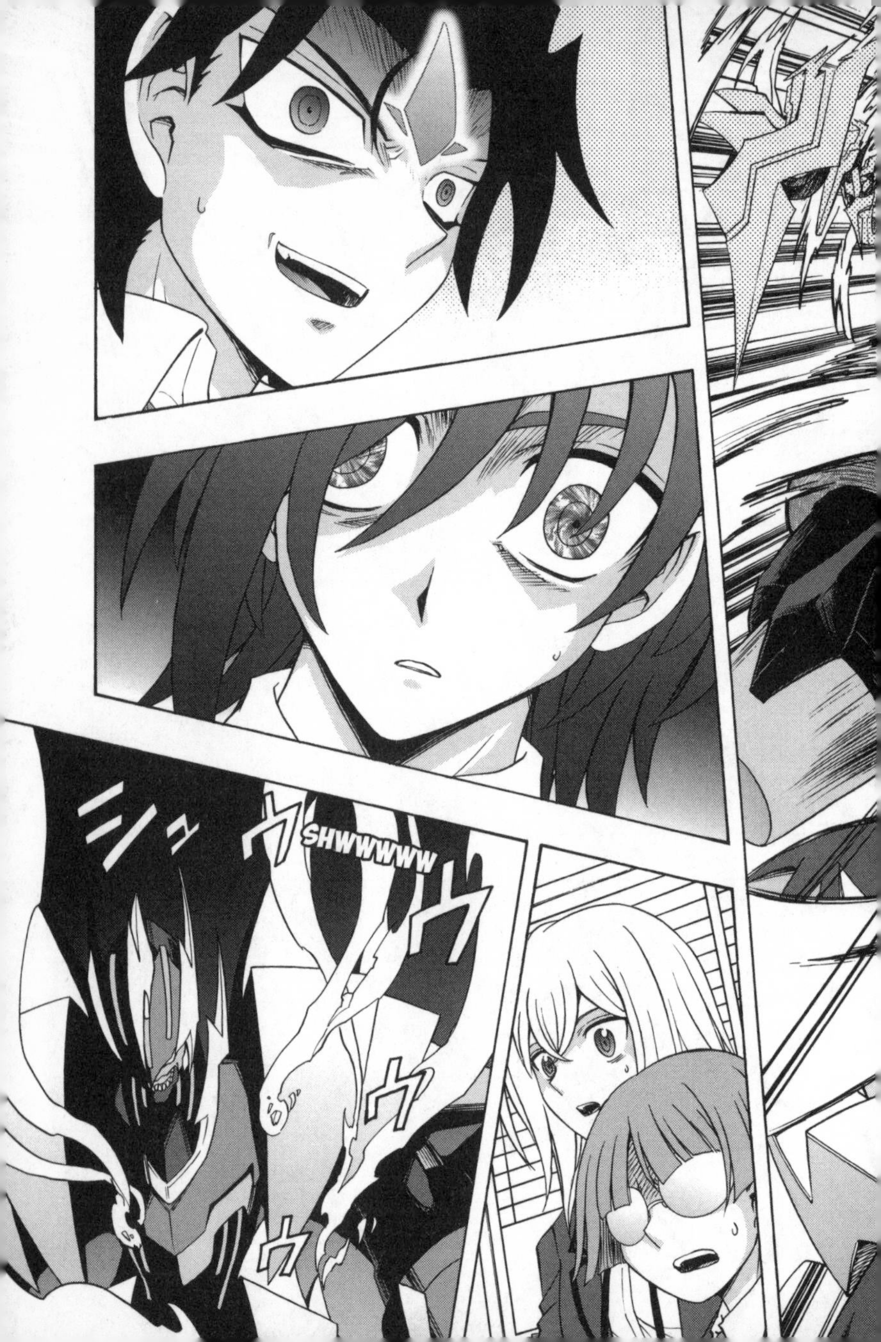
SHWWWWWW

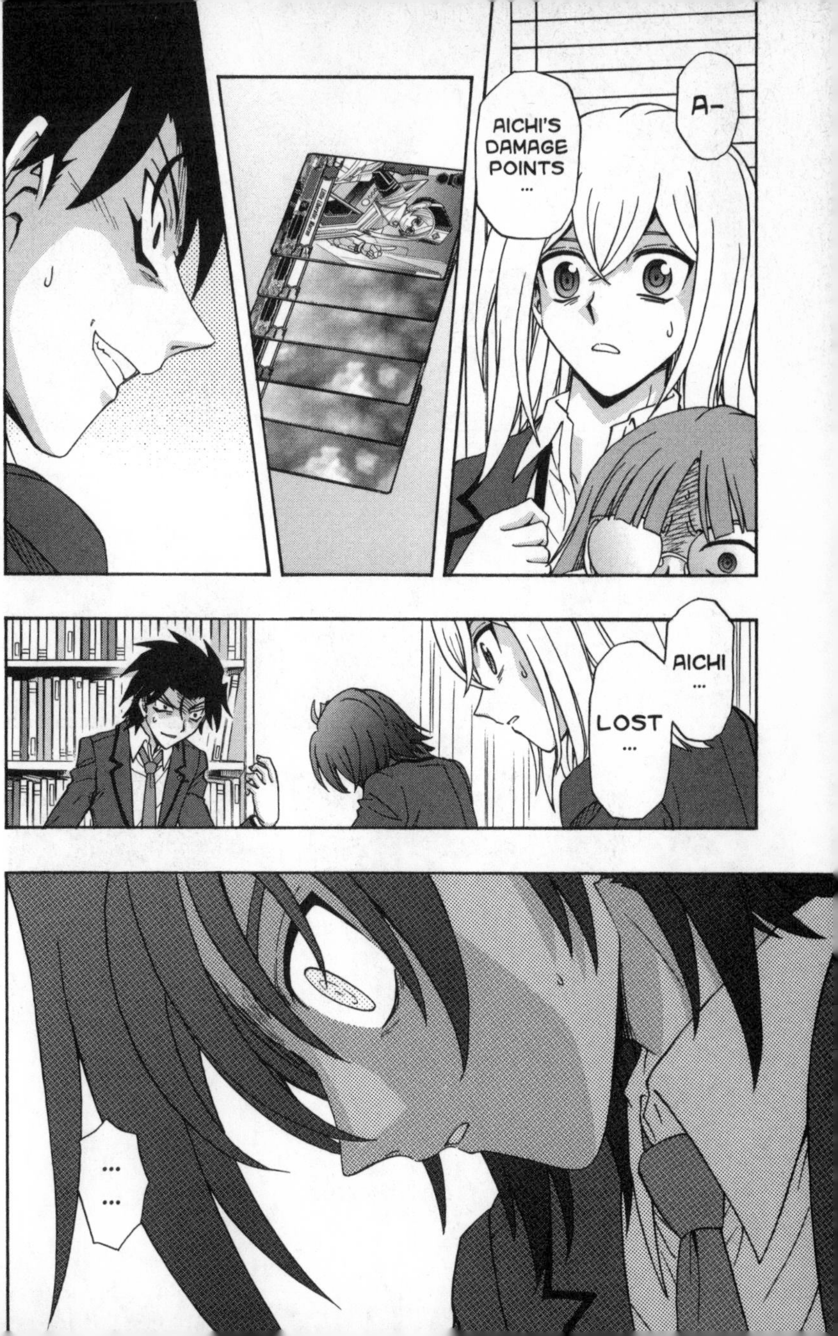
A-
AICHI'S DAMAGE POINTS ...
AICHI ... LOST ...
... ...

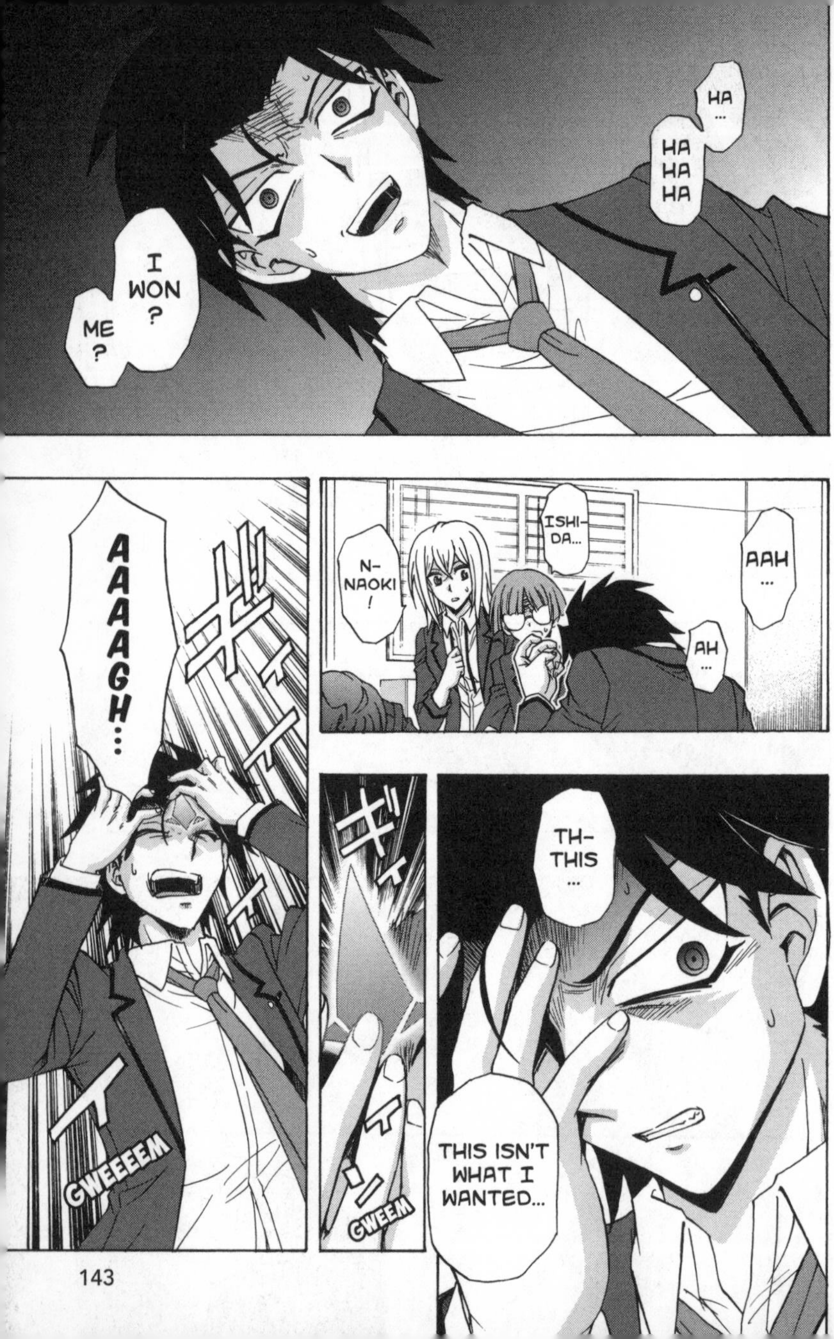
HA ...
HA HA HA
I WON ?
ME ?
AAH ...
AH ...
ISHI-DA...
N-NAOKI !
TH-THIS ...
THIS ISN'T WHAT I WANTED...
GWEEM
AAAAAAGH...
GWEEEEM

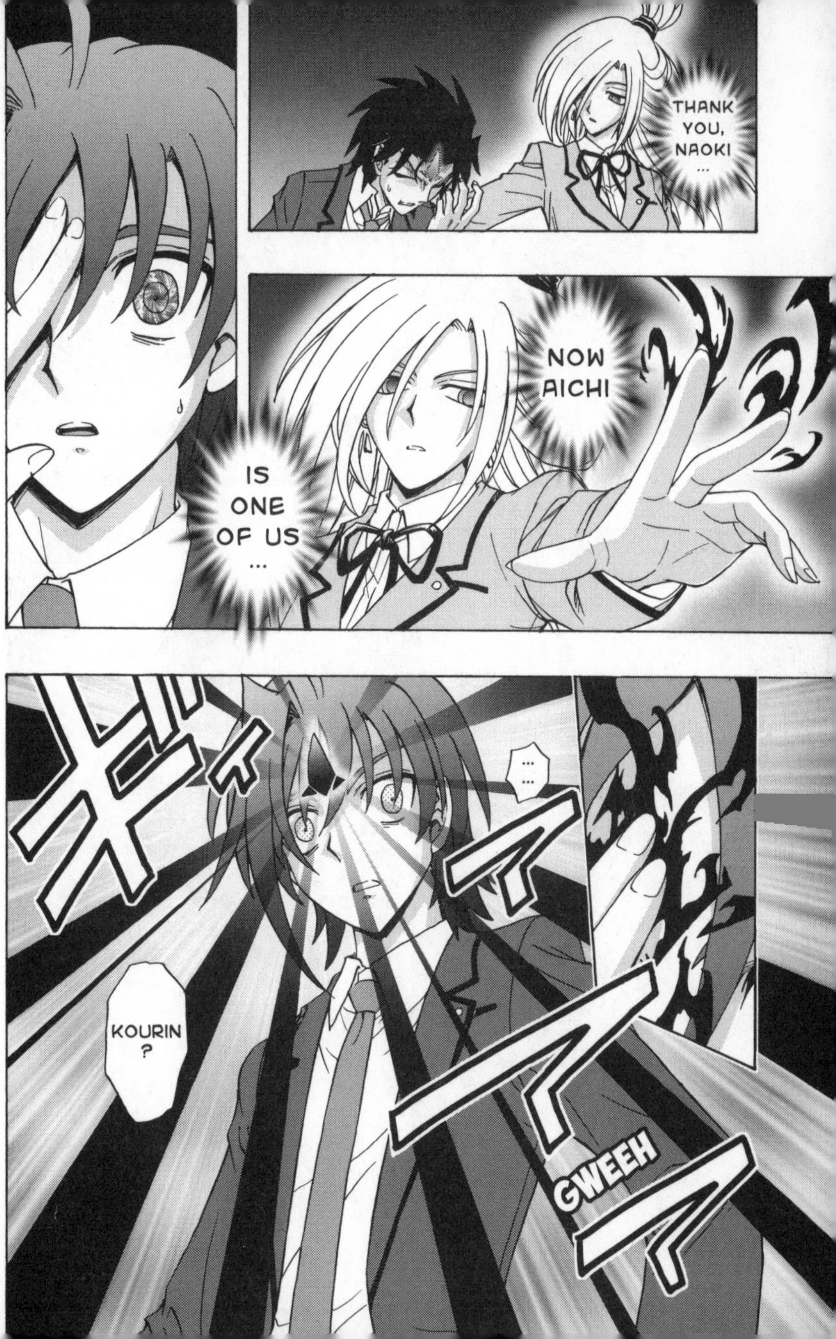
THANK YOU, NAOKI ...
NOW AICHI
IS ONE OF US ...
... ...
KOURIN ?
GWEEH

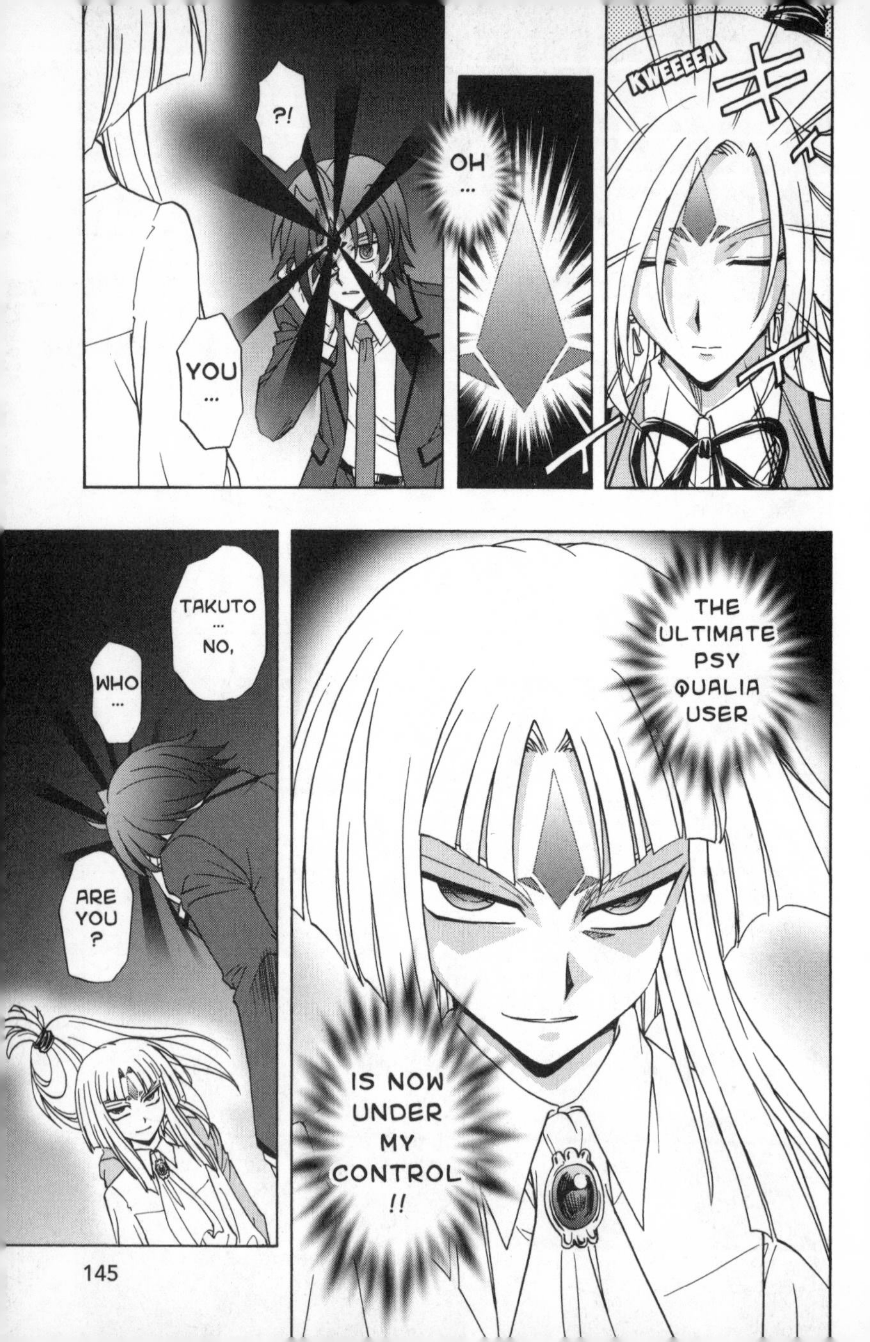
KWEEEEM
OH ...
?!
YOU ...
THE ULTIMATE PSY QUALIA USER
IS NOW UNDER MY CONTROL !!
TAKUTO ... NO,
WHO ...
ARE YOU ?

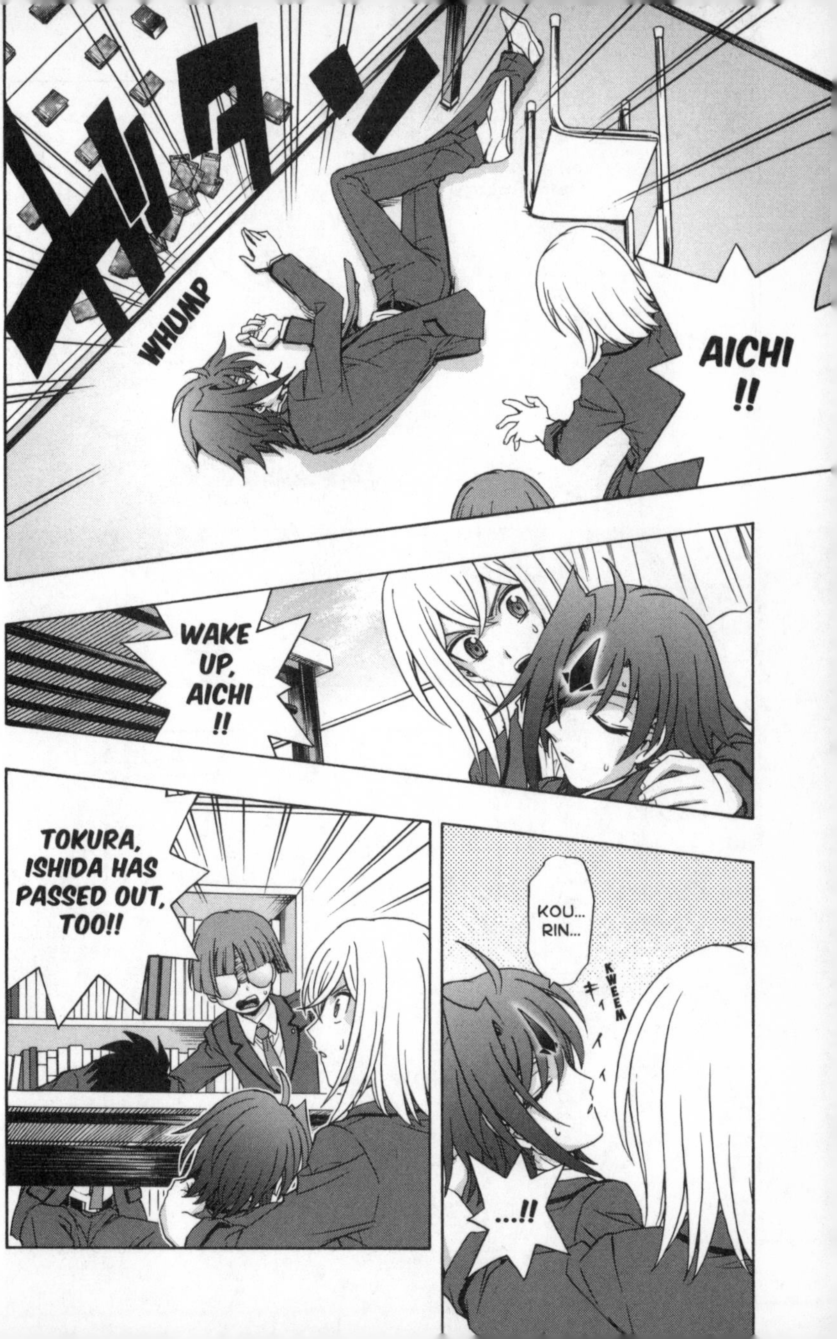
AICHI !!
WHUMP
WAKE UP, AICHI !!
KOU... RIN...
KWEEM
...!!
TOKURA, ISHIDA HAS PASSED OUT, TOO!!

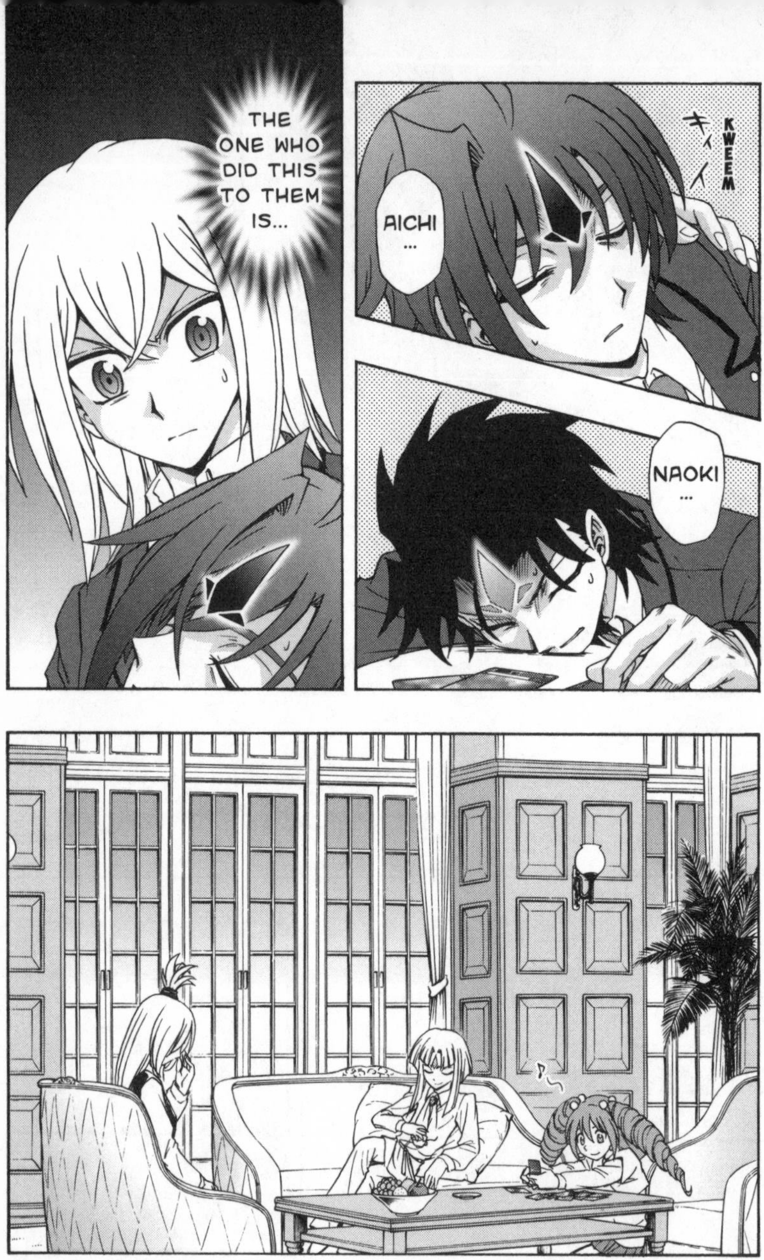
KWEEM
AICHI...
NAOKI...
THE ONE WHO DID THIS TO THEM IS...

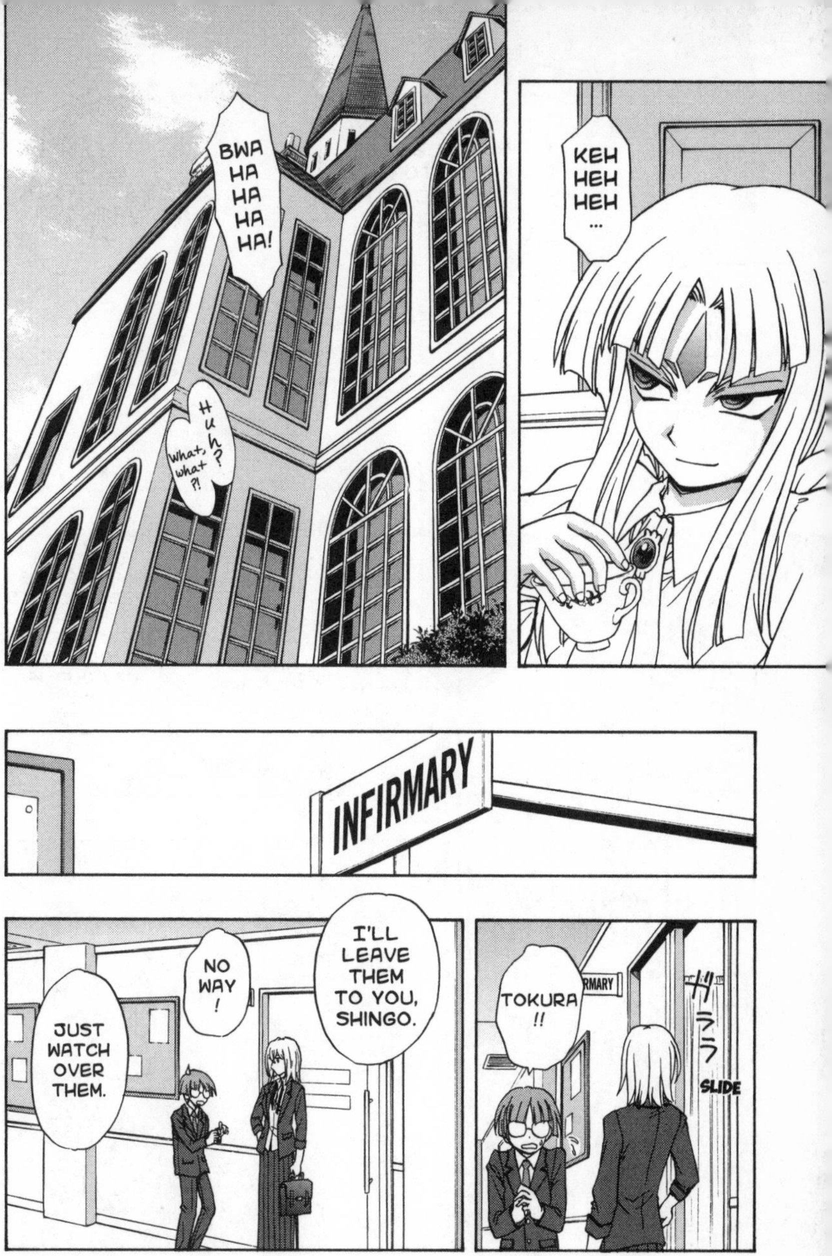
KEH HEH HEH ...
BWA HA HA HA HA!
Huh? what, what?!
INFIRMARY
SLIDE
TOKURA!!
I'LL LEAVE THEM TO YOU, SHINGO.
NO WAY!
JUST WATCH OVER THEM.

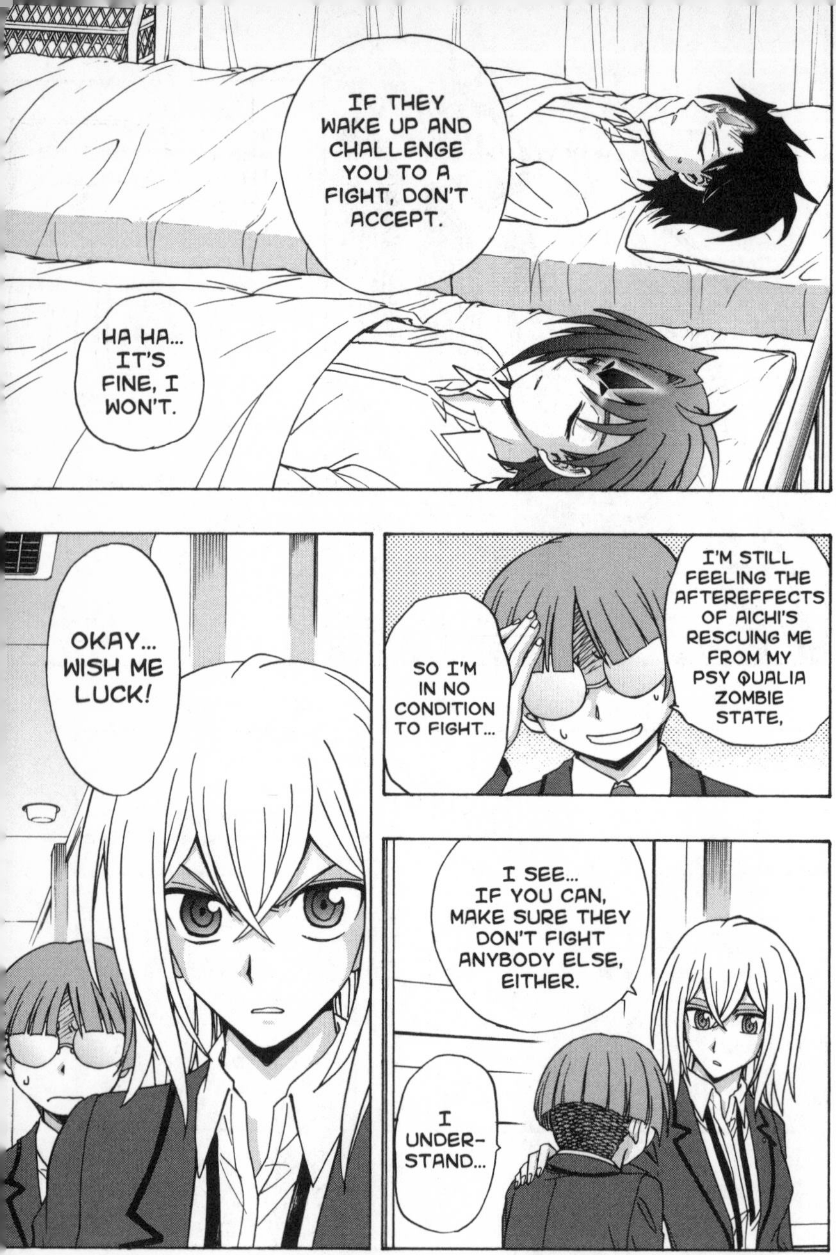
IF THEY WAKE UP AND CHALLENGE YOU TO A FIGHT, DON'T ACCEPT.
HA HA... IT'S FINE, I WON'T.
I'M STILL FEELING THE AFTEREFFECTS OF AICHI'S RESCUING ME FROM MY PSY QUALIA ZOMBIE STATE,
SO I'M IN NO CONDITION TO FIGHT...
I SEE... IF YOU CAN, MAKE SURE THEY DON'T FIGHT ANYBODY ELSE, EITHER.
I UNDERSTAND...
OKAY... WISH ME LUCK!

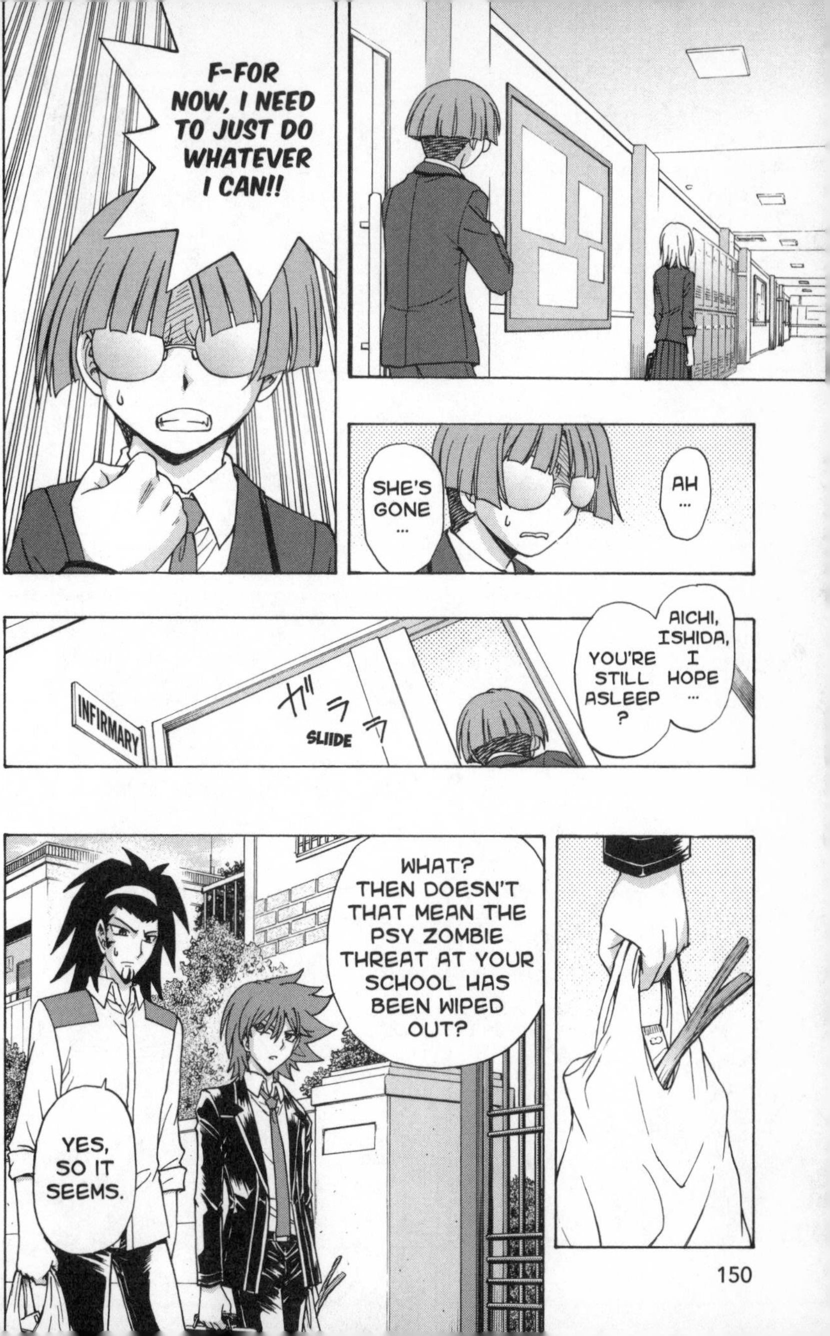
AH ...
SHE'S GONE ...
F-FOR NOW, I NEED TO JUST DO WHATEVER I CAN!!
AICHI, ISHIDA, I HOPE ...
YOU'RE STILL ASLEEP ?
INFIRMARY
SLIIDE
WHAT? THEN DOESN'T THAT MEAN THE PSY ZOMBIE THREAT AT YOUR SCHOOL HAS BEEN WIPED OUT?
YES, SO IT SEEMS.

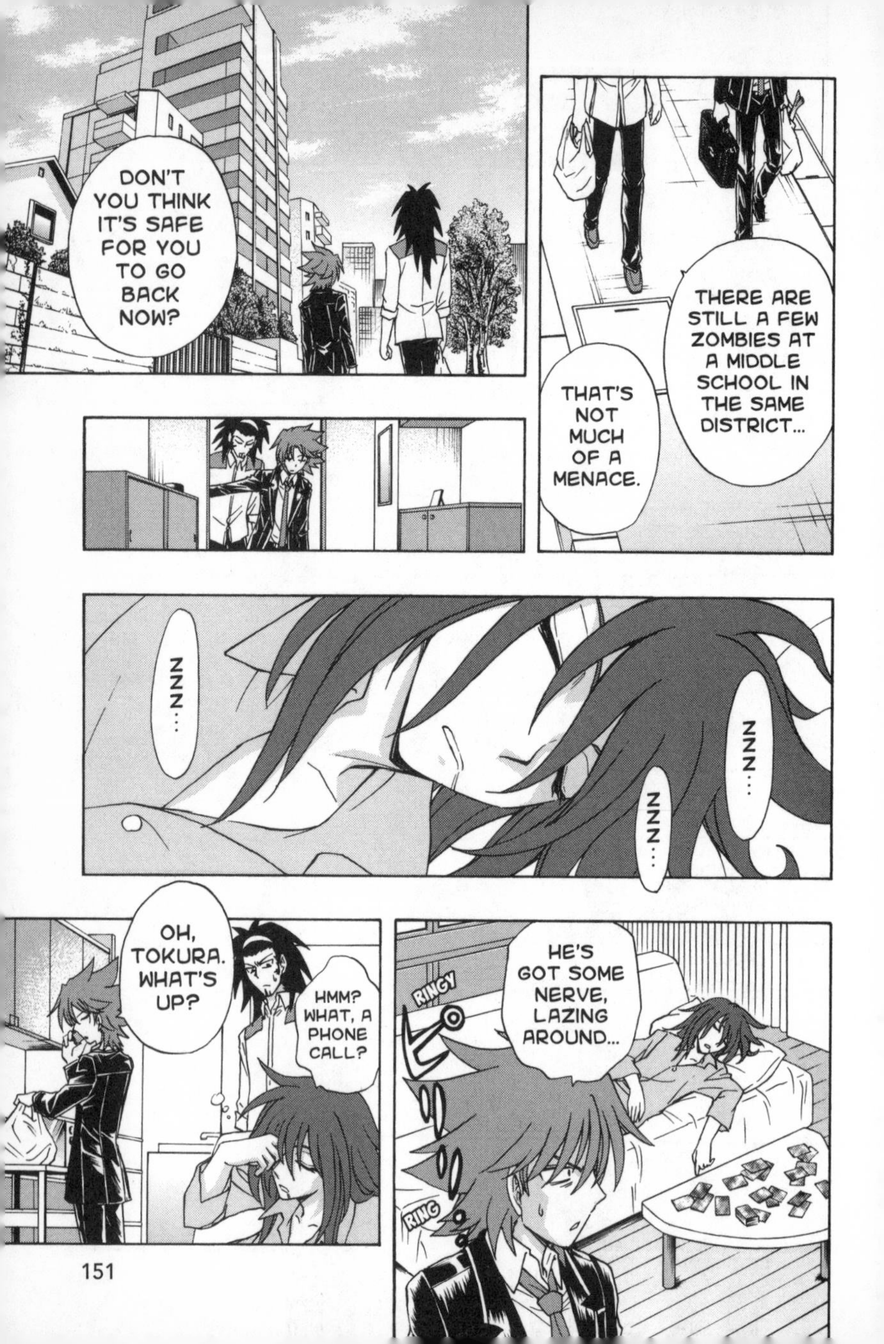

THERE ARE STILL A FEW ZOMBIES AT A MIDDLE SCHOOL IN THE SAME DISTRICT...
THAT'S NOT MUCH OF A MENACE.
DON'T YOU THINK IT'S SAFE FOR YOU TO GO BACK NOW?
ZZZ...
ZZZ...
ZZZ...
HE'S GOT SOME NERVE, LAZING AROUND...
RINGY
RING
HMM? WHAT, A PHONE CALL?
OH, TOKURA. WHAT'S UP?

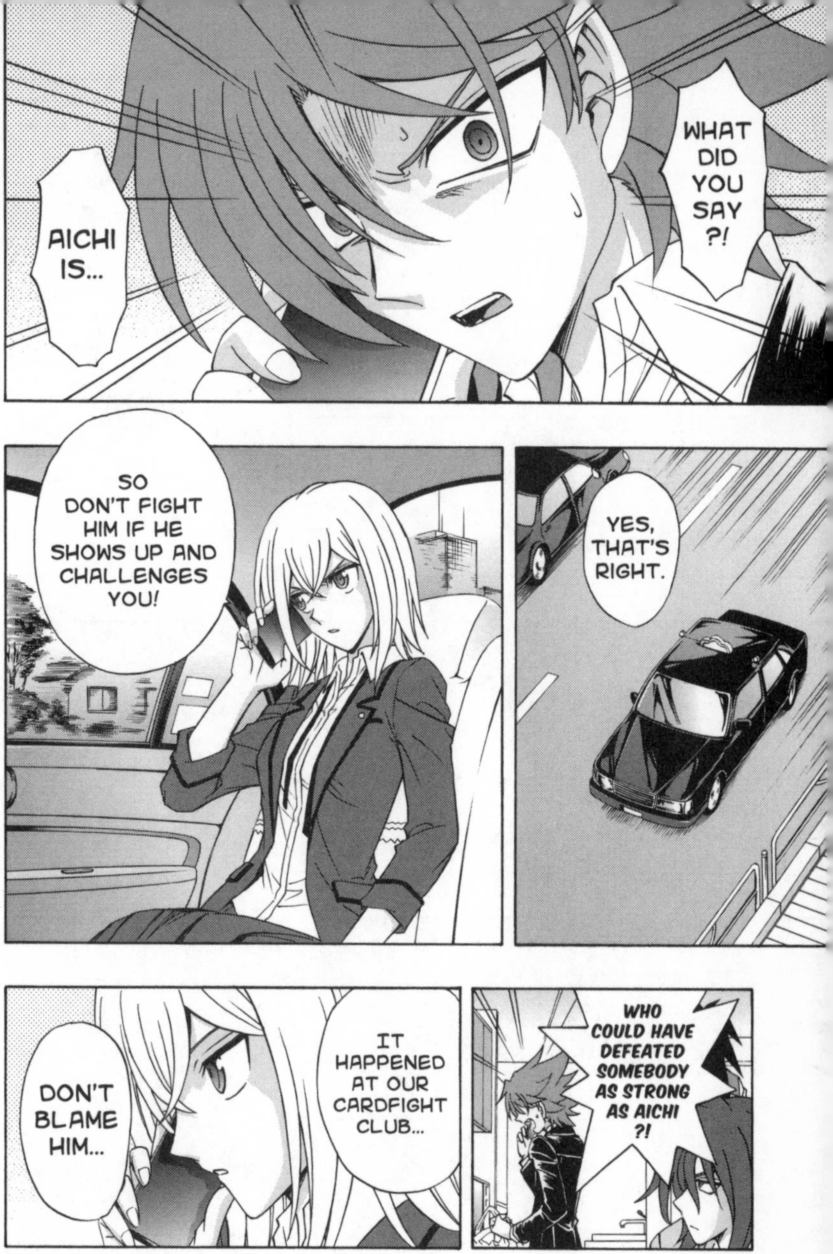
WHAT DID YOU SAY ?!
AICHI IS...
YES, THAT'S RIGHT.
SO DON'T FIGHT HIM IF HE SHOWS UP AND CHALLENGES YOU!
WHO COULD HAVE DEFEATED SOMEBODY AS STRONG AS AICHI ?!
IT HAPPENED AT OUR CARDFIGHT CLUB...
DON'T BLAME HIM...

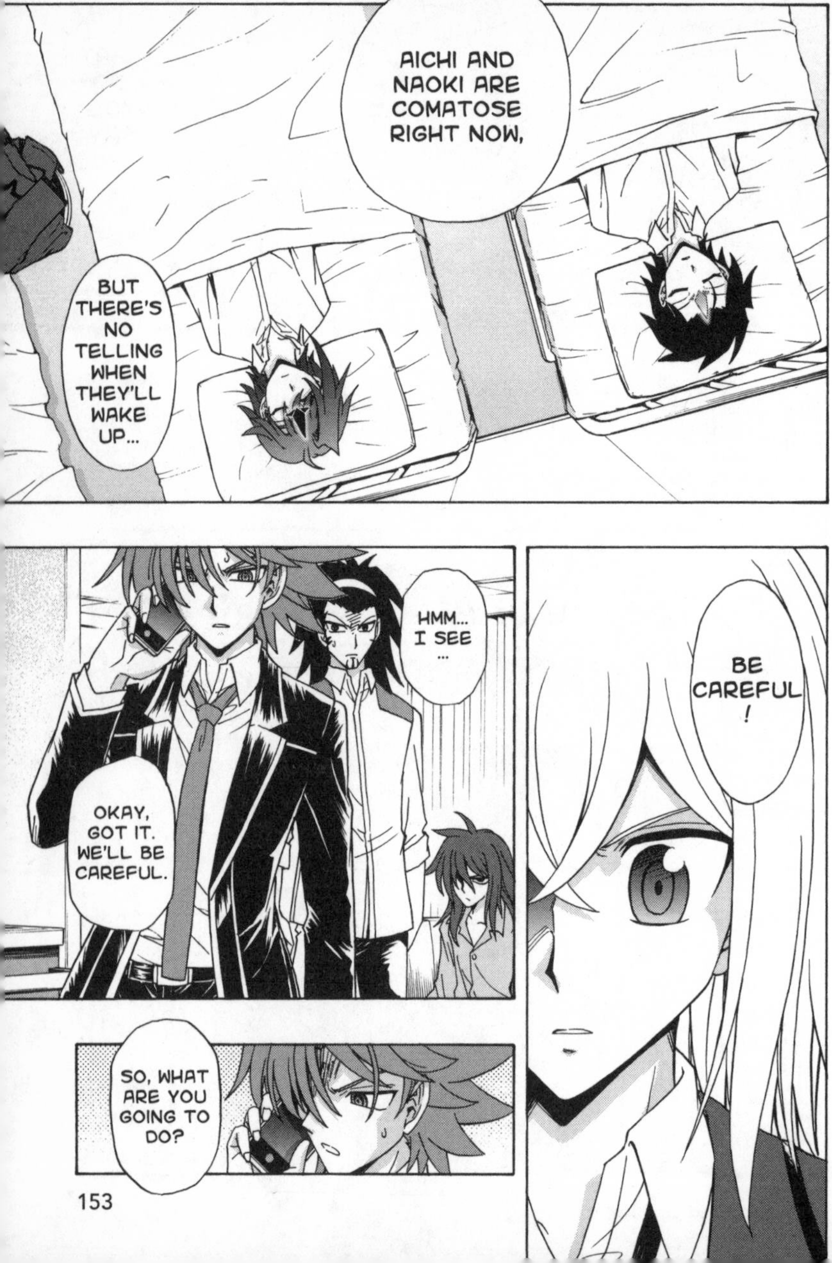
AICHI AND NAOKI ARE COMATOSE RIGHT NOW,
BUT THERE'S NO TELLING WHEN THEY'LL WAKE UP...
BE CAREFUL!
HMM... I SEE...
OKAY, GOT IT. WE'LL BE CAREFUL.
SO, WHAT ARE YOU GOING TO DO?

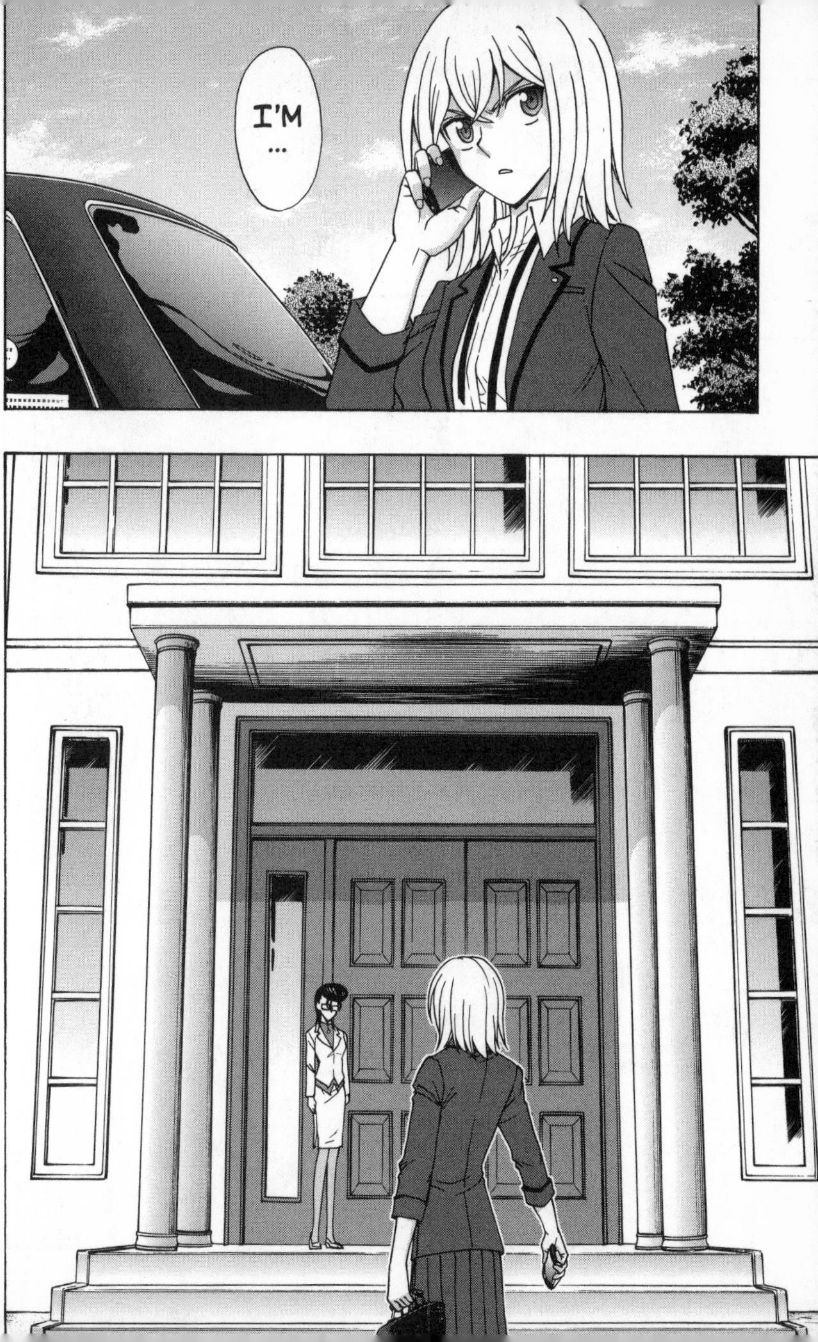
I'M ...

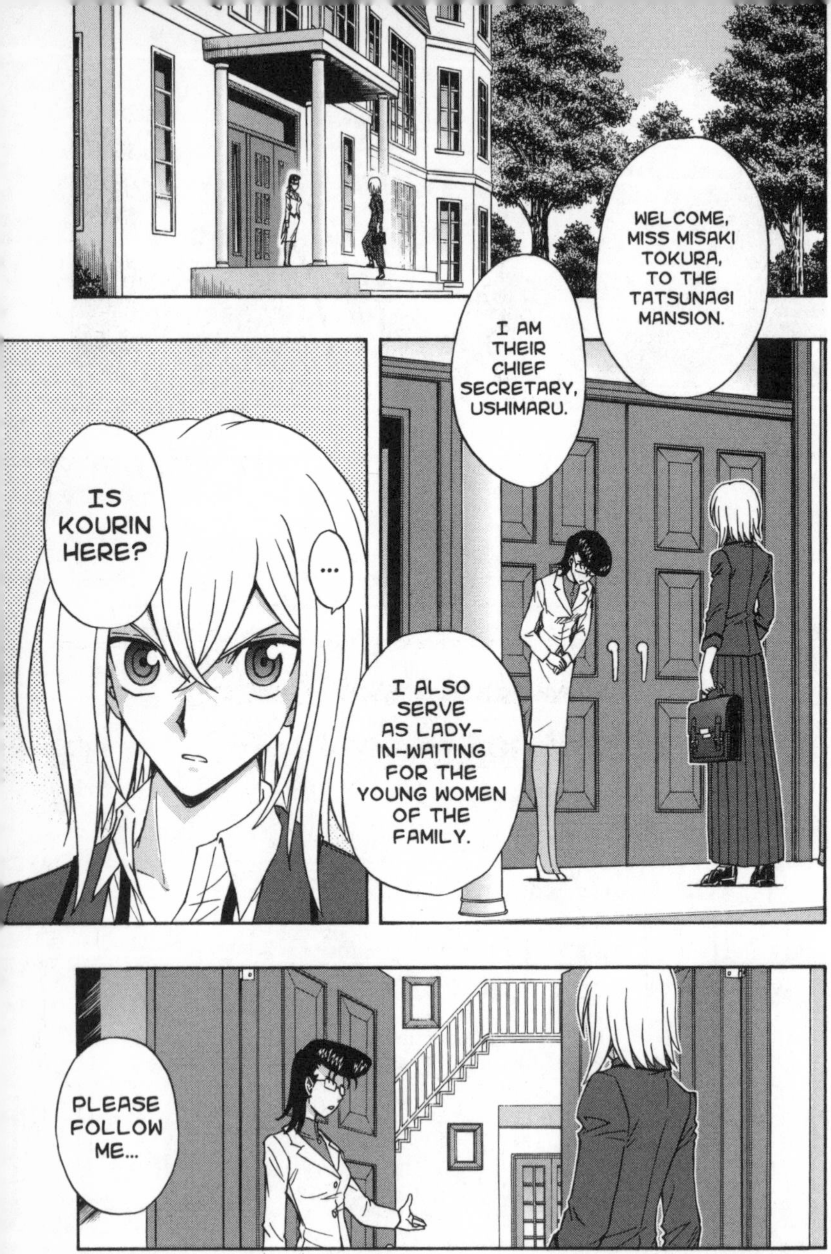
WELCOME, MISS MISAKI TOKURA, TO THE TATSUNAGI MANSION.
I AM THEIR CHIEF SECRETARY, USHIMARU.
I ALSO SERVE AS LADY-IN-WAITING FOR THE YOUNG WOMEN OF THE FAMILY.
...
IS KOURIN HERE?
PLEASE FOLLOW ME...

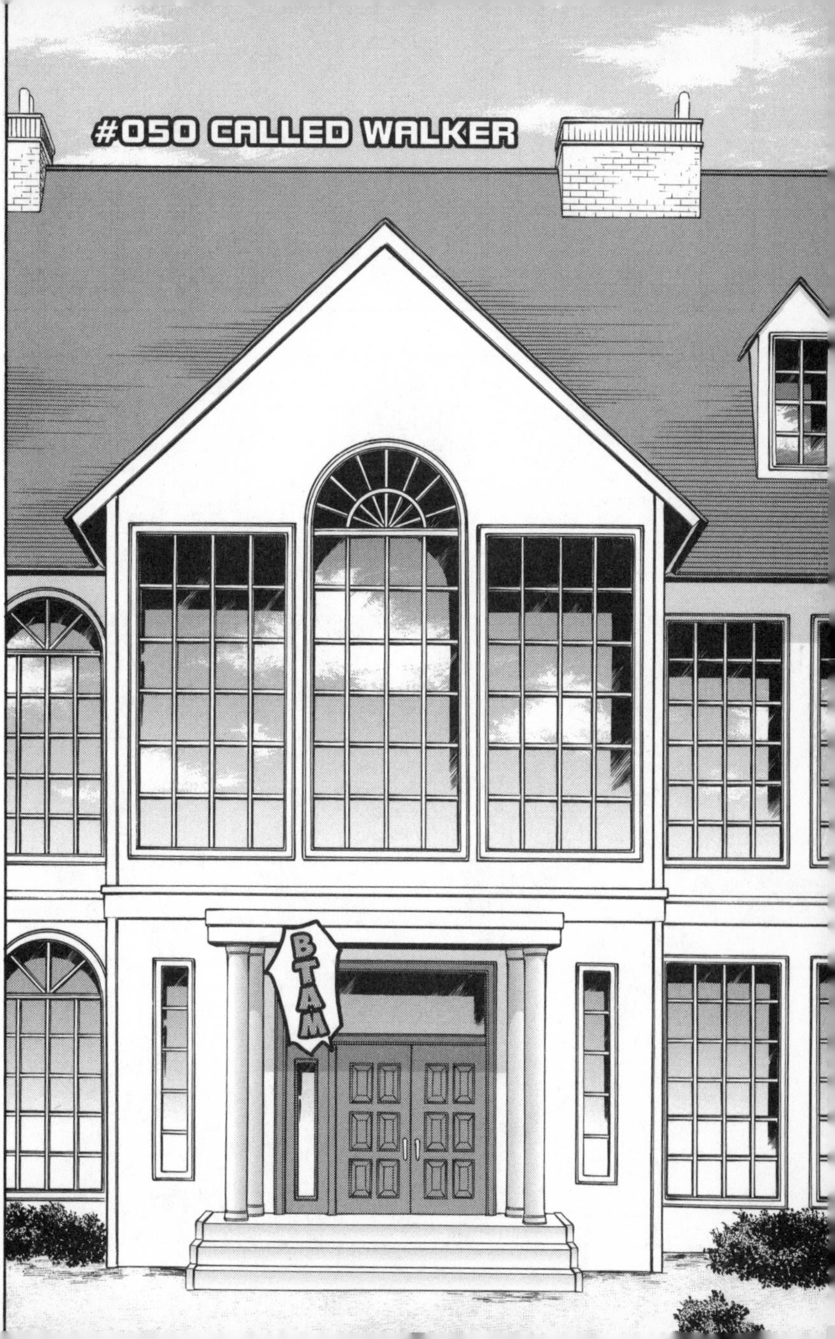
#050 CALLED WALKER
BTAM

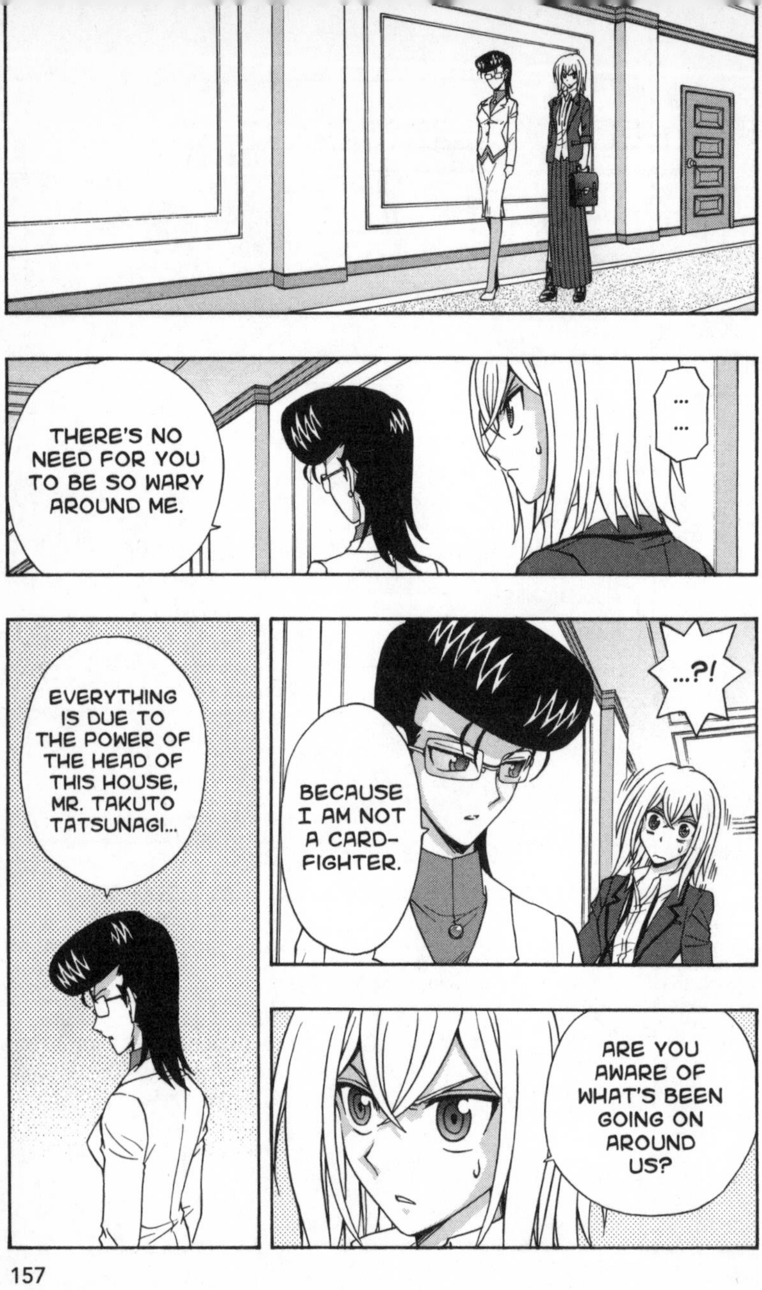
... ...
THERE'S NO NEED FOR YOU TO BE SO WARY AROUND ME.
...?!
BECAUSE I AM NOT A CARD-FIGHTER.
ARE YOU AWARE OF WHAT'S BEEN GOING ON AROUND US?
EVERYTHING IS DUE TO THE POWER OF THE HEAD OF THIS HOUSE, MR. TAKUTO TATSUNAGI...

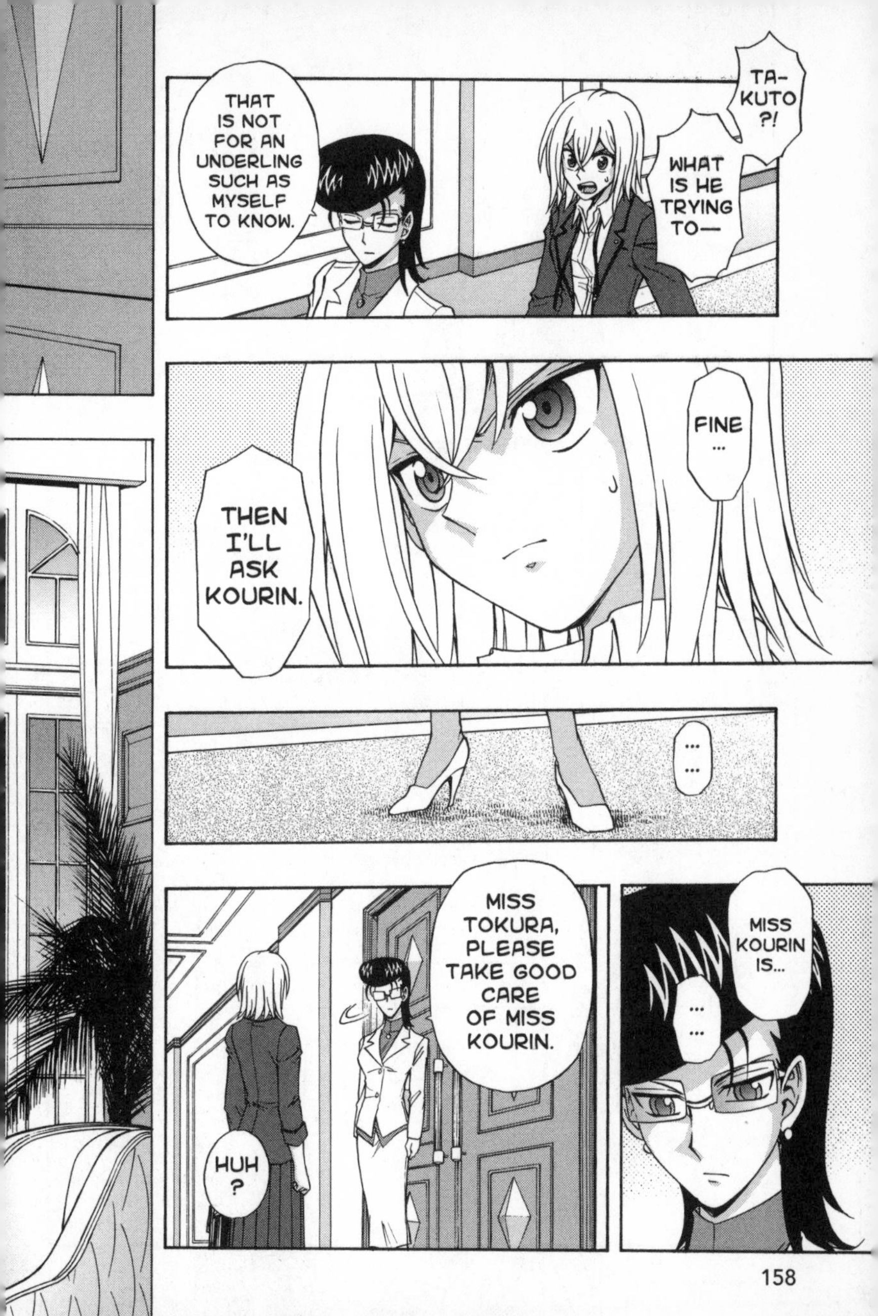
TA-KUTO?!
WHAT IS HE TRYING TO—
THAT IS NOT FOR AN UNDERLING SUCH AS MYSELF TO KNOW.
FINE...
THEN I'LL ASK KOURIN.
......
MISS KOURIN IS...
......
MISS TOKURA, PLEASE TAKE GOOD CARE OF MISS KOURIN.
HUH?

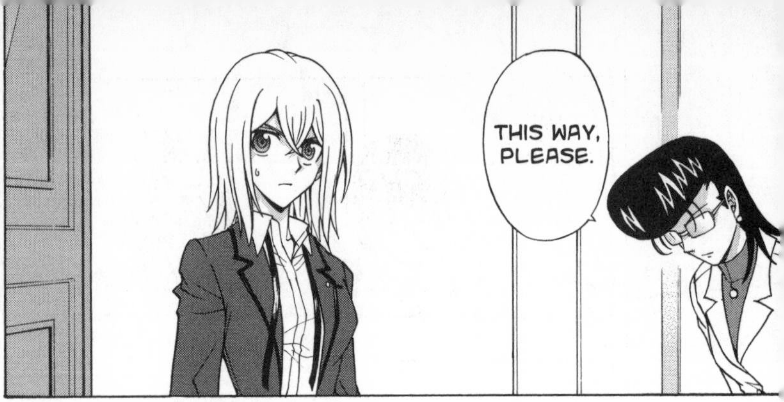
THIS WAY, PLEASE.
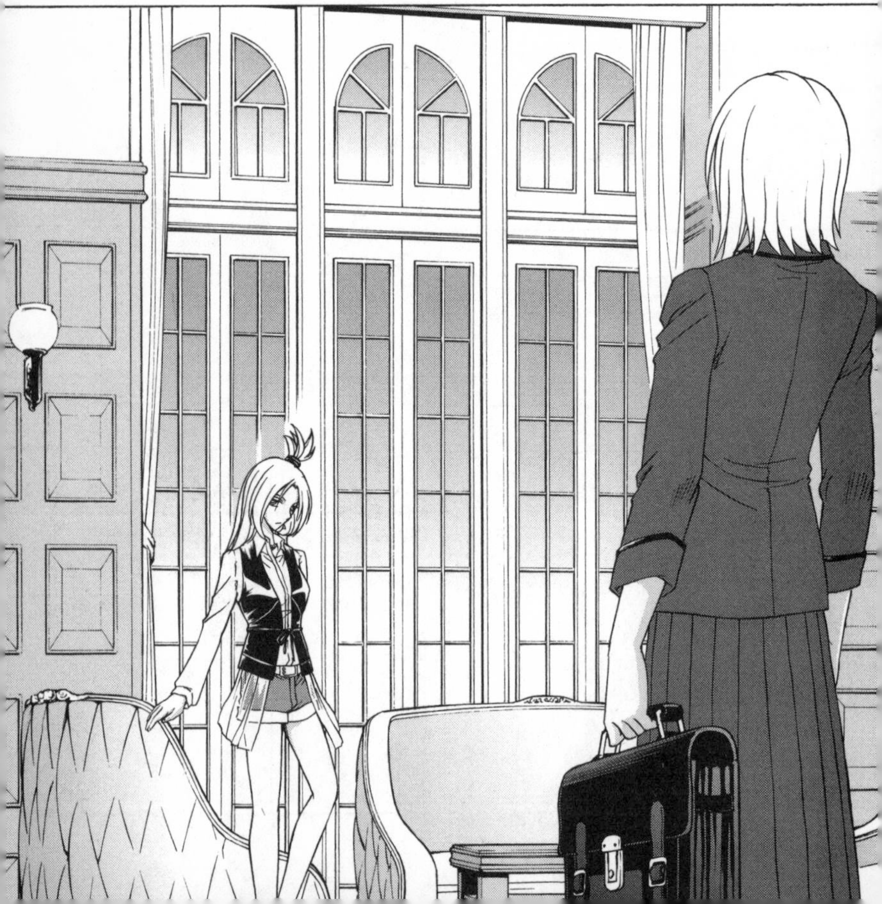

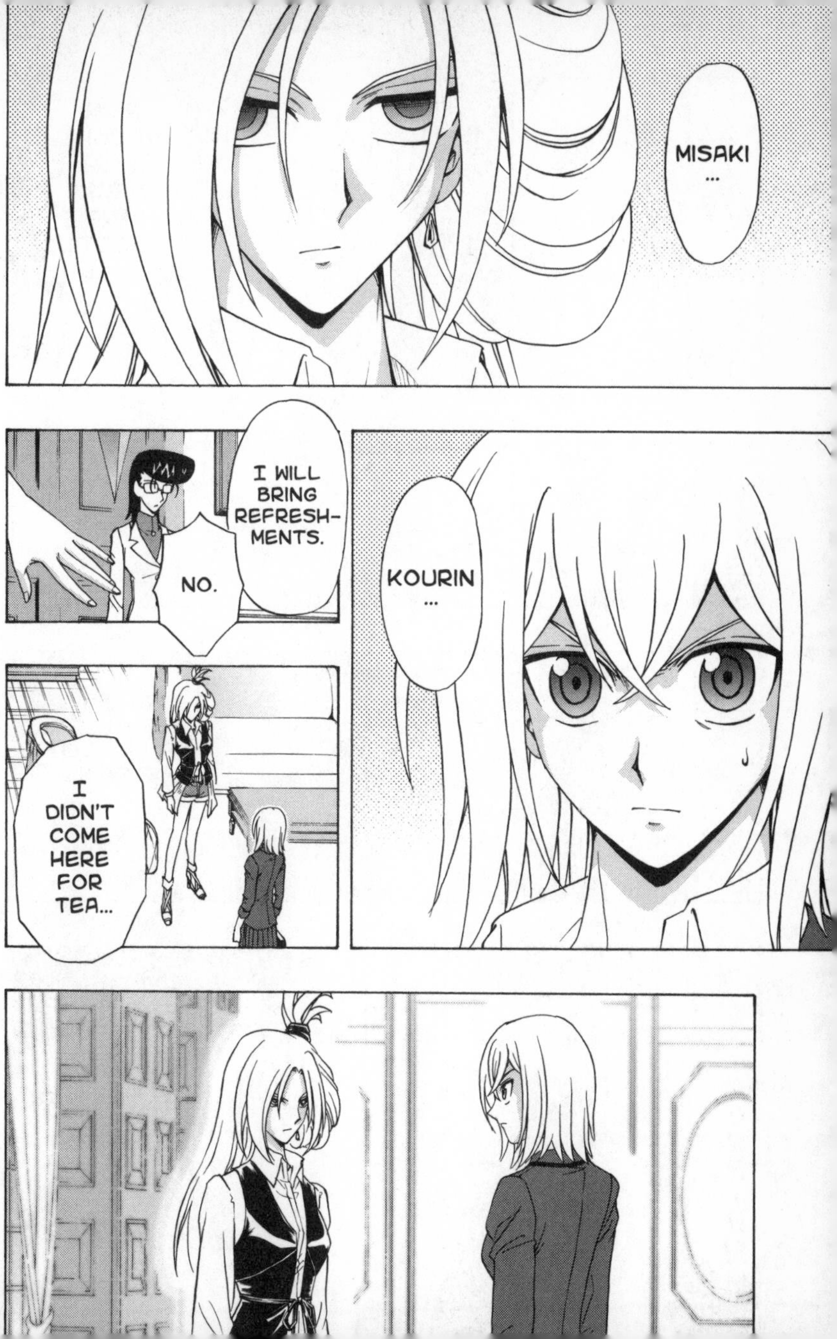
MISAKI ...
KOURIN ...
I WILL BRING REFRESH-MENTS.
NO.
I DIDN'T COME HERE FOR TEA...

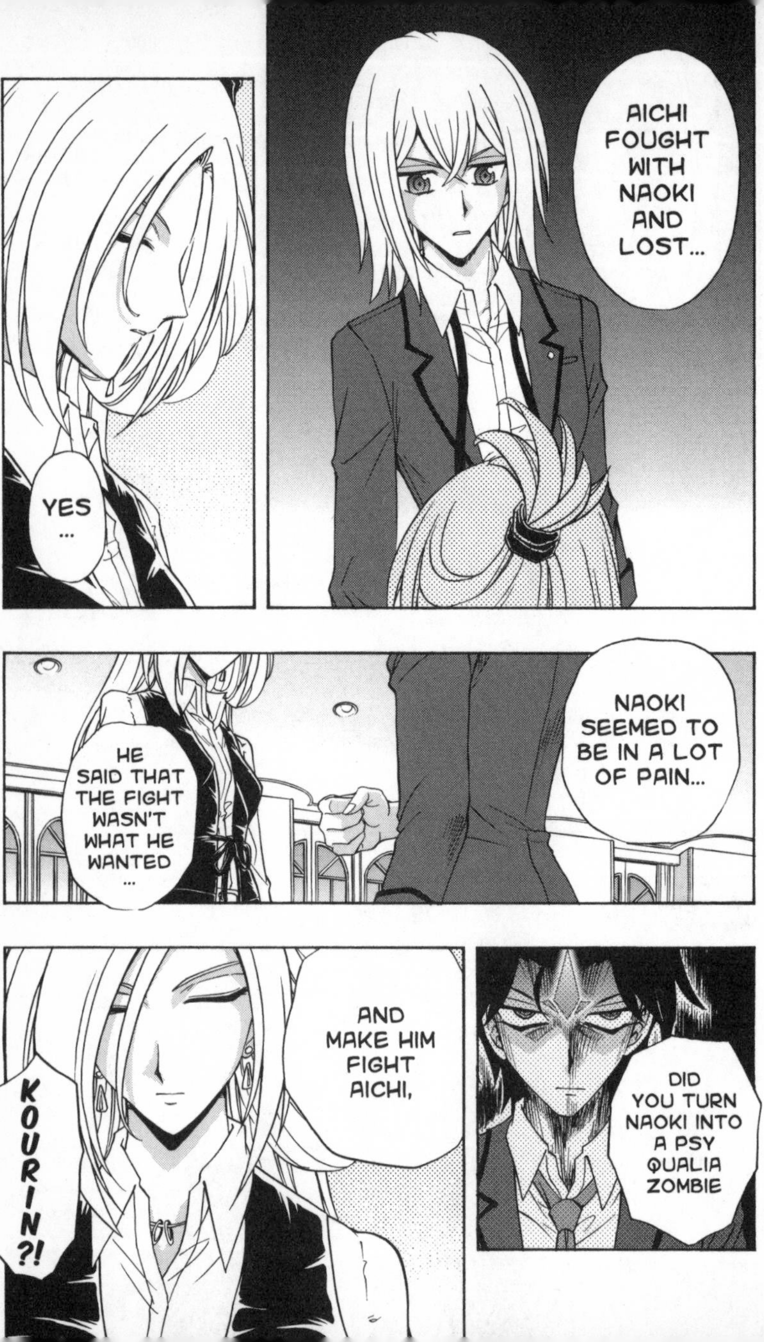
AICHI FOUGHT WITH NAOKI AND LOST...
YES ...
NAOKI SEEMED TO BE IN A LOT OF PAIN...
HE SAID THAT THE FIGHT WASN'T WHAT HE WANTED ...
DID YOU TURN NAOKI INTO A PSY QUALIA ZOMBIE
AND MAKE HIM FIGHT AICHI,
KOURIN?!

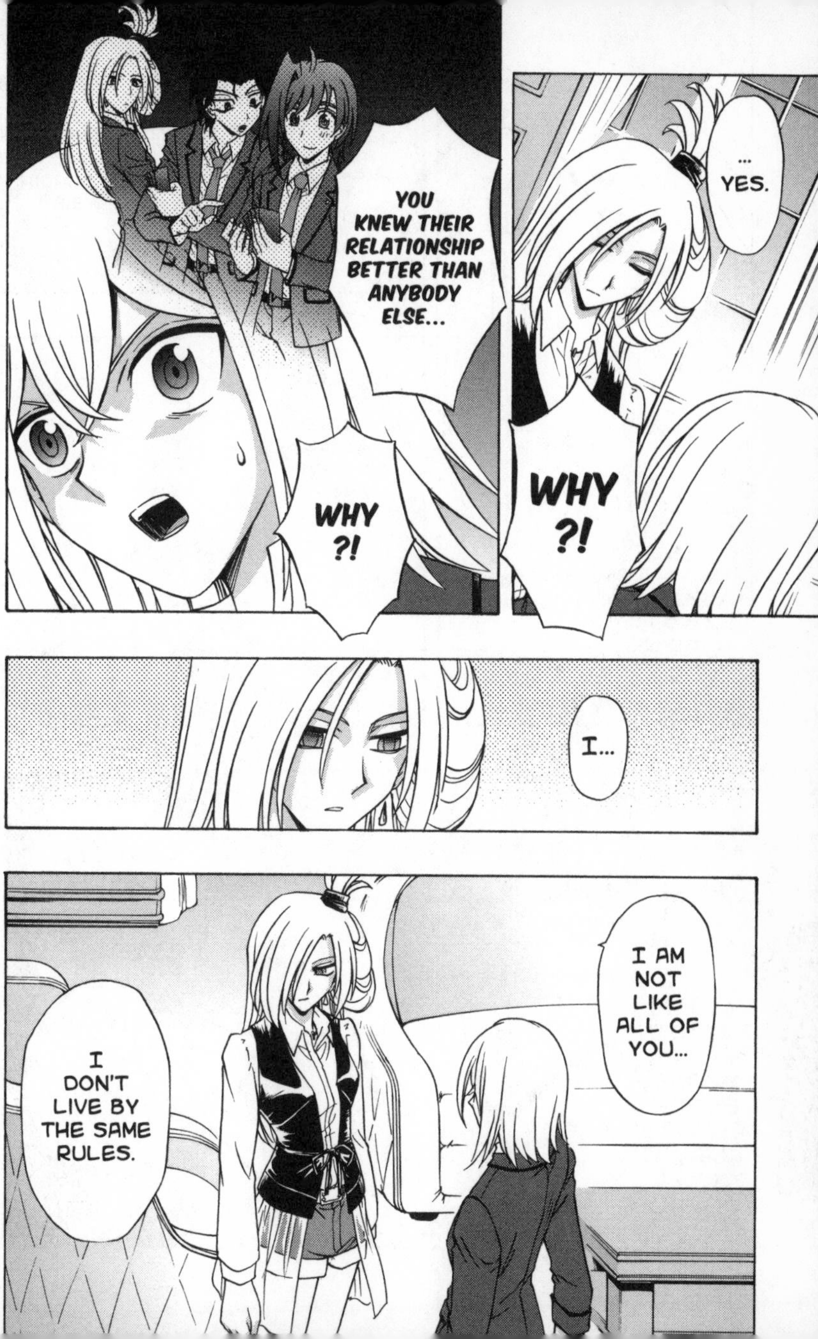
... YES.
WHY ?!
YOU KNEW THEIR RELATIONSHIP BETTER THAN ANYBODY ELSE...
WHY ?!
I...
I AM NOT LIKE ALL OF YOU...
I DON'T LIVE BY THE SAME RULES.

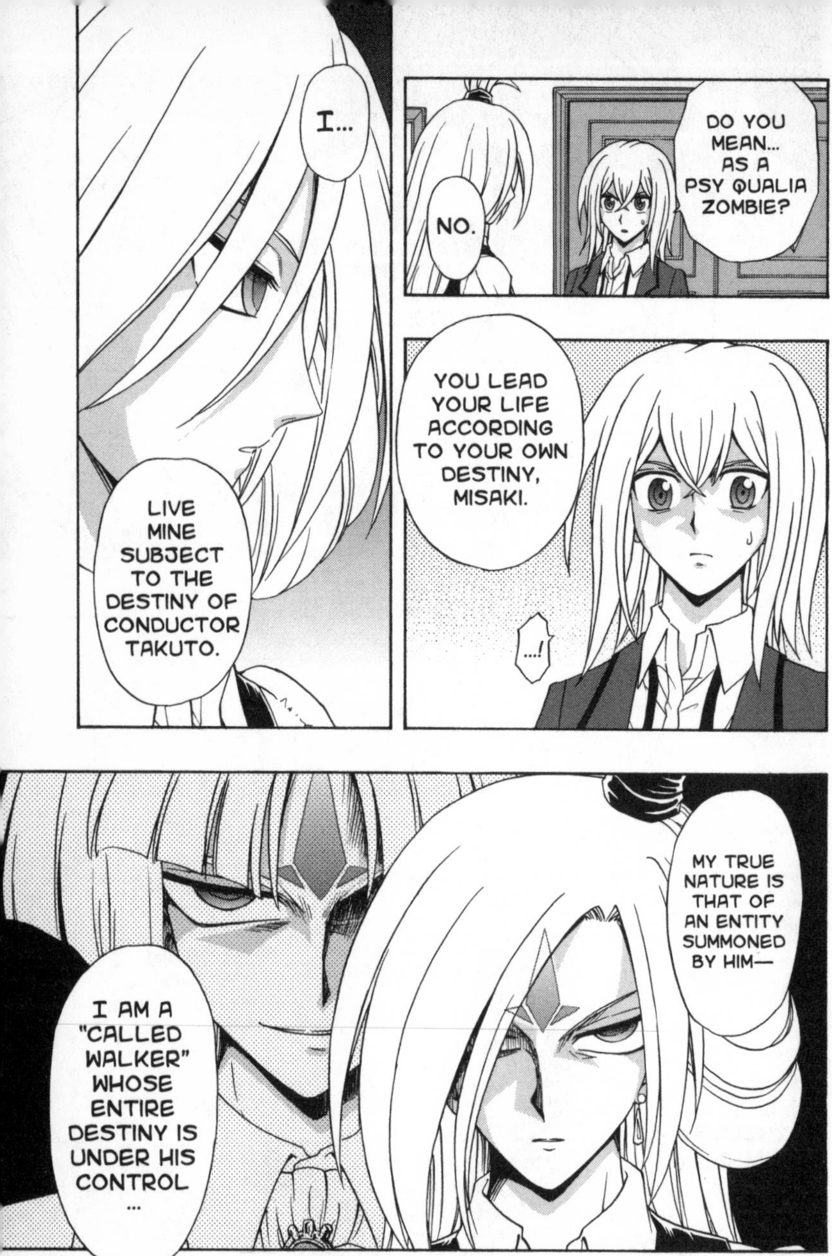
DO YOU MEAN... AS A PSY QUALIA ZOMBIE?
NO.
YOU LEAD YOUR LIFE ACCORDING TO YOUR OWN DESTINY, MISAKI.
...!
I...
LIVE MINE SUBJECT TO THE DESTINY OF CONDUCTOR TAKUTO.
MY TRUE NATURE IS THAT OF AN ENTITY SUMMONED BY HIM—
I AM A "CALLED WALKER" WHOSE ENTIRE DESTINY IS UNDER HIS CONTROL ...

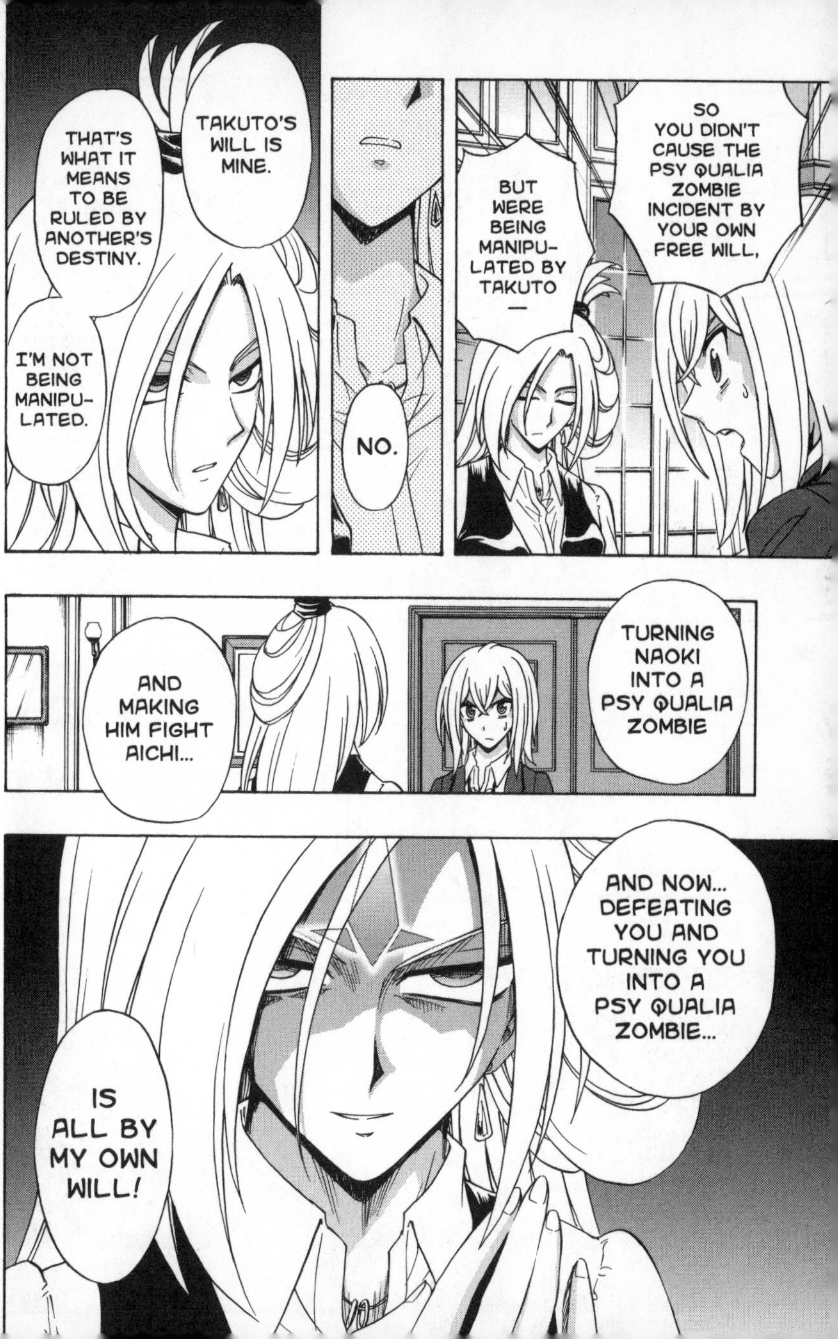

SO YOU DIDN'T CAUSE THE PSY QUALIA ZOMBIE INCIDENT BY YOUR OWN FREE WILL,
BUT WERE BEING MANIPU-LATED BY TAKUTO —
NO.
TAKUTO'S WILL IS MINE.
THAT'S WHAT IT MEANS TO BE RULED BY ANOTHER'S DESTINY.
I'M NOT BEING MANIPU-LATED.
TURNING NAOKI INTO A PSY QUALIA ZOMBIE
AND MAKING HIM FIGHT AICHI...
AND NOW... DEFEATING YOU AND TURNING YOU INTO A PSY QUALIA ZOMBIE...
IS ALL BY MY OWN WILL!

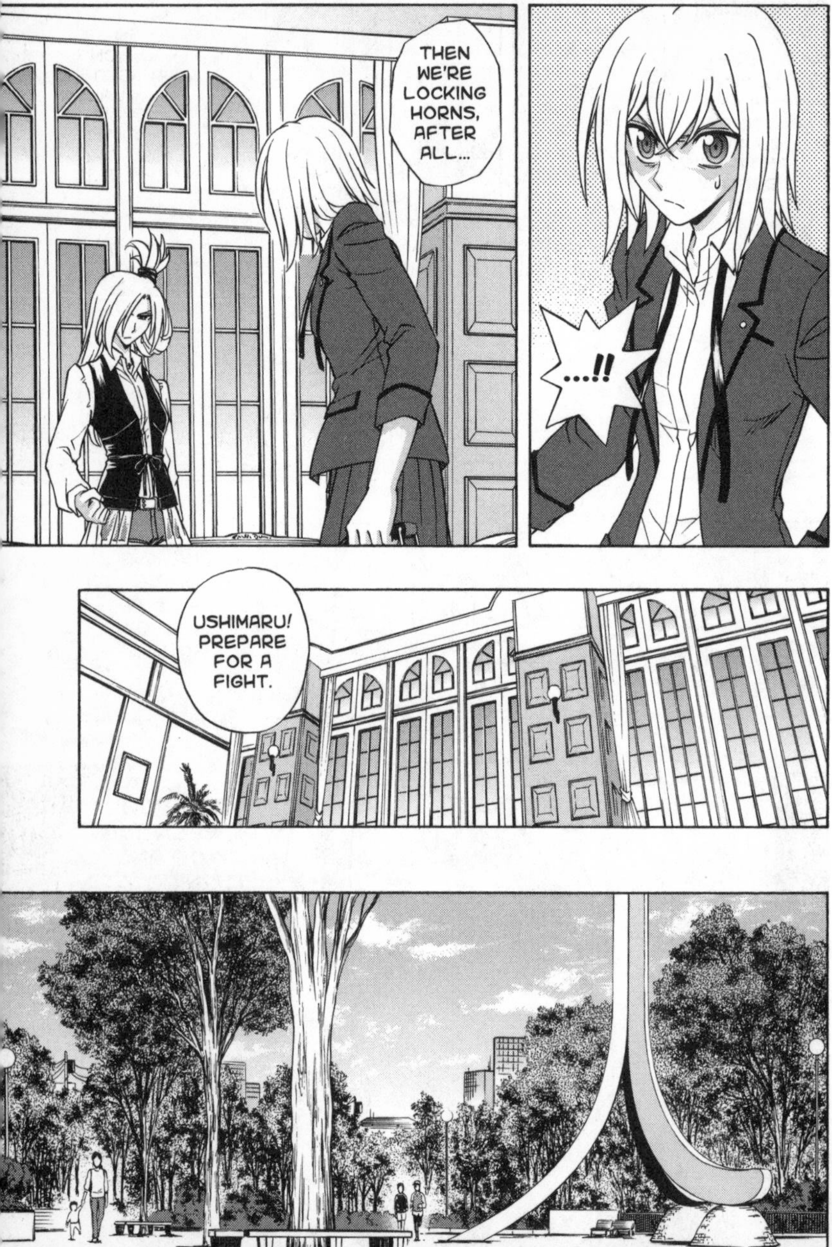
...!!
THEN WE'RE LOCKING HORNS, AFTER ALL...
USHIMARU! PREPARE FOR A FIGHT.

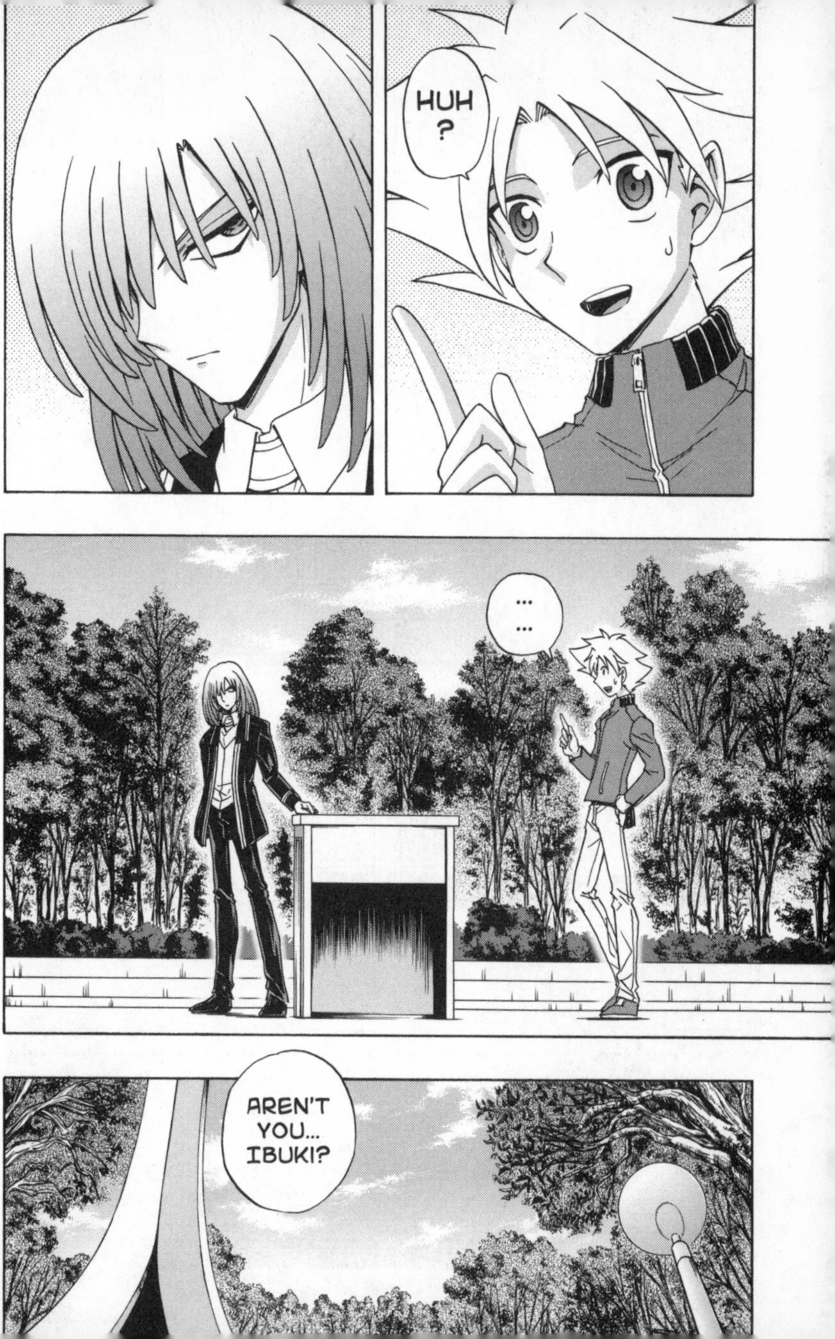
HUH?
……
AREN'T YOU... IBUKI?

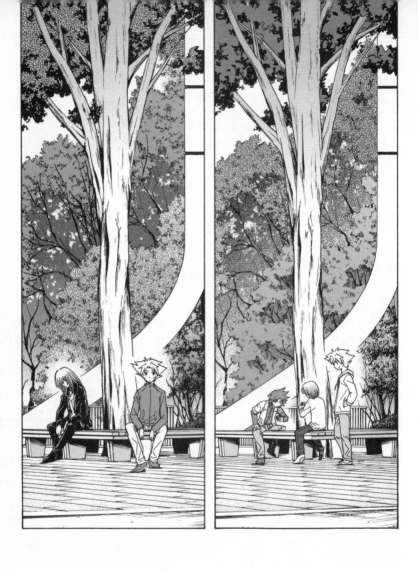

#051 MISAKI'S WISH

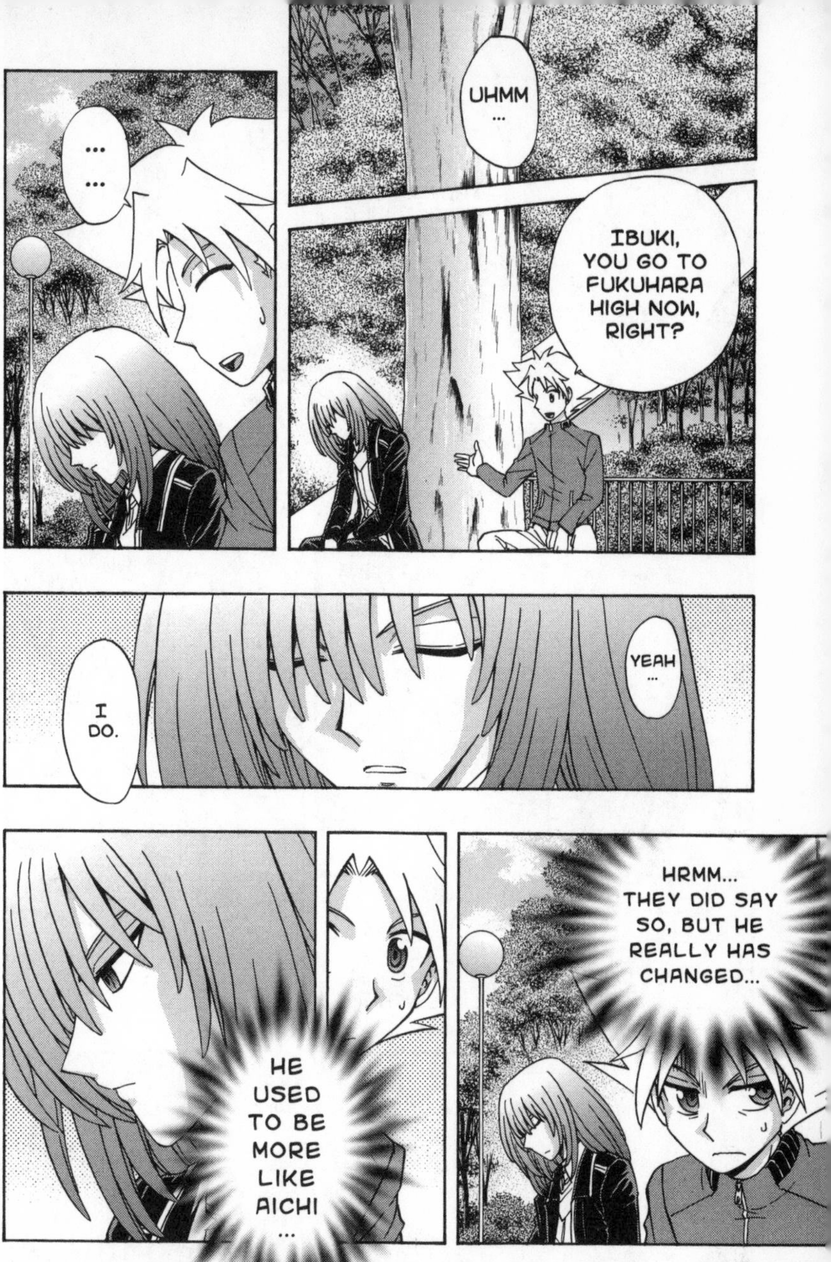
UHMM ...
IBUKI, YOU GO TO FUKUHARA HIGH NOW, RIGHT?
... ...
YEAH ...
I DO.
HRMM... THEY DID SAY SO, BUT HE REALLY HAS CHANGED...
HE USED TO BE MORE LIKE AICHI ...

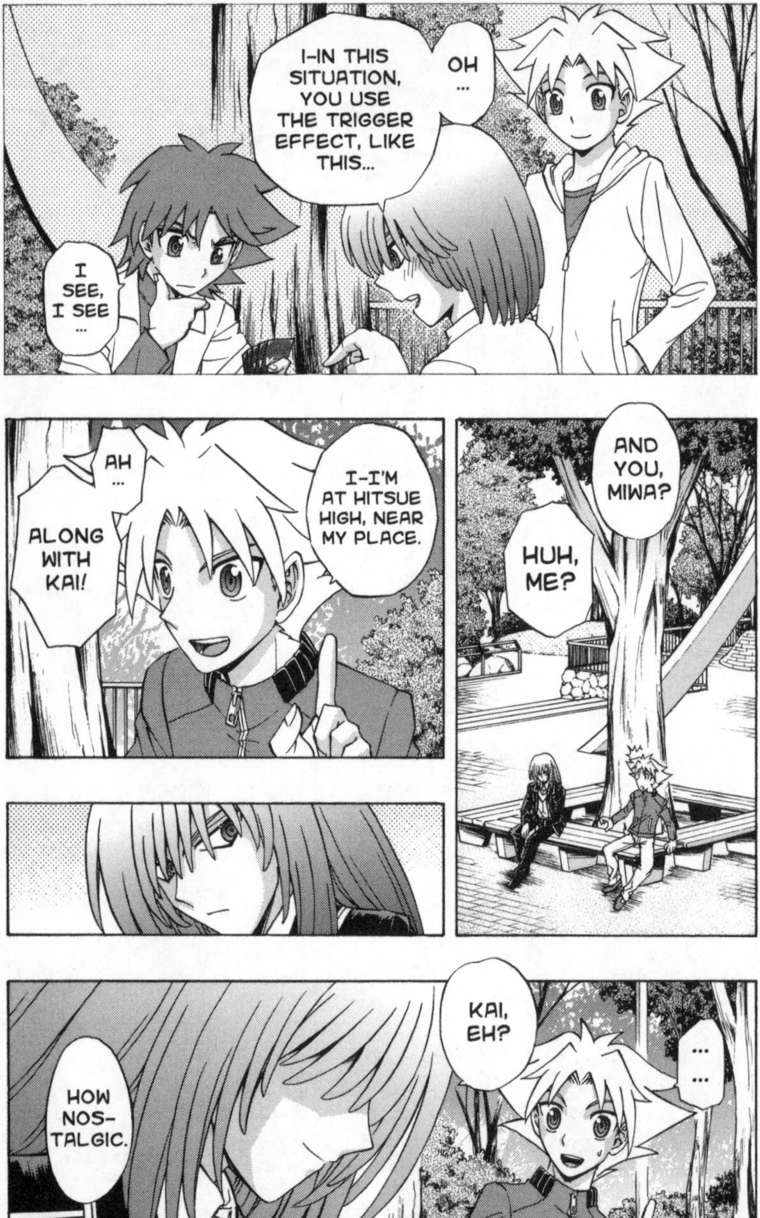
OH ...
I-IN THIS SITUATION, YOU USE THE TRIGGER EFFECT, LIKE THIS...
I SEE, I SEE ...
AND YOU, MIWA?
HUH, ME?
I-I'M AT HITSUE HIGH, NEAR MY PLACE.
AH ...
ALONG WITH KAI!
... ...
KAI, EH?
HOW NOS-TALGIC.

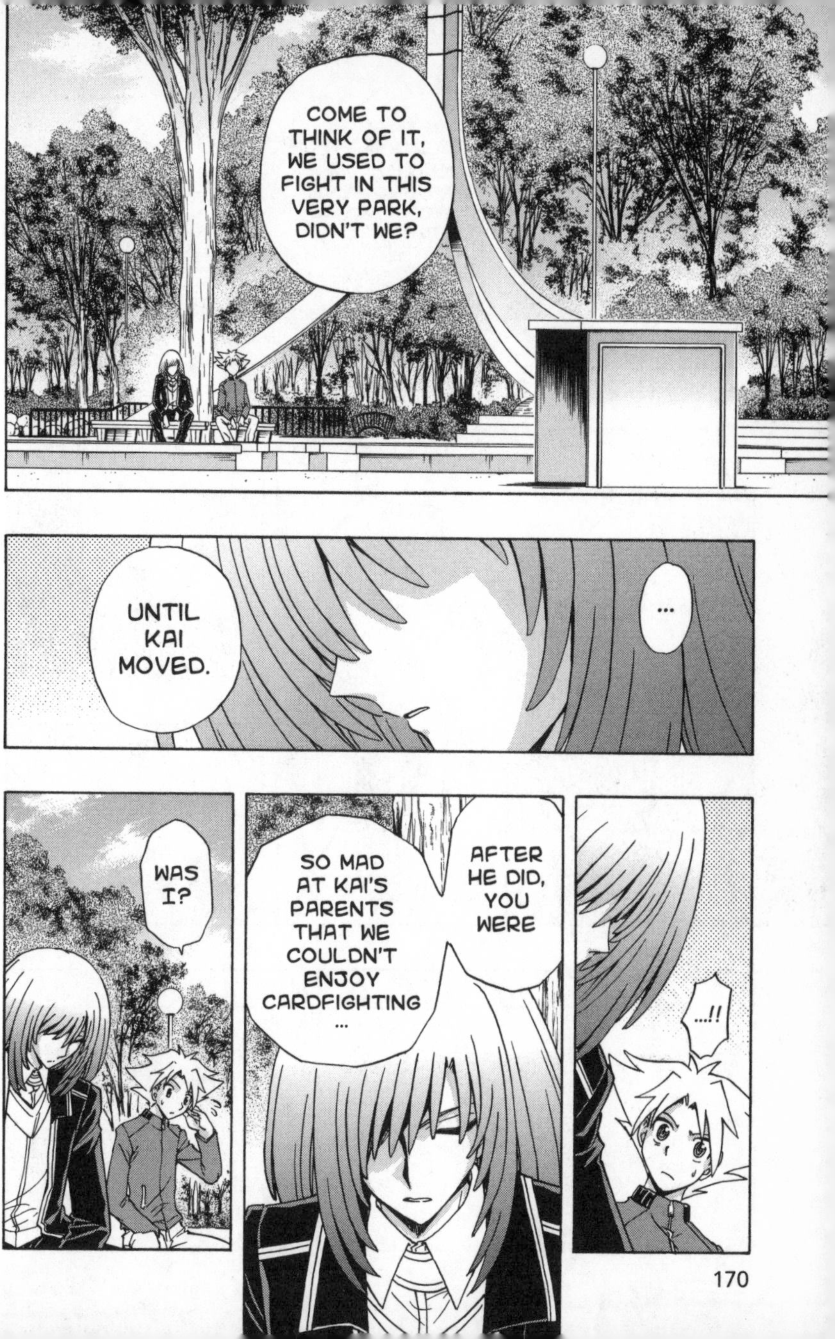
COME TO THINK OF IT, WE USED TO FIGHT IN THIS VERY PARK, DIDN'T WE?
...
UNTIL KAI MOVED.
...!!
AFTER HE DID, YOU WERE
SO MAD AT KAI'S PARENTS THAT WE COULDN'T ENJOY CARDFIGHTING ...
WAS I?

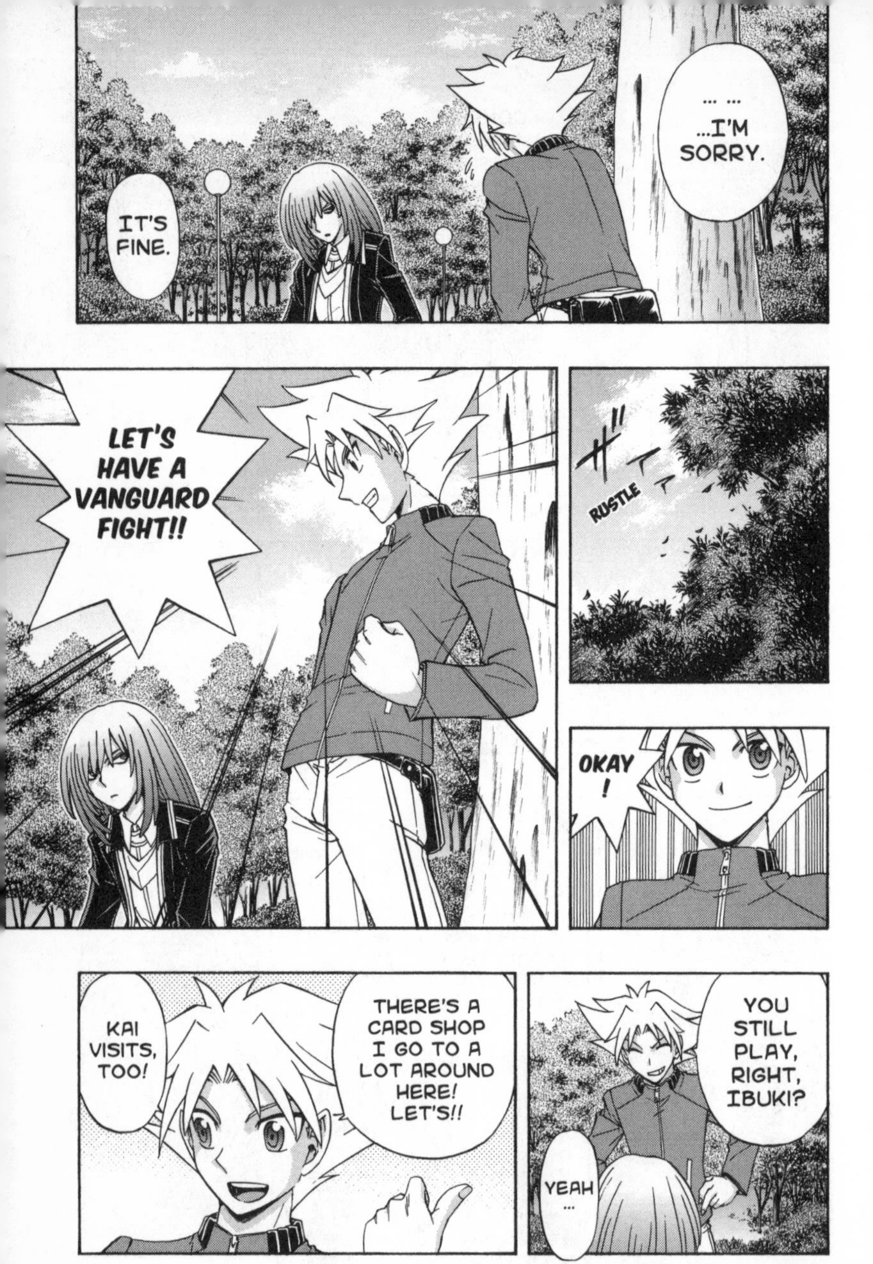
... ...
...I'M SORRY.
IT'S FINE.
RUSTLE
OKAY!
LET'S HAVE A VANGUARD FIGHT!!
YOU STILL PLAY, RIGHT, IBUKI?
YEAH...
THERE'S A CARD SHOP I GO TO A LOT AROUND HERE! LET'S!!
KAI VISITS, TOO!

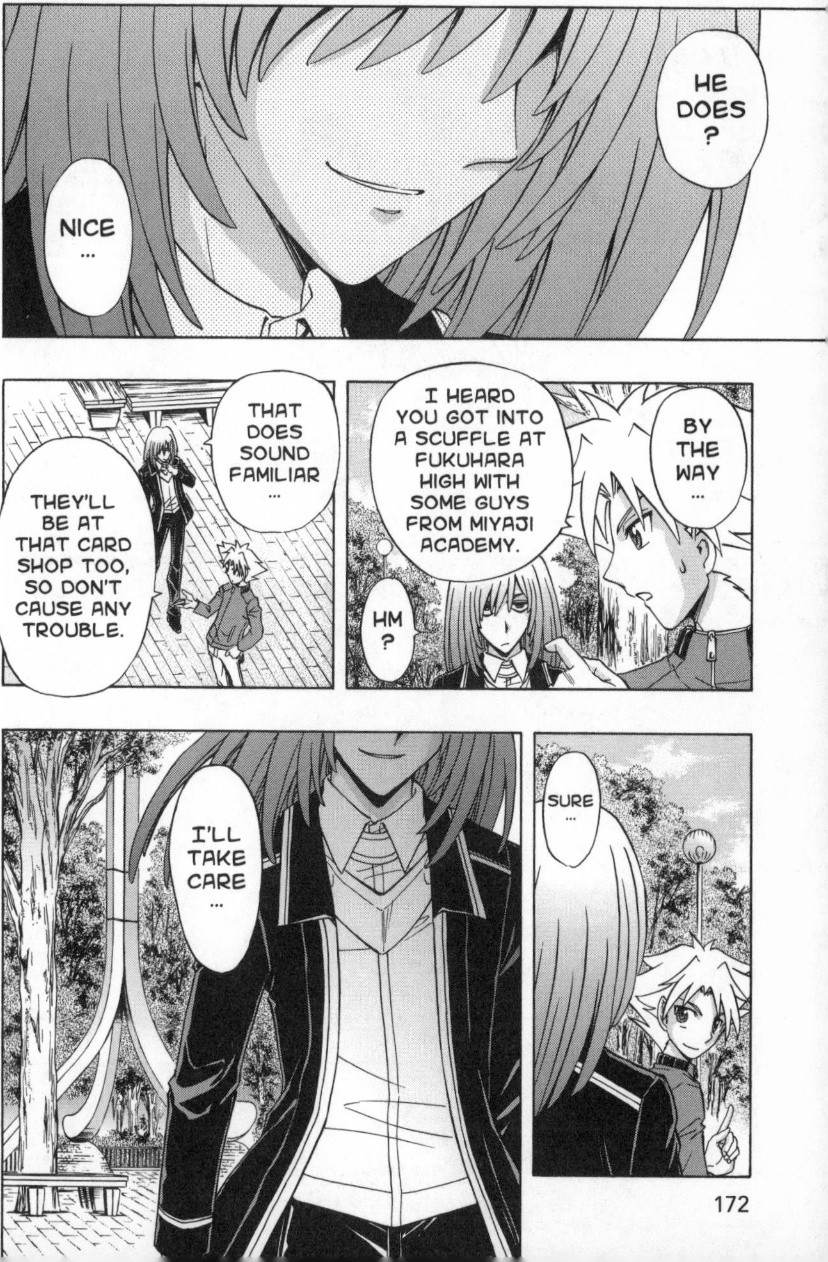
HE DOES ?
NICE ...
BY THE WAY ...
I HEARD YOU GOT INTO A SCUFFLE AT FUKUHARA HIGH WITH SOME GUYS FROM MIYAJI ACADEMY.
HM ?
THAT DOES SOUND FAMILIAR ...
THEY'LL BE AT THAT CARD SHOP TOO, SO DON'T CAUSE ANY TROUBLE.
SURE ...
I'LL TAKE CARE ...

...
...

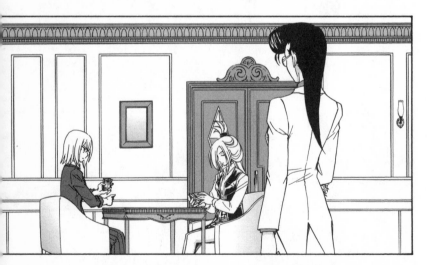

PAT

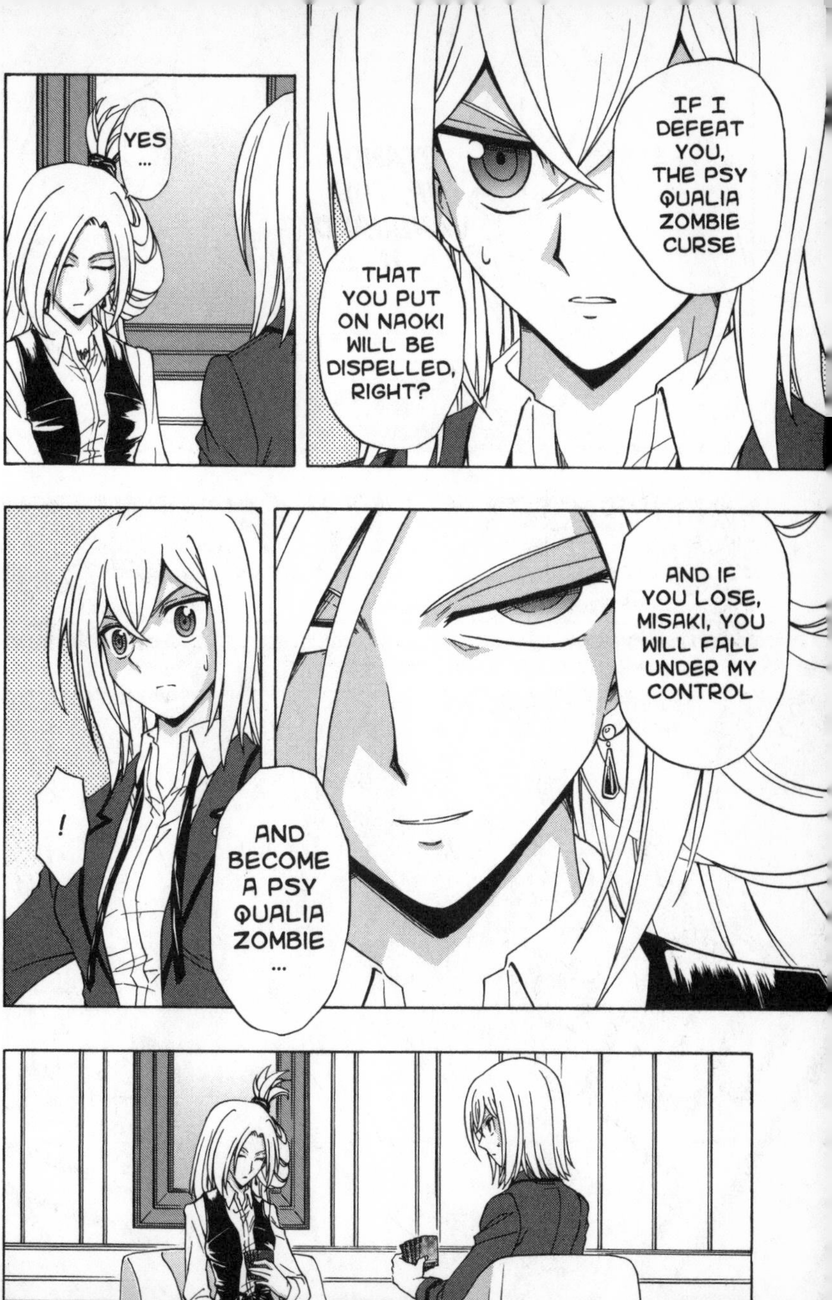
IF I DEFEAT YOU, THE PSY QUALIA ZOMBIE CURSE
THAT YOU PUT ON NAOKI WILL BE DISPELLED, RIGHT?
YES ...
AND IF YOU LOSE, MISAKI, YOU WILL FALL UNDER MY CONTROL
AND BECOME A PSY QUALIA ZOMBIE ...
!

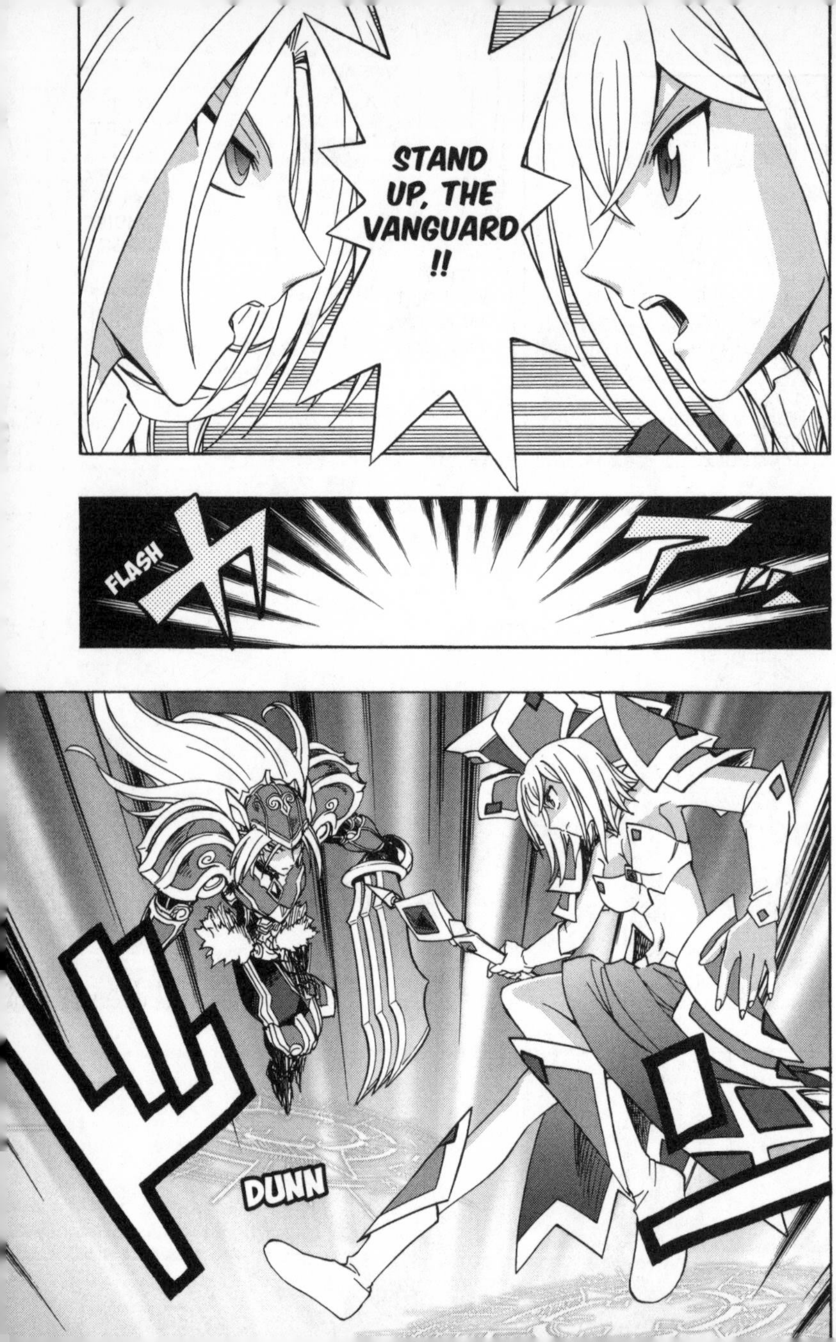
STAND UP, THE VANGUARD !!
FLASH
DUNN

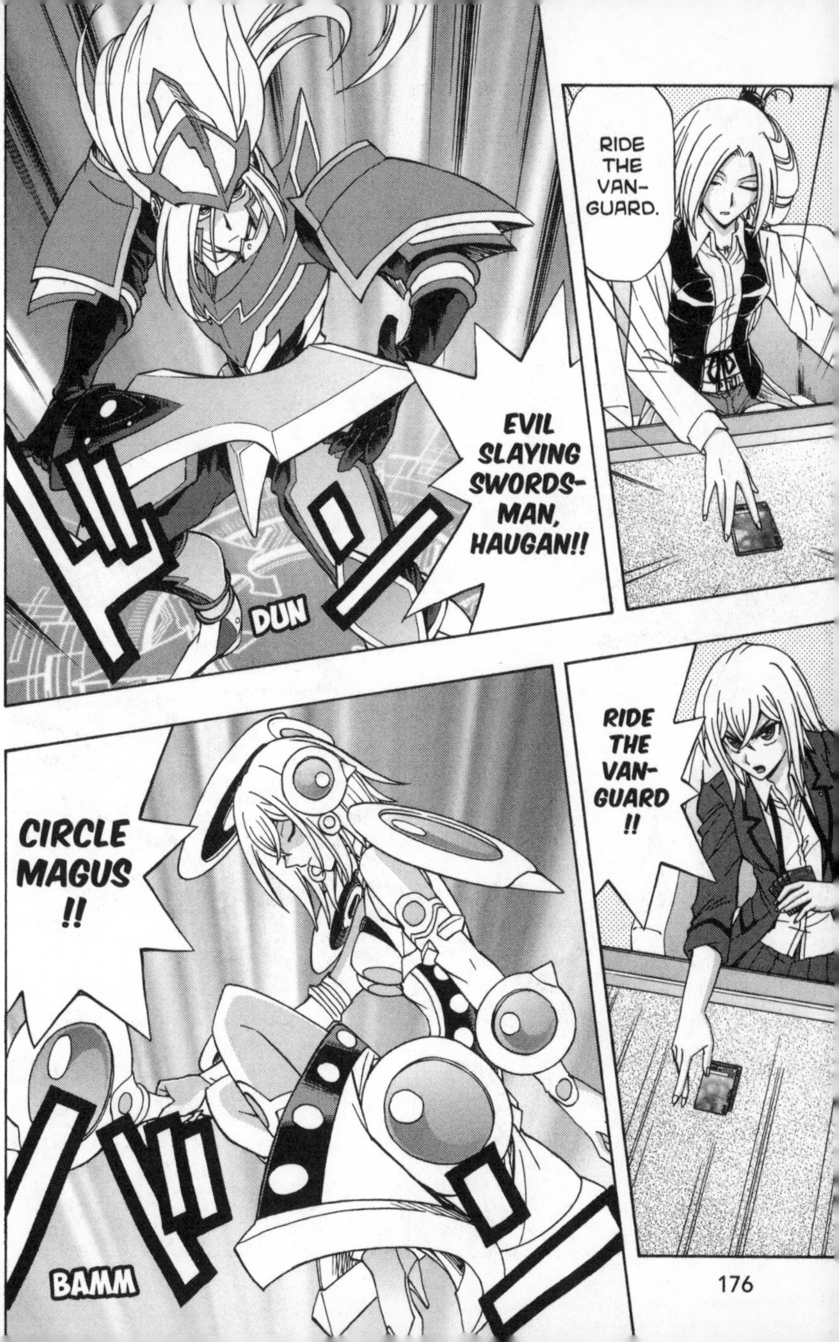
RIDE THE VAN-GUARD.
EVIL SLAYING SWORDS-MAN, HAUGAN!!
DUN
RIDE THE VAN-GUARD!!
CIRCLE MAGUS!!
BAMM

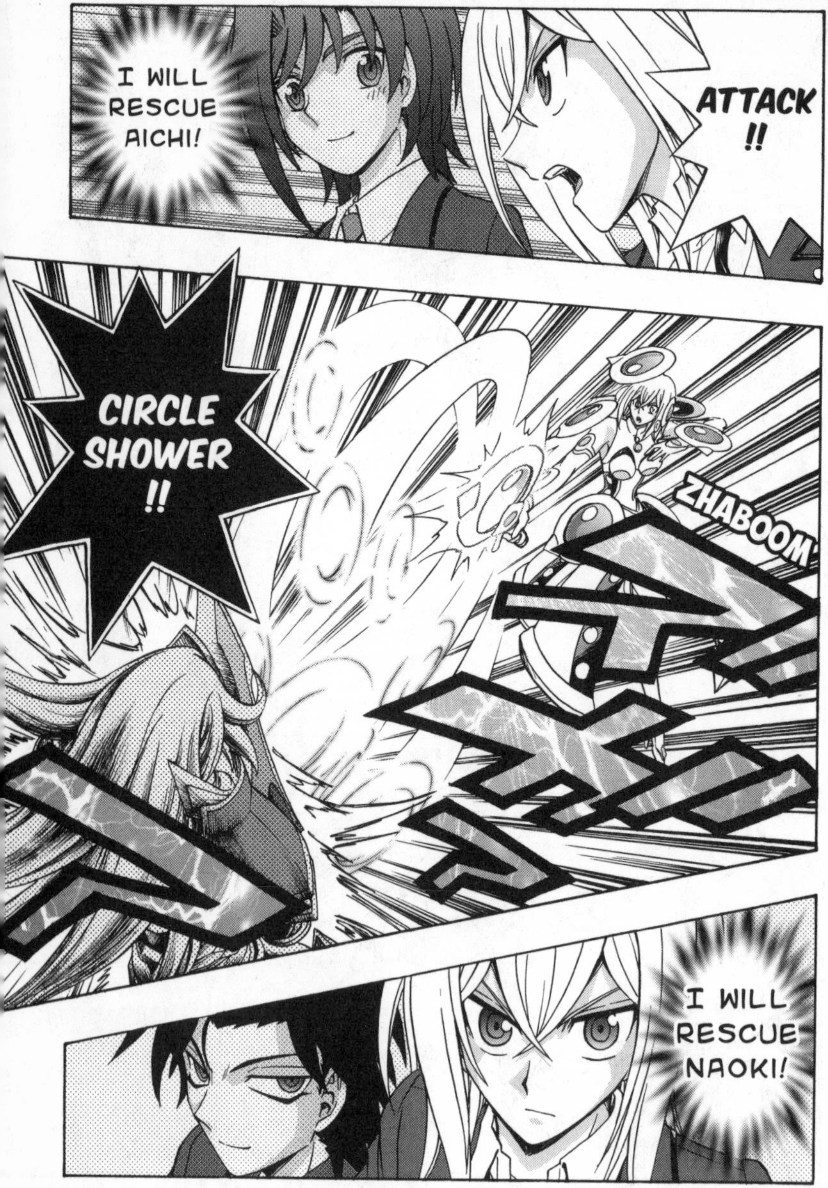
ATTACK !!
I WILL RESCUE AICHI!
ZHABOOM
CIRCLE SHOWER !!
I WILL RESCUE NAOKI!

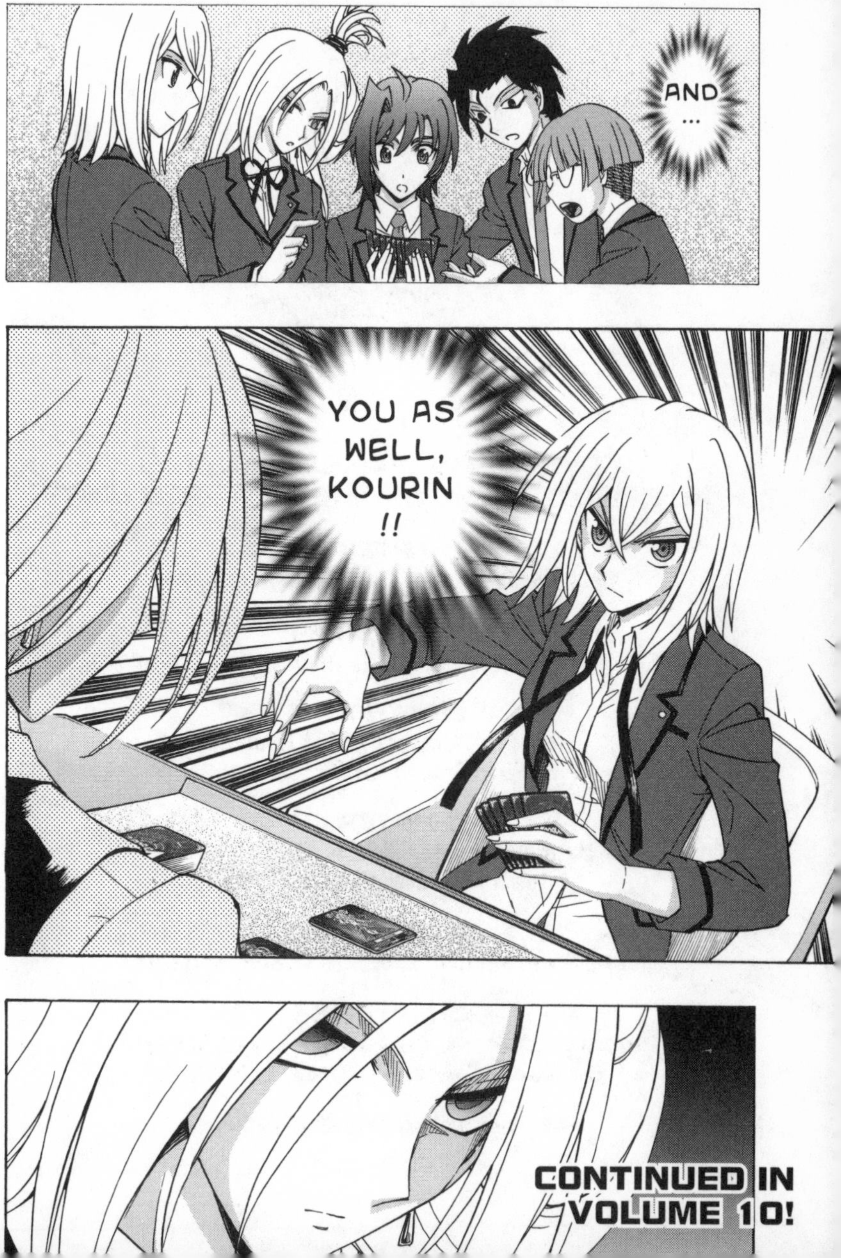
AND ...
YOU AS WELL, KOURIN !!
CONTINUED IN VOLUME 10!

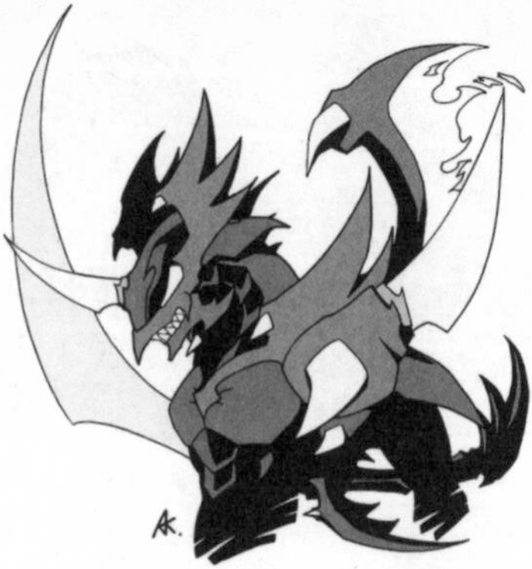
AK.

CARDFIGHT!! VANGUARD VOL. 9
ORIGINAL DESIGNS OF THE FEATURED UNITS

CHAPTER 43
Rough Seas Banshee / 萩谷薫 (Kaoru Hagiya)

CHAPTER 44
Stealth Beast, Hagakure / 強化新型 yutori (yutori Kyoukashingata)

CHAPTER 47
Red River Dragoon / 竜徹 (ryutetsu)
Eradicator, Demolition Dragon / 松島一夫 (Kazuo Matsushima)

CHAPTER 48
Malevolent Djinn / 仙田聡 (Satoru Senda)
Spark Edge Dracokid / 樹人(Kito)

CHAPTER 49
Little Sage, Marron / 山崎奈苗 (Nanae Yamazaki)

CHAPTER 51
Crimson Lion Cub, Kyrph / 村山竜大 (Ryota Murayama)
Evil Slaying Swordsman, Haugan / Hirokorin

All Other Units / 伊藤彰 (Akira Itou)

CARDFIGHT! VANGUARD
VOLUME 9

Translation: Yota Okutani
Production: Grace Lu
           Anthony Quintessenza

Copyright © Akira ITOU 2015
           © bushiroad All Rights Reserved.
First published in Japan in 2015 by KADOKAWA CORPORATION, Tokyo.
English translation rights arranged with KADOKAWA CORPORATION, Tokyo
through TUTTLE-MORI AGENCY, INC., Tokyo.
English language version produced by Vertical, Inc.

Translation provided by Vertical, Inc., 2017
Published by Vertical, Inc., New York

Originally published in Japanese as *Kaadofaito!! Vangaado 9* by KADOKAWA
CORPORATION
Kaadofaito!! Vangaado first serialized in *Young Ace*, 2011-

This is a work of fiction.

ISBN: 978-1-941220-51-1

Manufactured in Canada

First Edition

Vertical, Inc.
451 Park Avenue South
7th Floor
New York, NY 10016
www.vertical-inc.com

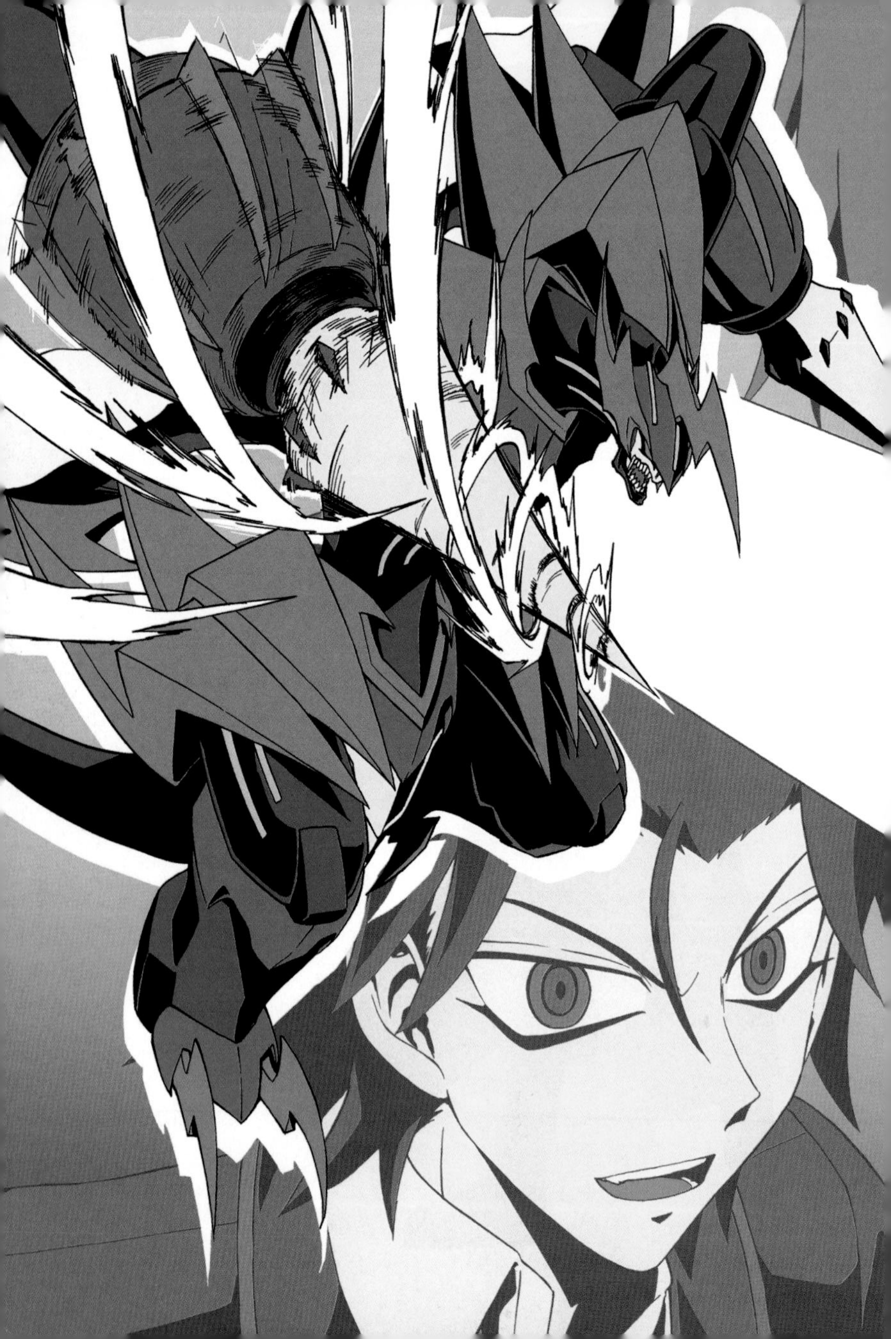

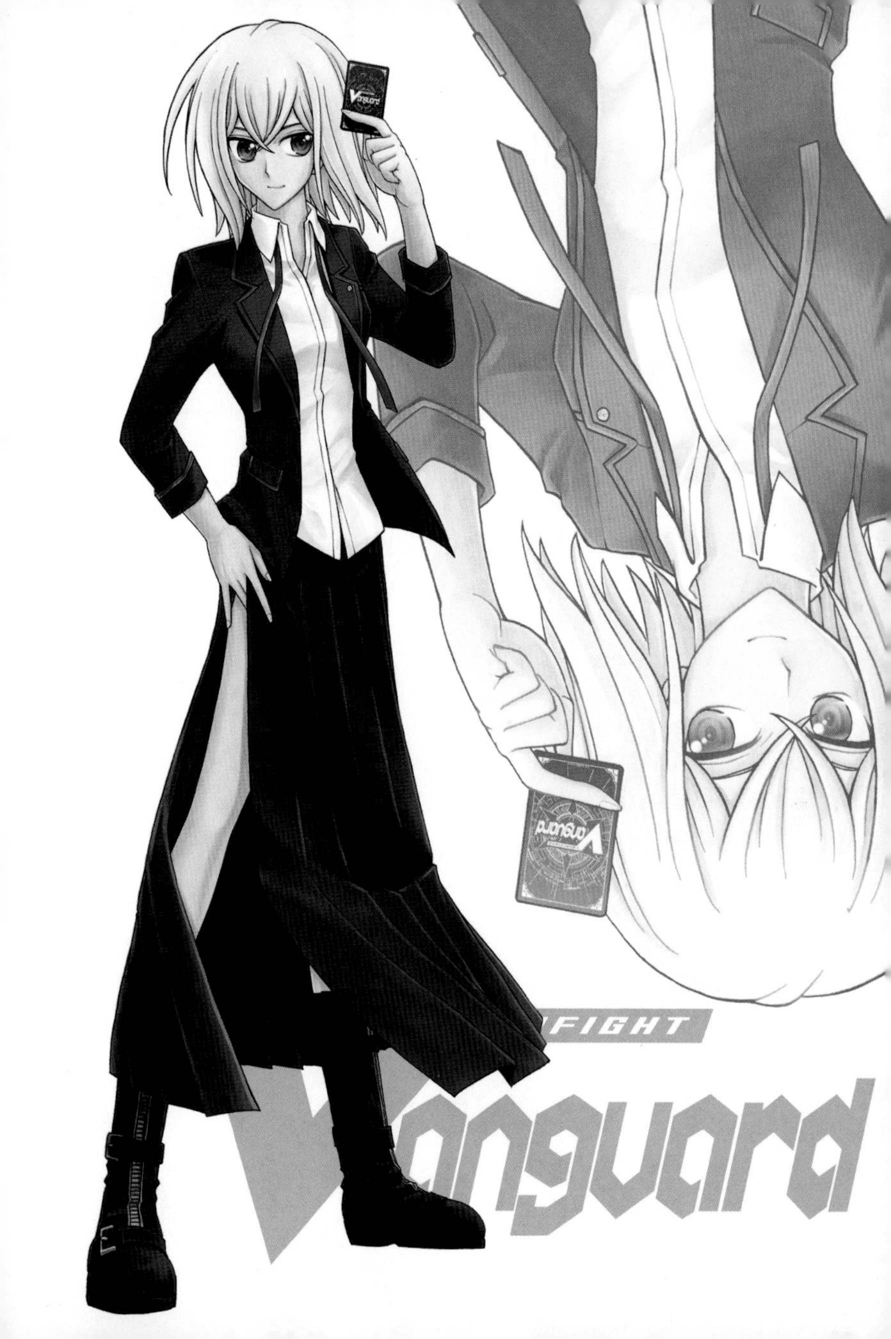
FIGHT
Vanguard

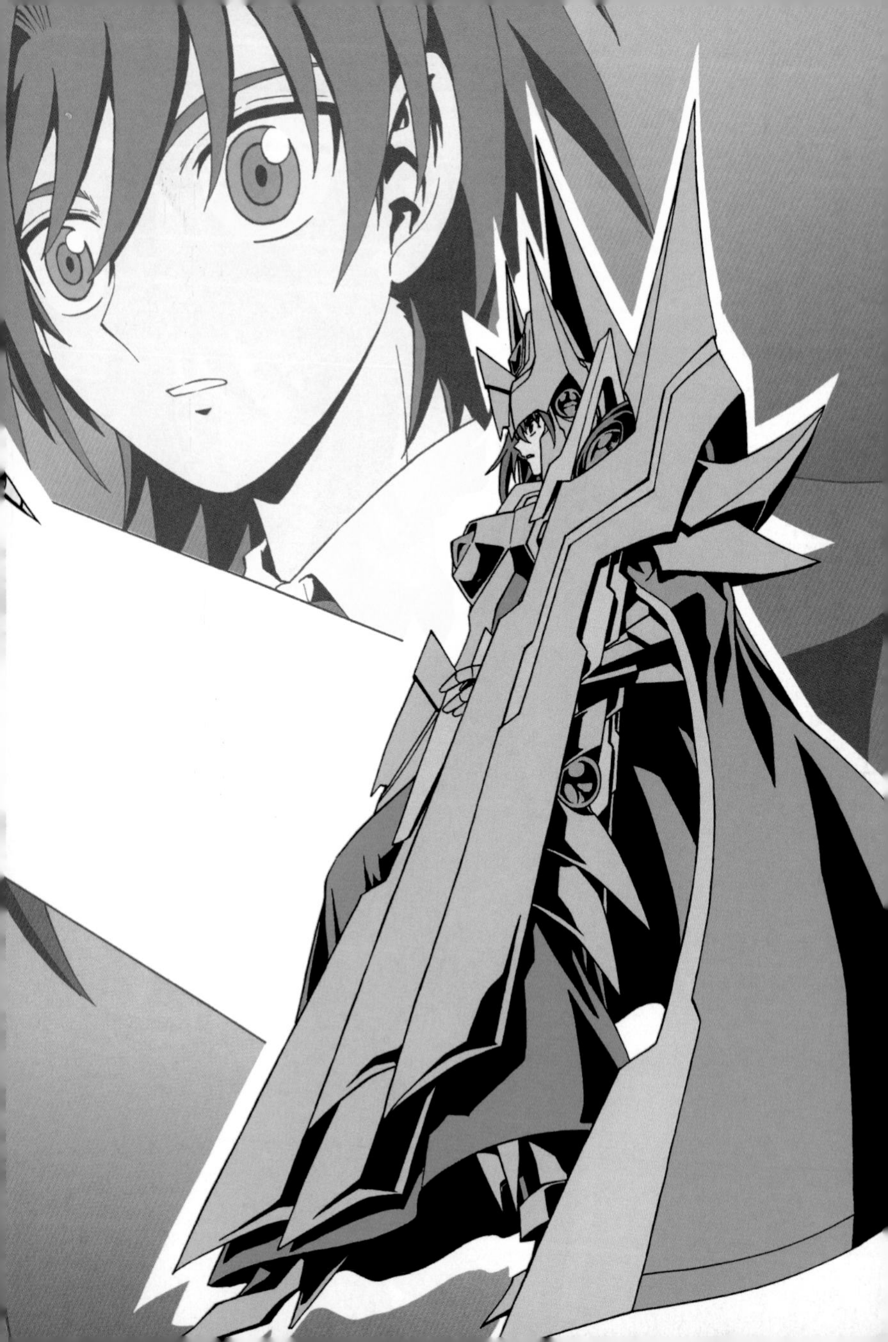

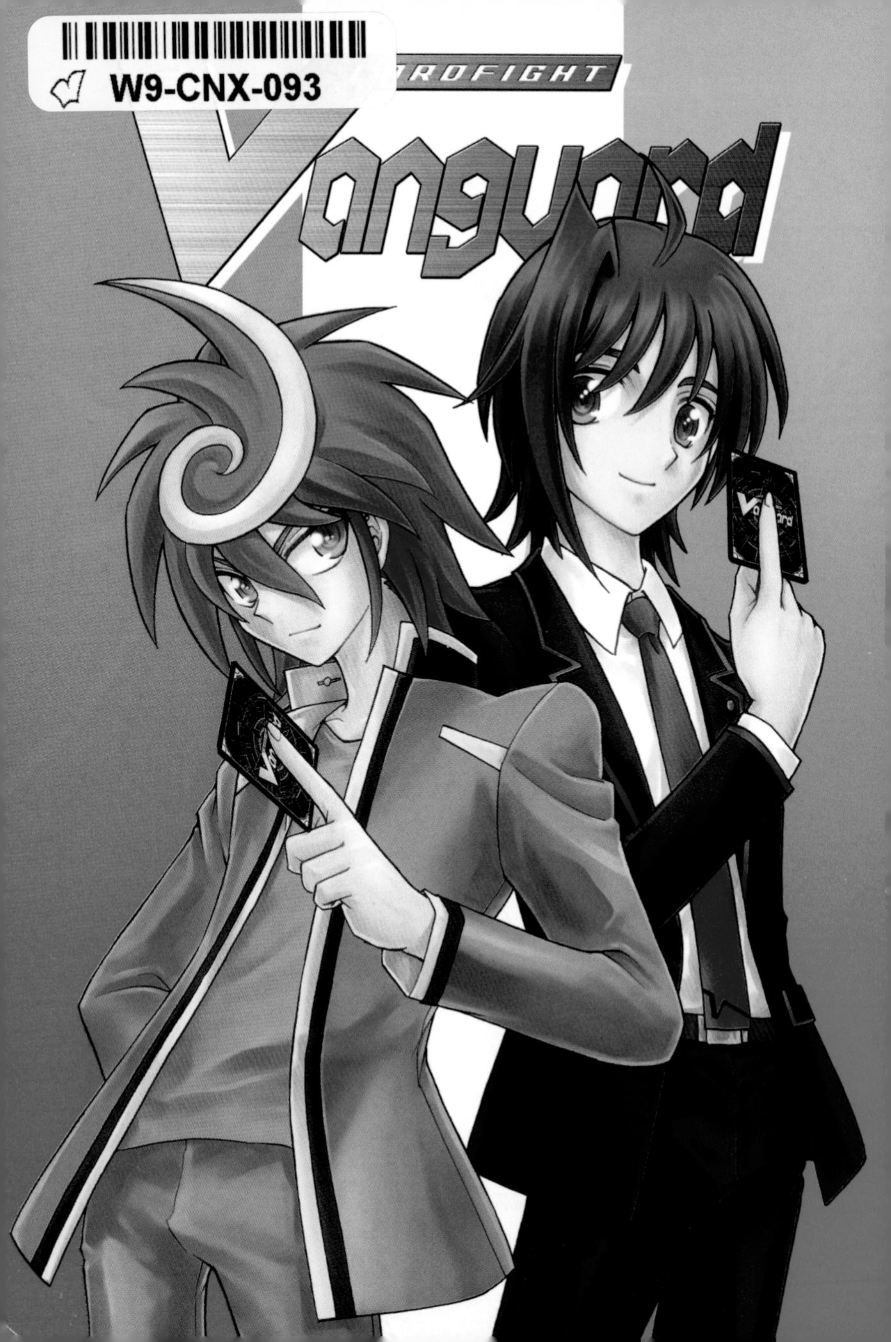
Vanguard